Merleau-Ponty and

Environmental Philosophy

SUNY series in the Philosophy of the Social Sciences

Lenore Langsdorf, editor

Merleau-Ponty and Environmental Philosophy

Dwelling on the Landscapes of Thought

Edited by

Suzanne L. Cataldi and

William S. Hamrick

State University of New York Press

Published by
State University of New York Press, Albany

© 2007 State University of New York

For information, address State University of New York Press,
194 Washington Avenue, Suite 305, Albany, NY 12210-2384

Production by Michael Haggett
Marketing by Michael Campochiaro

Library of Congress Cataloging-in-Publication Data

Merleau-Ponty and environmental philosophy : dwelling on the landscape of thought /
edited by Suzanne L. Cataldi, William S. Hamrick.
      p. cm—(SUNY series in the philosophy of the social sciences)
   Includes bibliographical references and index.
   ISBN-13: 978-0-7914-7051-0 (hardcover : alk. paper)
   ISBN-13: 978-0-7914-7052-7 (pbk. : alk. paper)
1. Merleau-Ponty, Maurice, 1908–1961.   2. Human ecology—Philosophy.   3. Ecology—
Philosophy.   I. Cataldi, Sue L., 1951–   II. Hamrick, William S.   III. Series.
   B.2430.M3764M4682   2007
   194—dc22   2006017859

10 9 8 7 6 5 4 3 2 1

For Martin C. ("Mike") Dillon: friend, insightful critic, constant source of encouragement, a founder and longtime General Secretary of the International Merleau-Ponty Circle, intellectual *agent provocateur par excellence*, and redoubtable sailor who knew the perils of an unintentional jibe both on the water and in philosophy.

What resists phenomenology within us—natural being, the "barbarous" source Schelling spoke of—cannot remain outside phenomenology and should have its place within it. The philosopher has his shadow, which is not simply the factual absence of future light.

—Maurice Merleau-Ponty, *Signs*

The whole life process is founded on this bipartite quality of that which we call matter and of that inner side, averted from our senses, that we intimate but do not discern. An image or inner spirit of life constantly emerges out of the corporeal and it always again becomes embodied through a reverse process.

—F. W. J. Schelling, *The Ages of the World*

Contents

Abbreviations   ix

Introduction   1

PART ONE
BUILDING, DWELLING, LIVING—
BORDERING ON THE NATURAL

1. A Little Knowledge of Dangerous Things:
   Human Vulnerability in a Changing Climate   19
   Robert Kirkman

2. An Inquiry into the Intercorporeal Relations Between
   Humans and the Earth   37
   Kenneth Liberman

3. The Liminal World of the Northwest Coast   51
   Patricia M. Locke

4. Borders and Boundaries: Edging into the Environment   67
   Edward S. Casey

5. Logos of Our Eco in the Feminine: An Approach Through
   Heidegger, Irigaray, and Merleau-Ponty   93
   Carol Bigwood

6. *Umwelt* and Nature in Merleau-Ponty's Ontology   117
   Duane H. Davis

7. Merleau-Ponty, Ecology, and Biosemiotics   133
   Maurita Harney

PART TWO.
EMBODIMENT, SOCIALITY, AND ECOLOGICAL VALUES

  8. Earth in Eclipse   149
        David Abram

  9. Lived Body and Ecological Value Cognition   177
        John R. White

10. "Fleshing" Out an Ethic of Diversity   191
        Molly Hadley Jensen

11. Social Ecology and the Flesh: Merleau-Ponty, Irigaray,
      and Ecocommunitarian Politics   203
        Sally Fischer

12. Harmony in a Dislocated World   217
        Jocelyn Dunphy-Blomfield

13. Merleau-Ponty's Transversal Geophilosophy and Sinic
      Aesthetics of Nature   235
        Hwa Yol Jung

14. Merleau-Ponty and the Ontology of Ecology
      or Apocalypse Later   259
        Martin C. Dillon

Contributors   273
Index   277

Abbreviations

AD   *Les Aventures de la dialectique.* Paris: Gallimard, 1955. Translated by Joseph Bien as *Adventures of the Dialectic.* Evanston: Northwestern University Press, 1973.

CAL   "La Conscience et l'acquisition du langage." 1964. *Bulletin de psychologie*, No. 236, XVIII, 3–6. Translated by Hugh Silverman as *Consciousness and the Acquisition of Language.* Evanston: Northwestern University Press, 1973.

EP   *Éloge de la Philosophie.* Paris: Gallimard, 1953. Translated by John Wild and James M. Edie as *In Praise of Philosophy.* Evanston: Northwestern University Press, 1973.

HT   *Humanisme et terreur.* Paris: Gallimard, 1947. Translated by John O'Neill as *Humanism and Terror.*

NC   *Notes de cours, 1959–1961.* Edited by Stéphanie Ménasé. Paris: Gallimard, 1996.

OE   *L'Œil et l'esprit.* Paris: Gallimard, 1964. Translated by Carleton Dallery as "Eye and Mind," in *The Primacy of Perception,* 159–190.

PhP   *Phénoménologie de la perception.* Paris: Gallimard, 1945. Translated by Colin Smith as *Phenomenology of Perception.* London: Routledge & Kegan Paul, 1962; New York: Humanities Press, 1962.

PM   *La Prose du monde.* Paris: Gallimard, 1969. Translated by John O'Neill as *The Prose of the World.* Evanston: Northwestern University Press, 1973; London: Heinemann, 1974.

PRI   *The Primary of Perception and Other Essays on Phenomenological Psychology, the Philosophy of Art, History and Politics.* Edited by James M. Edie. Evanston: Northwestern University Press, 1964.

RC   *Résumés de cours, Collège de France 1952–1960.* Paris: Gallimard, 1968. Translated by John O'Neill as *Themes from the Lectures at the Collège de France, 1952–1960.* Evanston: Northwestern University Press, 1970.

S   *Signes.* Paris: Gallimard, 1960. Translated by Richard C. McCleary as *Signs.* Evanston: Northwestern University Press, 1964.

SC   *La Structure du comportement.* Paris: Presses Universitaires de France, 1942. Translated by Alden Fisher as *The Structure of Behavior.* Boston: Beacon Press, 1963.

SNS   *Sens et non-sens.* Paris: Nagel, 1948; reprinted, Paris: Gallimard, 1996. Translated by Herbert L. Dreyfus and Patricia Allen Dreyfus as *Sense and Non-Sense* Evanston: Northwestern University Press, 1964.

VI   *Le Visible et l'invisible, suivi de notes de travail.* Edited by Claude Lefort. Paris: Gallimard, 1964. Translated by Alphonso Lingis as *The Visible and the Invisible, Followed by Working Notes.* Evanston: Northwestern University Press, 1968.

Introduction

This volume consists of a collection of essays that explore environmental questions in the context of the philosophy of Maurice Merleau-Ponty. From richly diverse perspectives the authors represented here attempt to flesh out Merleau-Ponty's vision in the direction of a coherent philosophical ecology.

In the "Preface" of his principal early work, *Phenomenology of Perception*, Maurice Merleau-Ponty (1908–1961) declares phenomenology to be, as Edmund Husserl had conceived it, a "study of essences," that is, the essential meanings of the phenomena, or what appears to us (PhP i/vii).[1] But it is likewise "a philosophy that puts essences in existence and does not think that one could understand man and the world otherwise than beginning from their 'facticity'" (ibid.). Phenomenology does aspire to be, in Husserl's words, "a strict science," but it also attempts "a direct description of our experience such as it is, and without regard to its psychological genesis and to the causal explications of it that the scientist, the historian, or the sociologist could provide" (ibid.). The task of phenomenology is "to describe, and not to explain or analyze" (PhP ii/viii); it is a method for describing all meaningful phenomena of the world of human life—the "life-world"—as they appear, in order to arrive at their essences.

Phenomenology is "a philosophy of consciousness" (S 225/178), but neither consciousness nor phenomena are to be understood in a radically subjective, idealist sense. As Husserl shows, consciousness is "intentional," and that intentionality means "the unique peculiarity of experiences 'to be the consciousness *of* something.'"[2] Therefore, to perceive is to perceive

1

something, to will is to will something, to love or hate is to love or hate something or someone, and so on. Consciousness and its object are given bilaterally and meant to be studied together. Hence, "phenomena" refers to both aspects of this concrete, unified subject-object structure.

On their objective side, phenomena are also to be understood in the widest sense possible as anything that can appear to us. It might be a perceptual object, a social movement, a public event, the Zeitgeist of a particular historical epoch, or any other meaningful appearance. Because of this enlarged scope, and because of the anticipations of the phenomenological method in previous philosophies, Merleau-Ponty holds that the method had actually been "en route for a long time," particularly "in Hegel and in Kierkegaard of course, but also in Marx, Nietzsche, and Freud" (PhP ii/viii.). It was thus "a movement before becoming a doctrine or a system" (PhP xvi/xxi), and this was no accident. Rather, like the work of "Balzac, Proust, Valéry, or of Cézanne," phenomenology is just as "painstaking" "by reason of the same kind of attention and wonder, the same demand for awareness, the same will to grasp the meaning of the world or of history aborning. In this way it merges with effort of modern thought" (ibid.).

Merleau-Ponty himself made significant and original use of the phenomenological method. Through his studies of normal and pathological perception and behavior, speech and language, history, sexuality, and political life, he made major, lasting contributions to twentieth-century philosophy. In addition, despite his distinction of phenomenology from the enterprise of science, he never rejected or refused to believe in science per se. Indeed, of all the phenomenologists of his generation, he was the most open and sympathetic to the sciences. Their methods and research results were, after all, equally phenomena of the life-world that solicited and nourished reflection. Thus, he concluded, how could "any philosopher aware of the philosophical tradition seriously propose to forbid philosophy to have anything to do with science? . . . Science is a set of means of perceiving, imagining, and, in short, living which are oriented toward the same truth of which our first experiences establish in us the need" (S 127, 128/101, 102; translation altered).

As a result, Nature (usually capitalized) is almost always present in his works from the earliest writings on, in one context or another. Moreover, in discussing what he finds to be an inevitable tension in Edmund Husserl's last writings between pure, constituting consciousness and its idealized meanings, and the life-world and Nature on which that consciousness and those meanings depend, Merleau-Ponty writes, ". . . the ultimate task of phenomenology as philosophy of consciousness is to understand its relationship to non-phenomenology. What resists phenomenology within us—natural being, the 'barbarous' source Schelling spoke of—cannot remain outside phenomenology and should have its place within it. The philosopher has his shadow, which is not simply the factual absence of future light" (S 225/178; translation altered).

For the greater part of his tragically short philosophical career, Merleau-Ponty stayed deliberately within the confines of "phenomenology as a philosophy of consciousness." And he more than once explicitly identified phenomenology with philosophy as such. Thus, although Nature was always there on the horizon to be understood, such comprehension was ineluctably shaped and limited by a philosophy of consciousness into which it was to be incorporated.

Thus, it came as a surprise to many when Merleau-Ponty chose "The Concept of Nature" as the subject of his 1956–1957 and 1957–1958 courses at the Collège de France and that he eventually came to reflect on Nature with a very different conception of philosophical method. For, during the last five or six years of his life, he turned from phenomenology, no longer identified *tout court* with philosophy, to ontology. He did not repudiate the validity of his phenomenological descriptions of the body, perception, language, and other phenomena of the life-world, but he did become convinced of the inadequacy of phenomenology as a method for doing philosophy. On his revised view, the earlier phenomenology could not provide a philosophically adequate alternative to a Cartesian mind-body dualism and, in general, a convincing account of the relation of body and consciousness, perception and intellect: "The problems posed in *Ph.P.* [*Phenomenology of Perception*] are insoluble because I start there from the 'consciousness'-'object' distinction. . . . Starting from this distinction, one will never understand that a given fact of the 'objective' order (a given cerebral lesion) could entail a given disturbance of the relation with the world—a massive disturbance, which seems to prove that the whole 'consciousness' is a function of the objective body" (VI 253/200).

Because of this shift, Merleau-Ponty abandons the contrasts in the early works between the lived-body with the objective body as described by science, and a body-consciousness with a Cartesian cogito. In the later writings, particularly in *Eye and Mind* and the incomplete, posthumously published manuscript of *The Visible and the Invisible*, Merleau-Ponty begins to develop an ontology of "flesh" (*la chair*), something for which traditional philosophy has no name. Flesh is not matter, in the sense of collections of corpuscles, and it is not "some 'psychic' material." Generally speaking, it is not a material or spiritual fact or collection of facts. Nor is it a mental representation. "The flesh is not matter, is not mind, is not substance. To designate it, we should need the old term 'element,' in the sense it was used to speak of water, air, earth, and fire, that is, in the sense of a *general thing*, midway between the spatio-temporal individual and the idea. . . . The flesh is in this sense an 'element' of Being" (VI 183–84/139).

Flesh includes my "self-sensing" flesh and the "sensible and not sentient" flesh of the world, and it is by means of the latter that the lived-body can be understood. The "flesh of the world" is "the Being-seen, i.e., a Being that is *eminently percipi*," and it is in and through that "being seen" that the seeing, the *percipere* of the lived-body, can become intelligible. It is "my body applying itself to the rest of the perceived," and this relationship in turn becomes both possible and comprehensible "because *there is* Being" (VI 304/250; italics in the original). Moreover, and this is a signal change from his earlier phenomenology, because flesh now explains the lived-body, the latter is an object in nature alongside other objects, made of the "same stuff": "Visible and mobile, my body is a thing among things. . . . Things are an annex or prolongation of itself; they are incrusted into its flesh, they are part of its full definition; the world is made of the same stuff as the body" (OE 19/163).

How are we to understand the relationship between our flesh and the flesh of the world? Jean-Paul Sartre once claimed that the "cardinal principle" of Merleau-Ponty's last writings was the notion of "envelopment" (1984, 132).[3] Merleau-Ponty articulates that envelopment in terms of what he terms an "intertwining" and "chiasm." That is, flesh has a reversibility such that to see is also to be seen, to touch is equally to be touched, and so on: "The chiasm, reversibility, is the idea that every perception doubled with a counter-perception . . . is an act with two faces, one no longer knows who speaks and who listens. Speaking-listening, seeing-being seen, perceiving-being perceived. . . . *Activity* = *passivity*" (VI 318/264–265).

There is also a "double and crossed situating of the visible in the tangible and of the tangible in the visible" (VI 177/134). Likewise, self and other cross over into each other's existence. "The experience of my own body and the experience of the other," Merleau-Ponty writes, "are themselves the two sides of one same Being" (VI 278/225). Soul and body similarly intertwine because "[t]here is a body of the mind, and a mind of the body and a chiasm between them" (VI 313/259). There is also a chiasm between thought and its object and equally an intertwining between the objective body and the lived-body—now called "the two 'sides' of our body, the body as sensible and the body as sentient" (VI 180/136)—just as there is between the thing perceived and the perceiving, the flesh of the world and the body's flesh. We exist, in short, at the intersection of these various reversibilities.

Merleau-Ponty's ontology of flesh has generated a heightened awareness of, and appreciation for, what his later texts say and imply about Nature and our place within it. This research has produced several illuminating contributions to environmental and ecological issues.[4] This is particularly true of those aspects of deep ecology that concern the intertwining and mutual well-being of all life forms, questions about the meaning of being human, and the refusal to value Nature solely in terms of its potential for human use. Indeed, apart from the process metaphysics of Alfred North Whitehead, it is difficult to imagine another philosophy that so completely supports environmental well-being and prepares for a coherent philosophical ecology.[5]

The essays collected here link Merleau-Ponty's ontology of Nature to contemporary environmental and ecological themes in richly varied ways. The volume is conceptually divided into two parts. Part I focuses on relations within the natural world. Part II connects aspects of Merleau-Ponty's philosophy to issues in environmental ethics.

Ecology studies relationships of organisms to each other and to their environment. Contributors understand ecology in a broad sense to include studies of these interrelations from the biological, physical, and social sciences. While Merleau-Ponty does not use the expression 'ecology,' much in his philosophy bears on it: for example, the centrality of relations in his work, his concept of the bond between humanity and nature; his thinking in terms of 'elements' and through expressions like 'animality' and 'brute' or 'wild' Being (L'Être sauvage); its accommodation of natural and social diversity; and of course, his thought on embodiment and Flesh. Several contributors both articulate and question the extent to which Merleau-Ponty's philosophy might help us understand and respond to increasing and alarming evidence of environmental degradation.

For example, in examining the question of why we fail to do more to avert threats to the environment, Robert Kirkman uses Merleau-Ponty's ontology of reversible flesh to articulate how human vulnerability as "a varied, multi-dimensional phenomenon of depths and hidden subtleties" applies to covert and relatively abstract environmental threats such as global warming. The recognition that we can be affected by the world precisely because as embodied organisms we are not separated from its 'flesh' ties into Merleau-Ponty's idea of sentient-sensibility. At the same time, nonsentient or invisible dimensions make it difficult to be able to "feel in my bones a threat as abstract and diffuse as global climate change."

Kirkman's phenomenology of the perception of threats also applies Merleau-Ponty's thesis of the fundamental ambiguity of perception to global climate change. At the same time, he uncovers several sources of the ambiguity. These sources make it difficult to discern whether the strange weather patterns we experience are pleasant anomalies or "the first inkling of an environmental catastrophe."

Ambiguity and the relation of perception to the natural sciences account for what Kirkman calls a plausible deniability on the issue of global climate change. He takes the argument a step further, however, and shows how Merleau-Ponty's philosophy can be used to challenge this very position. An inescapable fact of incarnate life, the primordial perception of vulnerability can help focus our attention on the suffering that will surely ensue if certain predictions are borne out. This vulnerability can thus serve as a justifiable basis for an appropriate level of alarm and motivation to act concerning, as he puts it, even the mere possibility that global climate change will negatively affect our dependence on steady and predictable weather cycles.

Applications of Merleau-Ponty's reversibility thesis and perceptions of human vulnerability and limitations continue into Kenneth Liberman's reflection on wilderness experiences. Liberman uses an expansive sense of agency, one "that belongs to both the earth and to ourselves," to fathom and flesh out Merleau-Ponty's contention that "Nature is what has a sense without this sense being posited by thought." Merleau-Ponty's notion of flesh as intercorporeal "fabric that pre-exists . . . but also includes us" is developed in Ken Liberman's inquiry into why—and how—people seek primitive contact with the earth.

Liberman contrasts the wilderness experience of abiding with the landscape with explorations intended to survey or conquer the terrain. In the process, he describes a deep sort of knowing, one often lost or ignored in political discussions on the subject of the environment. It involves a relinquishment of human agency and a cultivation of reciprocal relations born of our bodily engagements with the earth. "The earth draws us out of ourselves, not just to explore the terrain in order to dominate it but to learn from our contact with it, and from the resistance it offers us." What we come to comprehend through intimate bodily contact with the earth is a sense of our own obscurity: "the principal legacy of the wilderness experience."

This felt sense of obscurity is an experience of depth; it is evocative of the depth of deep ecology movements and our deep, intercorporeal belonging to the sensible Merleau-Ponty tries to capture with his claim that visibility and invisibility are intimately entwined in the "flesh" of the world. Patricia M. Locke analyzes this sense of obscurity in ecological terms as "straits" and in embodied terms as "skin"—a perceptibly imperceptible gap or tissue between interior and exterior horizons. She turns to the world of the Haida Indians on the Pacific Northwest Coast "for a sense of what it is like to live in the straits."

Just as Liberman calls attention to the restorative potential derivable from cultivating reciprocal relations with the earth, Patricia Locke brings Merleau-Ponty's pre-reflective "wild" meanings (VI 155) to life in her depictions of the complex and dynamic reciprocities between earth, sea, sky, human beings, animals and inanimate entities in the Haida's "non-Cartesian yet highly developed social world." We see through her descriptions how the art and architecture of their great plank houses "echoes our corporeality and defines its natural surroundings," enveloping its inhabitants "but is also a defining feature of the landscape outside." These native communal household dwellings illustrate a dynamic sense of reversible flesh, a fluidity of boundaries and a "wild" multiplicity of criss-crossed images that give to the perceiver an experience of being "always on the verge, the border between touching and being touched, between human and animal."

Locke borrows a saying from the culture that captures the precarious positioning of their houses on a "thin blade of treeless land" above the sea as well as the "fragile balance of the remaining fragments of the Haida world." In its time and for the native Northcoast Indians, the metaphor of the "world as sharp as a knife" signified the narrow margin between life and death, a reminder of how easily and quickly one might slip and fall off that "edge." Their saying and their sense for "living in the straits" reminds us of our own vulnerability and the possibility that we may indeed be risking everything we value unless we restore a sense of ecological balance to our complex and contemporary relationships with our natural surroundings.

Images of borders, boundaries, and edges are taken up again in Edward S. Casey's contribution. Allowing that edges or borders are "oppressive and restrictive in many contexts," he shows how they may also be comforting and constructive presences in others. In his depiction of their role in natural landscapes and urban environments, Casey reflects on ways that fixed, determinate borders may intermingle with fluid indeterminate boundaries to bring invisible connections to light and delineate moving senses of the ecological. These revived senses are expansive and dynamic enough to include spontaneously evolving formations of birds staking a territory out of thin air and the layout of Central Park where "what is boundary and what is border" have become as intertangled as what is natural and what is contrived.

Casey defines boundaries as porous regions of transitional back and forth movements. He points out a limitation in Merleau-Ponty's philosophical commitments to transitional movements within a "closely woven" and continuous fabric of flesh; namely "his aversion to treating the *ends of things*"—edges where "something comes to an abrupt and decisive termination." Aversion to edges is natural, Casey contends, given that edges are often occasions for possible or hidden violence, masking threats that may be lurking around corners and which, by the way they may suddenly and surprisingly come into view, "flay" our glances and expectations. Ecological sensitivity requires that we overcome our aversion to thinking about edges in their discomfiting and disconnecting aspects. It requires paying attention to human practices that contribute to the deadly endings of things, practices like the use of agri-chemicals in farming, that lead us and others into *dire* straits, generating deadly zones where life can no longer be sustained or supported.

Carol Bigwood's moving meditation on the arts of constructing and cultivating contrasts violent farming and biotechnological methods with nonviolent ones. She draws ecofeminist and phenomenological thought (Heidegger's and Irigaray's) into an understanding of ecology and a deeper appreciation of Flesh.

Etymologically, "ecology" stems from the Greek word (*oikos*) for household or dwelling. From Merleau-Ponty, Bigwood develops "an understanding of the body as primal ecological home": a place where we touch and are touched. Through arts of cultivation such as nurturing and healing, she relates Flesh to a dynamic tending of generativity: "Cultivation is fidelity to growth, responding to the generativity of the living world with attuned questioning touch." The body is central to Bigwood's discussion. The nurturing self is an embodied self who makes a skill of touch.

Despite the skill involved in cultivating, it is often invisible, taken for granted work. Globally it is still performed predominantly by women "who do most of the farming, healing the sick with herbs and medicines, and taking care of the young and the home." Bigwood underscores the importance of women forming a central part of environmental solutions. She helps us to see how crucial the arts of healing and nurturing are for "understanding our human being in a healthier way and for our very survival."

Bigwood questions why Merleau-Ponty's prime examples of touching are not examples of touching another. The intelligent feeling in the empathic, tender, and questioning touch she describes is a touching without grasping, the sort of touch that can help guide us to an ethos of organic sensitivity and a cultivation of compassion we will need to tend and heal our world home earth.

The relation of human beings to nature is one of openness, and this entails vulnerability, not only on our part but on the part of nature as well. As Duane H. Davis, the next author, states: "We could destroy the earth— perhaps that is what we are doing. But this same openness allows for us to care for it."

In examining the question of transcendental reflection on the environment, Davis also addresses the question of what it means to be at home in nature and how being at home requires construction. "We build against the threats of nature because we are also not at home there."

Davis compares Merleau-Ponty to two thinkers championed by environmentalists for their powerful descriptions of nature. He shows how Merleau-Ponty's account of nature as lived from within an unstable perceptible field avoids "two errors of transcendentalisms": Henry David Thoreau's, which "betrays a nostalgic or even mystical return to nature-as-provider," and Martin Heidegger's, which dwells on "the strangeness (*Unheimlichkeit*) from nature that we are."

Davis believes that Merleau-Ponty would cast our relationship to nature as more of a struggle than a romantic sentiment, "a struggle to define and redefine our relation to Nature," and that his situating transcendence in a latent intentionality—a divergence (*écart*) or spread of differentiation across a open field which is not a monolithic unity—captures the sense in which we are, and are not, at home in nature. As Davis says, "we redefine ourselves and nature as we live there. The redefining presents a threat and provides a home—thus it calls for respect. Perhaps we can more wisely choose actions and policies that respect nature as threat and home, as origin and product."

The next contributor, Maurita Harney, also focuses attention on how radical shifts in Merleau-Ponty's understanding of intentionality, progressively generalized to the point where it "becomes 'globalized' to the world of which I am a part," may be viewed as stage setting for the development of a philosophical ecology. She compares aspects of Merleau-Ponty's views of intentionality with Charles Sanders Peirce's notion of sign and its development within the field of biosemiotics.

Biosemiotics studies processes by which signs are generated and communicated. Harney shows how taken together, both approaches may prove useful in developing a philosophical ecology where "the relationship between organism and environment is more like a reciprocal, communicative interaction than the action-reaction of a subject and an inert, passive world." For, as she points out, in neither approach "can meaning or significance be reduced to sets of causal events in the physical world."

Contributors in Part II of the volume relate ideas in Merleau-Ponty's philosophy of nature to issues in environmental ethics. David Abram's contribution updates Merleau-Ponty's thesis of the primacy of perception by describing the "astonishing proliferation of worlds" in twenty-first century life. He questions how we can maintain a sense of ecological balance, coherence and integrity in the context of our "tumbling" between a multiplicity of micro- and macrocosmic worlds, environments that are more of or less corporeal, incongruous, and hidden from each other. The fathomless, digital domain cyberspace, where bodiless minds "meet" and communicate is considered along with other (technological, scientific, transcendent) realms.

Abram believes that the proliferation of these less corporeal worlds perpetuate a historical (philosophical, religious, scientific) disparagement of sensorial reality. He attributes the contemporary erosion of ecological values to the lack of a common ground or sense, which has resulted in a reckless disregard, a "trashing" of the directly experienced world. Abram recalls attention, as Merleau-Ponty's philosophy and other chapters in this volume do, to the sensuous body's world at the heart of the others. It is the world where we learn, or are socialized out of, a somatic empathy with others.

John R. White, the next author, connects Max Scheler's notion of vital sympathy, "our sympathetic entry into another's vital experience," to a notion of vital values derivable from Merleau-Ponty's view of sensing as a vital process. White defines vital values as those which contribute to the flourishing of ecosystems and their living members. His essay explores how they are given through lived bodily experience and shows why a body-ethic is required for a comprehensive environmental ethics.

White discusses vital values in connection with social formations and bodily praxes that may alienate us from our own animality and interfere with our experiencing ecological values *as* values. This is a key and crucial point, for unless we perceive ecological values as valuable, what reason do we have to defend the environment? White's thesis and the use he makes of Scheler's differentiation in value ranks also helps to shed light on why "even persons highly sensitive to other morally relevant values might fail to grasp the significance of ecological values."

To illustrate his thesis, White points to effects of contemporary American capitalism on lived body experiencing. The example provides a model for how the inclusion of a body-ethic, an ethic of the socialized living body, into a comprehensive environmental ethic can help us apprehend how "it could be that the 'outer' devastation of the environment is in the end a projection of the 'inner' alienation we experience from our own animality."

In her exploration of its ethical ramifications, Molly Hadley Jensen connects Merleau-Ponty's thematic focus on differentiation in nature to the ecologically vital value of diversity. Merleau-Ponty's view of the sensed and sensing body-self as fundamentally polymorphic, communicative, elementally open and reciprocally involved with others is, as she says, "an ethically potent reinterpretation."

Through its double-belongingness to sentience and sensibility, Flesh is characterized by a difference that itself is "never collapsed" and that enables sense perception. Furthermore, in Merleau-Ponty's understanding, "difference need not imply separation or opposition: difference and diversity are a basis for coherence." Just as isolation and seclusion dull the senses, so too one who "is separate, isolated, and removed from others lacks the capacity for sharing with, feeling for, and responding to others." Body-selves flourish through intercorporeal relations. Thus the flesh ontology "undermines the assumption that difference poses a threat to self or community" and "conceives of the possibility that human and more-than-human cohere for the flourishing of life."

In Jensen's view a fleshed-out ethic of diversity understood as a life-sustaining matrix can "offer ethical guidelines for confronting ecological threats." It can, for example, challenge models of "development" that suppress diversity; help counter "a prevailing logic of sameness, a logic that legitimates dominance of one species to the detriment of diverse others";

and help to revise Kantian-styled ethics based on rational, autonomous egos.

Sally Fischer also finds in Merleau-Ponty's thought an ecologically beneficial alternative to the individualistic subject of modernity. She makes a case for a Merleau-Pontyan social ontology that moves from "egology," "which emphasizes the individualism of subjectivity along with its technological control and power over/against objectivity" to a socially "ecological" way of understanding self/other relations in nonhierarchical terms. She follows Merleau-Ponty in his attempts to reevaluate radically the most fundamental presuppositions of Western metaphysics: "our ontological categories of thought, thing, selfhood, and alterity," a project for which she finds important support in Luce Irigaray's works, and she wishes to place the latter's thought and Merleau-Ponty's ontology of flesh in the service of re-creating "socially and ecologically sound ideologies and institutions." She argues for "a Merleau-Pontyan social ecology" based on this changed notion of self and others, and she views these changed conceptions politically "as a kind of ecocommunitarian politics" accomplished "through the dialectic of concrete intersubjectivity." However, this politics, and this intersubjectivity are, in turn, possible only because of the *dialogical* intentionality implicit in Merleau-Ponty's phenomenology of perception, an intentionality that allows others to be "recognized as real others, rather than as universal subjects." Inherent in this dialogical intentionality is a type of "consummate reciprocity," which in turn generates a "reciprocal recognition that 'I am not everything.'"

Jocelyn Dunphy-Blomfield is also concerned about questions of dominance, problems of communication, and power in maintaining a stable world-order and personal relationships amidst environmental destabilization by industry and economic development. She takes up Enzo Paci's analysis of Merleau-Ponty as "preeminently a philosopher of relations" and David Abram's emphasis on our inclusion within ecological systems, and she attempts to bring these themes to bear on Merleau-Ponty's philosophy of action in social and political life. She shows how Merleau-Ponty's writings on psychology interweave both a philosophy of nature and of human action, and that "his study of love as both union and oppression" in "The Child's Relations with Others" form equally a connection between nature and action and an access to ecology. In both we can see "the principles of truth and freedom as fragile," and never more so than when attempting to justify torture in order to stop terrorism. The essay ends with an examination of Merleau-Ponty's remarks about the use of torture in French Algeria, remarks that are as pertinent today as they were in 1958.

Hwa Yol Jung's essay on "Merleau-Ponty's Transversal Geophilosophy and Sinic Aesthetics of Nature" picks up themes common to both Jensen and Dunphy-Blomfield's essays, and situates them a very different context. Seeking to overcome "our human-induced ecological crisis," Jung finds in Merleau-Ponty's "intercorporeal ontology" the means to establish and secure the beginnings of a foundation for "the edifice of geophilosophy *as if the earth really matters."* The core of what Merleau-Ponty can offer to geophilosophy, for Jung, is his "carnal ontology which provides us with the earthly comprehension that all relationships necessarily begin with the intercorporeality or interweaving of lived bodies both human and nonhuman."

Moreover, Jung appropriates Merleau-Ponty's concept of "lateral universals" in developing the notion of transversality, which consists of a fundamentally "new way of facilitating *lateral* border-crossings by decentering all the centers from one culture to another (intercultural), from one species to another (interspeciesistic), from one discipline to another (interdisciplinary) and from one sense to another (intersensorial)." Transversality "deconstructs and replaces universality as a Eurocentric idea," and "unpacks anthropocentrism (as well as egocentrism), which regards man as the apex of all creation and the measure of all things and as such is the cause of wanton ecological destruction and the accelerated disappearance of biodiversity." This discussion invokes, among other things, Irigaray's turning to Eastern thought in her efforts to transcend logocentrism, Eurocentrism, and phallocentrism, and provides an insightful application of Sinism— "expressed in the corporeal language of ideography," and which includes Taoism, Buddhism, and Confucianism—to the construction of geophilosophy. Jung reflects on the rich expression of geophilosophical ideas in Sinic eco-art forms such as bonsai, haiku poetry, and feng-shui, "widely practiced as an art of everyday living" that "sanctifies and ritualizes" an inseparable bond between humans, the land and cosmic 'elemental' energy (ch'i)."

Finally, Martin C. Dillon's essay stands apart, as he so often did in life, as an insistent, vigorous counterpoint to all others in this volume. He believes that there are "fundamental flaws in the conceptual structures that inconspicuously inform contemporary discourse about our environment." One is that the "very word 'ecology' is misleading and should be abandoned" because the Earth is our dwelling place, but not our house (*oikos*). Houses are things we build for protection from our surroundings and the elements. The belief that the Earth is our home "reflects the familiar desire to influence by worship, supplication, and arcane rites the powers whose sendings take our destinies out of our hands."

Instead of ecology, which he sees as underwritten by primitive superstition, Dillon prefers *phronesis*, or practical wisdom, conceived as the task of discovering "how the world works," and then incarnating that knowledge in our actions "with the hope that it will produce consequences more to our liking" than those that flow from ignorance or superstition. Key to this *phronesis* is Merleau-Ponty's "ontology of becoming," with its emphasis on overflowing meaning that is sometimes not compatible with human needs and a world that imposes limits on our freedom that we have no choice but to accept, even though we are largely ignorant of the fate of this world and "bereft of reliable information about any origin or destiny it might or might not have." Noteworthy also in this context is the fact that Dillon is the only author present here who takes the sea as a theme for extended analysis.

Temporality is an important part of Dillon's appreciation of Merleau-Ponty's ontology, both in terms of lived-time described in Merleau-Ponty's earlier phenomenological writings and natural time that appears in his later ontology of flesh. Dillon also applies these ontological insights to public policy issues such as conservation and the restoration of nature, and he states that the essential question facing us is "How, then, do we stand—how should we stand—with regard to the world in which we dwell?" He seeks an answer to this question in Merleau-Ponty's ontology as well as in a Heideggerean resoluteness and *poeisis,* and seems to hold out a faint hope for *phronesis* avoiding the misuse of technology in war and human annihilation. It is a hope that the editors and all the authors represented here endorse.

Suzanne L. Cataldi

William S. Hamrick

NOTES

1. As with all the citations to Merleau-Ponty's works in this book, when dual pagination is provided, the original French pagination precedes that of the English translation. Single pagination will always be that of the English translation.

2. Edmund Husserl, *Ideas I*, § 84, "Intentionality as the Main Phenomenological Theme," trans. W. R. Boyce Gibson (London: George Allen & Unwin, Ltd., 1931), p. 242.

3. "Merleau-Ponty [I]." Trans. William S. Hamrick. *Journal of the British Society for Phenomenology*, vol. XV, no. 2 (May 1984), 123–154, at p. 132. This previously unpublished manuscript was the initial version of the well-known memorial article for Merleau-Ponty that appeared in the October 1961 issue of *Les Temps modernes* and was reprinted in *Situations IV.*

4. See, for example, David Abram, "Merleau-Ponty and the Voice of the Earth," *Environmental Ethics* 10 (1988), 101–120 and *The Spell of the Sensuous: Perception and Language in a More-than-Human World* (New York: Pantheon Books, 1996); Renaud Barbaras, "Merleau-Ponty and Nature," *Research in Phenomenology* 31 (2001), 22–38; Carol Bigwood, "Renaturalizing the Body (With a Little Help from Merleau-Ponty)," *Hypatia: A Journal of Feminist Philosophy* (Fall 1991), 54–73; Helen Fielding, "The Finitude of Nature: Rethinking the Ethics of Biotechnology," *Medicine, Health Care and Philosophy: A European Journal* 4 (2001), 327–334; Sally Fischer, "Ecology of the Flesh: Gestalt Ontology in Merleau-Ponty and Naess," *International Studies in Philosophy* 34 (2002), 53–67; Eleanor Godway, "The Being Which Is Behind Us: Merleau-Ponty and the Question of Nature," *International Studies in Philosophy* 30 (1) (1998), 47–56; Nancy J. Holland, "'With One Headlight': Merleau-Ponty and the Philosophy of Science," *Philosophy Today* 46 (2002), 28–33; Monika Langer, "Merleau-Ponty and Deep Ecology," in Galen A. Johnson and Michael B. Smith, eds. *Ontology and Alterity in Merleau-Ponty* (Evanston: Northwestern University Press, 1991); Irene Klaver, "Phenomenology on (the) Rocks," *Research in Phenomenology* 31 (2001), 173–186; Glen A. Mazis, *Earthbodies, Rediscovering Our Planetary Senses* (Albany, NY: State University of New York Press, 2002); John Russon, "Embodiment and Responsibility: Merleau-Ponty and the Ontology of Nature," *Man and World: An International Philosophical Review* 27 (3) (1994), 291–308; Ted Toadvine, "Naturalizing Phenomenology," *Philosophy Today* 43 (1999), 124–131; and Ted Toadvine and Charles S. Brown, eds. *Eco-Phenomenology: Back to the Earth Itself* (Albany, NY: State University of New York Press, 2003).

5. This interest increased dramatically after the 1995 publication of anonymous student notes taken during the 1956–1957 and 1957–1958 courses at the Collège de France. These notes came to light when the library of the École Normale Supérieure de Saint Cloud was moved. The French editor, Dominique Séglard, annotated and published the notes, with certain spelling and other corrections, along with Merleau-Ponty's own notes for his 1959–1960 course on "The Concept of Nature, Nature and Logos: The Human Body," under the title of *La Nature, Notes de Cours du Collège de France*. This work, essential for anyone with a serious interest in Merleau-Ponty's thought, illuminates the development of that thought and makes it clear that the previously published *Résumés de cours* for those years includes only a brief sketch of what *La Nature* elaborates. For example, there are extremely detailed reflections on Descartes's view of nature, on Schelling and Bergson—a chapter titled "The Romantic Conception of Nature"—and on Kant—"The Humanist Conception of Nature." Also, whereas the original *Résumés de cours* provided only one thin reference to Alfred North Whitehead, *La Nature* contains an entire thirteen-page essay ("The Idea of Nature for Whitehead") as well as other scattered references. Also, the third lecture course manifests much more completely the development of Merleau-Ponty's later thought as it eventually appeared in *Signs, Eye and Mind*, and especially in *The Visible and the Invisible*.

PART ONE

Building, Dwelling, Living—Bordering on the Natural

A Little Knowledge of Dangerous Things

Human Vulnerability in a Changing Climate

Robert Kirkman

In January 2001, the Intergovernmental Panel on Climate Change (IPCC) released its Third Assessment Report. The report from Working Group I indicates, among other things, that "the global average surface temperature . . . has increased since 1861. Over the 20th century the increase has been 0.6±0.2°C" (IPCC 2001b, 2). Other indicators of change are decreases in snow cover and ice extent, a rise in sea level, and an increase in ocean heat content. The report also musters evidence that concentrations of greenhouse gases are increasing as a consequence of human activities, especially the combustion of fossil fuels. Consider, for example, that "the atmospheric concentration of carbon dioxide (CO_2) has increased by 31 percent since 1750. The present CO_2 concentration has not been exceeded during the past 420,000 years and likely not during the past 20 million years. The current rate of increase is unprecedented during at least the past 20,000 years" (IPCC 2001b, 7).

While Working Group I of the IPCC is charged with measuring and projecting changes in climate, Working Group II is charged with measuring the actual and potential impact of climate change on biological and human systems. In their 2001 report, Working Group II summarized its findings on human systems that are especially sensitive to changes in climate, including "water resources; agriculture (especially food security) and forestry; coastal zones and marine systems (fisheries); human settlements, energy and industry; insurance and other financial services; and human health" (IPCC 2001a, 5). Consider one striking passage from the report:

> The vulnerability of human societies and natural systems to cli-
> mate extremes is demonstrated by the damage, hardship, and
> death caused by events such as droughts, floods, heat waves, ava-
> lanches, and windstorms. While there are uncertainties attached
> to estimates of such changes, some extreme events are projected
> to increase in frequency and/or severity during the 21st century
> due to changes in the mean and/or variability of climate, so it can
> be expected that the severity of their impacts will also increase in
> concert with global warming. (IPCC 2001a, 6)

Put simply, if the most severe projections of climate change are borne out, then many human beings would be likely to suffer as a result.

Whatever their technical merits, descriptions and projections of global climate change by scientists on the IPCC may be deceptive, in a subtle but important sense. The objective detachment of scientific lan-guage can give the impression that the threat of global climate change is precisely the same as any other threat: a falling tree, a charging bear, a loaded gun, a dose of cyanide, a cloud of smog, or an asteroid hurtling toward Earth. All of these are supposed to be taken as objective threats to our objective existence as organisms. If these threats are all alike in this sense, then it follows that our reaction to any one of them should be about the same, assuming that we are being rational: we should act immediately to avert the danger. So, given that there is widespread consensus on the objective account of global climate change, why do we not act immedi-ately and unanimously to avert the threat it poses?

It would not be fair to assume that the problem is simply one of irra-tionality. While evasion and denial probably contribute a great deal to the sluggishness of both the domestic and international responses to climate change, it is nonetheless possible for intelligent and thoughtful people to disagree about both the seriousness of the threat and the scope and timing of the appropriate response. More to the point, while denial may seem irrational from an objectivist point of view, it may be that our lived expe-rience of the threat of global climate change gives it what might be called "plausible deniability." From the point of view of everyday life in the world, all threats are not equal. The processes that drive the climate seem remote from us in time and space, and so we go about our lives attending to what seem to us to be more immediate and pressing threats, such as a sudden spike in the price of gasoline that makes it more expensive to earn a living.

The objectivist approach seems also to assume that we *should* care about the possibility of human-induced global climate change. But why should we? At least part of the answer lies in our own vulnerability. As living organisms, we find ourselves in an inescapable predicament. We must act in order to live, and in acting we change our environment. Our knowledge is necessarily limited, so we must choose how to act without being able to foresee all the consequences of our actions. As living organisms, we are dependent on our environment for the basic services that support our civilization and our very lives. Because we are dependent on our environment, any changes in our environment—including those we ourselves bring about—could pose a direct threat to everything we value, up to and including the continued existence of our species.

Here again the objectivist account of human vulnerability seems to leave something out. If we are to be motivated to avert a threat, we must perceive the threat; we must feel it in our bones. But how do we experience our own vulnerability? This question sets my first task, which is to articulate our lived experience of vulnerability, especially in the face of specific threats of various kinds. As a first point of entry into this task I turn to Maurice Merleau-Ponty's ontology of flesh as he developed it in *The Visible and the Invisible,* especially in the pivotal chapter on "The Chiasm." What I find there, in short, is that to perceive the world is to be perceptible within it: I perceive the world only because the flesh of my body intertwines with the flesh of the world. This intertwining is not always benign, however, and the overlapping or even collision of flesh on flesh can harm me even to the point of obliterating perception itself. Vulnerability is the price of perception.

My second task is to consider what kind of threat global climate change might be or, more to the point, how we experience global climate change as a threat given that we can only know about it through the apparatus of the natural sciences. This task requires a broader phenomenology of climate change, with a particular emphasis on the character of the natural sciences and on the relation of scientific theory to embodied perception. There are clues to be found throughout *The Visible and the Invisible,* as Merleau-Ponty lays plans to reconceive science as a particular kind of embodied action in the world, but it has been left to more recent phenomenologists to draw out these implications. In the end, there is at least the possibility of feeling the threat of climate change, but in a manner that is necessarily ambiguous and prone to distortion. Then again, it may be that the very ambiguity and uncertainty of our perception of climate change is itself reason to worry.

Flesh and Vulnerability

As a college student home on summer vacation, I took a job at a department store in the nearest mall. On occasions when I had to go to the upper stockroom, I would often take time to look down onto the sales floor through a two-way mirror that had been installed in an alcove that was enclosed by black curtains; the mirror was intended for use by the store's security personnel. For a few minutes, from that vantage point, I could see without being seen. It is a rare privilege for any organism to look out upon some part of the world with such detachment, and with such a sense of security, comfort, and even power.

Of course, this sense of security was as fragile as it was exceptional. If the truth be told, it was also largely illusory. It is true that, while I gazed down from the upper stockroom, people on the sales floor could not gaze back at me; even so, usually after only a few minutes, I would be overcome by the sense that I was myself being watched or approached from behind, and I would have to leave the alcove. I was never only a pair of eyes looking out through the glass. While I looked, there was still the curtain at my back, and behind it the stockroom; someone could have been sneaking up from behind with ill intent. For that matter, something else could have happened to me, alone in the stock room, and no one would have known or been able to help: a portion of the ceiling could have collapsed, a shelf laden with men's sportswear could have fallen over. Oddly enough, to be alone and unseen by others is also dangerous; in most circumstances, there is safety in numbers.

"Yes or no," asks Merleau-Ponty in *The Visible and the Invisible,* "do we have a body—that is not a permanent object of thought, but a flesh that suffers when it is wounded, hands that touch?" (VI 181–182/137). His own answer, of course, is a resounding "Yes!" but notice that the body is a flesh that suffers when it is wounded. It is only as flesh, as a sensible sentient, that I participate in the world, and yet it is through this very element of flesh that I am vulnerable to the slings and arrows that fly at me, from time to time, out of the depths of that same world. There is always the latent possibility of pain and suffering, of wounds, of sickness, and—at the farthest horizon—of death and dissolution, when this individual fold in the flesh of the world is smoothed out and rendered merely visible to other eyes.[1]

Short of death, there is no escape from this vulnerability of flesh. I can never rise above the world in order to look down on it with magisterial detachment from a perfectly secure viewpoint. Even behind a two-way mirror, in a locked room to which only I hold the key, I would still be a being of flesh in the midst of the world of flesh. I would either have to leave that room and go out into the midst of things, if only to eat, excrete, and take fresh air, or I would have to trust others to provide what I would need to go on living as I gazed through the glass. Even if all my fleshly needs were met within the locked room, and even if the room itself endured the unseen forces that would tear it open and expose me to the world, I would still be there within the visible and tangible walls of the room, and I would still be subject to my own tendency toward illness, age, and infirmity.

The purpose of such a room would be to minimize the dangers of being seen by other people. To be seen by another can be dangerous because I and the other both belong to the flesh of the world or, as Merleau-Ponty puts it, because the "anonymous visibility inhabits both of us." There is a synergy among different organisms, "their landscapes interweave, their actions and their passions fit together exactly" (VI 187/142). The other extends a hand to clasp mine: I touch and am touched by the hand of the other, and the other's hand touches and is touched by mine; I am both active and passive in relation to the other. There is no need to construe this synergy as harmony, however, as the same principle applies if the other throws a left hook at my right eye: my face feels the impact even as my face is felt by the fist of the other; as a sensible sentient I am both active and passive, even if as a passive agent I have been overwhelmed by the activity of the other and so begin to suffer. Through the fist of the other, the bone structure of my face becomes fully tangible to me, albeit in a blinding flash of pain, and I am likely to spend the next few days acutely aware of my own eye and of the occlusion of its vision. (I might, perhaps, take some grim satisfaction in the thought that the other may have split a knuckle.)

In many places in the contemporary world I can pass freely among others, fully exposed to them, and trust that they will not do me harm. Most of the time, I can count on others to come to my aid if some alien threat should present itself. I and my fellow citizens have even hired people to stand by, ready to come to our aid when any of us needs it. The deliberate impact of flesh against flesh remains a latent possibility, however, whether in the fists, feet, or teeth of the other, or in some implement that the other wields against me: a baseball bat, a knife, a handgun, an automobile, an airplane. That possibility may be more or less evident, closer or farther from becoming an actuality, depending on time, place and circumstance—and, of course, it is possible for me to misjudge a situation, to see a threat where none exists, or fail to see one that is racing toward me out of a clear blue sky.

But the possibility that the other can wield a tool against me, that there might be an intermediary between the other's active passivity and my passive activity, opens up another dimension of vulnerability: threats to my body are not all directed at me by other people. Rather, the latent possibility of suffering and death lies in my relation to the world as such, as the coiling over of flesh on flesh. Merleau-Ponty writes of the "fundamental narcissism of all vision" by which "I feel myself looked at by the things" (VI 183/139). I am both active and passive not only in relation to other people, but in relation to the visible as such. To see is "to be seen by the outside, to exist within it . . . so that the seer and the visible reciprocate one another and we no longer know which sees and which is seen" (VI 183/139). To acknowledge this narcissism of vision is not to fall into animism: the things of the world around me need not be themselves sentient for me to be visible and tangible before them. I see a brick wall, and I am at the same time made visible before the brick wall: it stands there in its brute facticity; I cannot walk through it, and it would hurt to try. I gaze down from a high balcony to a marble floor several hundred feet below, and in that moment of vertigo I am for myself a fragile being of bone and sinew and weight. A rusty nail, a broken window, a falling coconut, a flight of stairs, the water in a swimming pool, a bolt of lightning, a landslide—in seeing each of these things I am made more sharply aware of my own fleshly life and the ease with which I can be pierced, sliced, drowned, burned, and crushed.

In one sense, vulnerability is monolithic: it is the one overwhelming and inescapable fact of incarnate life. At the same time, vulnerability is a varied, multidimensional phenomenon of depths and hidden subtleties. Already, a rough taxonomy of threats suggests itself: a threat may be overt or covert, and its source may be sentient or nonsentient. To these dimensions I would add that a threat may be focused or dispersed. A face-to-face threat from a human or other sentient animal is overt and focused, as is the threat from poison ivy or a rusty nail. The tingling on the back of my neck as I walk through the woods at night, or the tingling in my limbs and belly when I swim in the ocean, suggest a covert threat from a focused, sentient source: a latter-day bandit in the woods, or a shark in the ocean. The *Salmonella* growing on a the rind of a melon together constitute a nonsentient variant of the covert, focused threat. The cloud of smog that triggers an asthma attack is overt but dispersed through the whole of the sensible. The widespread dispersal of persistent organic chemicals like polychlorinated biphenyls (PCBs), the depletion of stratospheric ozone, and human-induced climate change are dispersed but covert. What is odd about cases of pollution is that, even though they may find their origins in human activities, they act in our experience as nonsentient threats that rise up against us in their brute facticity, like a brick wall.

I would add two observations to this taxonomy, the first of which is that my sense of vulnerability need not arise exclusively from threats to my own body. Those I love are also vulnerable, which is a source of constant worry and occasional grief. Consider the worry of parents for their children. When she was two, the elder of my daughters contracted *Salmonella* from a contaminated cantaloupe—a covert threat from a nonsentient, focused source. At the time, we were unaware that cantaloupe could harbor *Salmonella*. The bacteria found their way into our daughter's bloodstream and, even though she made a full recovery, she did so only after five days in isolation at a hospital near our home, five days of dread and impatience punctuated by occasional trauma. Objectively speaking, only our daughter was in danger, only she was suffering. Nevertheless, her suffering was transitive, crossing over into her parents so that we suffered for and with her, the flesh of our flesh. This transitivity need not be limited to those we love, or even to those we know: even the suffering of strangers can find its echo in our own flesh.

The second observation is that perception of all of these threats requires at least a little knowledge. I know better than to walk into walls, or to balance on the rail of a high balcony, or (now, at least) to cut a cantaloupe without scrubbing it first. I am informed by my past experience, and by the spoken and written knowledge of humanity, a knowledge that itself rises from and resides in the flesh of the world. I also know that I do not know everything, that the world is large and complex, and that prediction is difficult: however much I know, there remains always the possibility of unpleasant surprises.

CLIMATE CHANGE AS A THEORETICAL THREAT

Our knowledge of many of the threats that confront us is due to the natural sciences. Without microscopes and germ theory, and without the equipment of modern medical laboratories, I would not have known that a microscopic organism growing on a melon had caused my daughter's illness even though I could see with my own eyes that she was ill. To this extent, the threat posed by *Salmonella* is theoretical, hidden in the invisible depths of the world.

Global climate change is a theoretical threat par excellence in that even its symptoms are hidden. If it were not for the various media by which scientific knowledge is conveyed to the public, I would have had no idea that the air I breathe now contains 31 percent more carbon dioxide than the air breathed by my eighteenth-century ancestors, and I would not have known that sea level has been rising steadily by about a millimeter a year. If it were not for the concerted efforts of scientists around the world, disparate events—an unusually warm winter here, a particularly strong hurricane there—would have remained disparate events, with no possibility of their adding up to a single environmental threat with a clear set of causes. At some later point, a change in the climate might become obvious, like a fever in a young child, but that we know what might be happening before that point seems to be a remarkable achievement on the part of the natural sciences.

Then again, this is precisely the problem I started with: How does theoretical knowledge play itself out in my experience? Is it possible for me to feel in my bones a threat as abstract and diffuse as global climate change?

Before I can address these questions, I need to make a further distinction within the taxonomy of dangerous things: not all covert threats are so in the same sense. Some covert threats are simply hidden, like a concealed handgun. I can discover the handgun by acting in the world, moving in a particular way in relation to the other—patting down the pockets of the other's coat, for example. The end result of this activity could well be that I can see and feel the handgun itself. Global climate change is a covert threat in a somewhat different sense. The discovery of elevated levels of carbon dioxide requires activity of a different order and, even if I claim to have discovered it, I still will not actually see, or feel, or even smell the carbon dioxide. It is as though some threats are covert in practice, while others are covert in principle. Perhaps it would be better to say that some covert threats are potentially visible, while others are invisible by their very nature.

Now, the necessity of theoretical knowledge seems to lie in the fact that the threat of global climate change is a threat that is invisible by its nature, but that is also dispersed along two different dimensions.

First, the effects of climate change are dispersed in time. Climate is not weather: I cannot look out the window and tell you what the climate is. Rather, climate can only be perceived, if at all, over a long period of time as that which binds together the weather in a given place, or over the surface of the Earth as a whole; it might be described as the cyclical style or mood of the weather, or as the habitual relation of weather to the seasons. If there is a permanent change in the climate, then it will be visible to us, if at all, as a kind of background radiation that pervades the whole of the visible. The effects of a change in global climate would be more directly perceptible, but they would be scattered through an array of events—a flood, a dry spell, a storm—that are not connected together in a way that is obvious on the face of things. If I am content simply to observe the weather, I might eventually come to grasp that the mood of things has changed, but perhaps only vaguely, and perhaps with a sense that the mood might yet change back. To connect such events together in a systematic way, and to grasp that the change in climate is accelerating and irreversible, requires something more than unaided perception.

Much the same can be said of the physical and chemical causes of climate change, the second dimension along which the threat is dispersed. Here the difficulty is to relate human activities that are not otherwise connected, from flipping on a light switch to raising cattle.[2] The challenge of grasping the threat theoretically, then, is to connect together my actions now with diverse and often subtle changes in observable weather patterns years or even decades from now. The connection between them passes out of sight, into the depths of the world. In effect, climate researchers claim to peer into the invisible depths of the world, to espy the hidden order of real objects that explains the shifting and apparently disconnected fragments of our lived experience.

There is often a presumption that in order to peer into the depths scientists must make a radical break with ordinary experience and so enter into a world of mathematical abstraction. This objective realm is supposed to open up to us when we filter out all of the vagaries and idiosyncrasies of any merely individual perspective. In the objectivist account of the natural sciences, this process of filtration is portrayed as a purely intellectual exercise, designed to detach the scientist from the details of ordinary life, to make the scientist into an approximation of a pure, disembodied subject hovering over and attempting to master the realm of pure objects purportedly revealed by the precise algorithms of theory.

The problem with the objectivist account is precisely that this disembodiment can never be complete. The retreat to objectivism is the equivalent of locking oneself in a room with a two-way mirror: the objectivist pretends to gaze out at the world with magisterial detachment, but remains nonetheless a creature of flesh in a world of flesh. In one of his working notes for *The Visible and the Invisible,* Merleau-Ponty reminds himself to "justify science as an operation within the given situation of knowledge," and to "characterize the scientific treatment of being, time, evolution, and so on, as a locating of 'features' of the Universe or of 'features' of Beings, a systematic explanation of what they imply in the virtue of their role as *hinges.*" Scientists are participants in the flesh of the world, even if they do have highly specialized ways of speaking and acting in the world. It is only as participants that they can make any headway in revealing the structures of the world, its hinges or "*pivots,*" as Merleau-Ponty also calls them, "certain traits of the inner framework of the world" (VI 279/225).

Scientists participate in the world and engage in specialized forms of activity within it, but these activities are always mediated by tools of various kinds. In taking up the question of whether phenomenologists could detect a "greenhouse effect," Don Ihde has faulted Husserl for falling into precisely the same "theory-weighted" interpretation of science as that adopted by the logical positivists, an interpretation that assumes a radical break between the mathematized abstractions of theory and the details of experience. "Of course science requires measurement, quantification, and the processes of analysis that occur in mathematization," writes Ihde, "but it equally requires a material relation with the 'things themselves' and this occurs in actually embodied science. That embodiment is the technological extension of primary perception through instrumentation." From this interpretation of scientific research, which he has dubbed "technoscience," Ihde concludes that "CFCs, CO2 [*sic.*], and Ozone are not pure shapes, but are instrumentally presentable, material entities through science's increasingly sophisticated technological embodiments" (Ihde 1997, 129).

So, scientists interact with one another and with their instruments as they develop and test models of the invisible world that underpins the visible; as a consequence, even though it is still the case that none of us can *see* carbon dioxide, scientists can detect its presence, measure its prevalence, and trace the trends of its accumulation. In principle then, there should be little trouble perceiving the theoretical threat of global climate change, as long as we have access to the appropriate instruments, and as long as we have an effective model for interpreting the data those instruments produce.

In practice, matters are not so clear. The winter of 2001-2002 was unusually warm for much of the United States. I was living in mid-Michigan at the time, where sixty-degree weather in January was met with equal measures of disbelief, discomfiture, and delight. Even with the growing technical sophistication of climate research, the experience of strange weather remains fundamentally ambiguous: Was it just a pleasant anomaly, a fine contrast with the harsh winter of the year before, or was it the first inkling of an environmental catastrophe?

This ambiguity itself has several distinct sources. First, however sophisticated scientists become at plumbing the depths of the world, the natural sciences will always be overshadowed by uncertainty. A scientific theory is always only a partial glimpse of what the hidden armature of the visible world might be, subject always to dispute and sudden reversals. Even if there is a broad consensus among scientists concerning the outlines of a theory, there might still be credible grounds for disagreement over the finer points of the theory and over the predictions that are to be derived from it. In practical terms this means that however many scientists think it is highly likely that a human-induced change in the climate is looming, no scientist can say so with absolute certainty. Then again, no scientist can say with absolute certainty that such a change is *not* looming. Even if climate change is widely regarded as likely, there is bound to be disagreement over the degree and consequences of that change. It is difficult enough to agree on a five-day weather forecast when the climate is presumed to be stable.

A second source of ambiguity lies in the relation between scientists and the public. Both the causes and effects of climate change are dispersed, the connections between them hidden in the invisible depths of the world; the path from a particular cause to a particular effect is tortuous. Consider a hot and rainless summer day on the east coast of the United States. What does it take to see, and feel in my bones, that this rainless day is part of a prolonged drought, and that this drought is the result of a shift in the global climate, and that this shift in global climate has been brought about by an increase in the concentrations of carbon dioxide and other gases in the atmosphere, and that this increase in concentration has been brought about by human activities, including my use of an air conditioner to remain comfortable on a hot and rainless summer day? Put simply, to see all of these connections, I would need to know what I was looking for, which would require a good deal of theoretical and technological sophistication. Even if I had such sophistication, the ramifications of the resulting knowledge would boggle the imagination.

The natural sciences are highly specialized forms of activity, which means that it takes well-trained specialists to practice them well. Few non-scientists have the time or the resources available to actively engage the details of scientific findings and so, for most people, the perception of climate change becomes a matter of communication and trust. Even if scientists all agreed that projections of climate change were highly probable, their message can all too easily be lost or garbled in transmission to the public, sometimes through deliberate distortion. Even if the message came across clearly and without distortion, the public still might not know how to see what the scientists are talking about. For many, global climate change remains an abstraction, "only a theory," with no obvious relation to their own lives in the world.

A third source of ambiguity lies in the problem of perspective: that which is closest to us seems to be the most important. For my own part, I like to think that I have a pretty good grasp of the theory behind projections of global climate change, and from time to time I am acutely aware of the connections between cause and effect. On my way to work one day in March 2002, when I was still living in Michigan, I was stopped at a railroad crossing by a mile-long train of coal hoppers on its way to the power plant I could see from the backyard of my house in Lansing. As the train sped by, I imagined the coal being ripped from some mountainside in Kentucky or West Virginia and loaded onto the train for Michigan; I imagined the power plant pumping carbon dioxide into the air over the city; I pondered the unusually warm winter weather. And yet, there I was, idling my car at the railroad crossing, on my way from one computer to another, nourished by food that was preserved and prepared using power from that same coal-fired plant. Global climate change remains a covert threat, lurking over some far horizon; there are always more immediate, visible, and tangible concerns that get in the way. For many people on this planet, the theoretical threats trumpeted by scientists from the developed world are entirely obscured by the ever-present threats of starvation, disease, and warfare. Even those of us with comfortable and relatively secure lives are subject to the attenuating effects of perspective: seen from the here and now, the risk of global climate change can be much less urgent than the risk of being stranded in the suburbs without a car.

A fourth source of ambiguity concerns the question of whether a change in the climate really constitutes a threat. This is a matter of evaluation, and someone could argue that climate change is neither good nor bad in itself. Rather, the argument might go, it is actually little more than the hidden causal process behind a developing syndrome, and that even the individual symptoms that make up that syndrome do not necessarily constitute a threat. On this basis, we might even conclude that we are in for nothing more than a change in the weather, and we might then acknowledge that, in some times and places, the change might be for the better.[3] This argument has some merit: it would be a mistake to assume that climate change is bad simply because it is a change. Nevertheless, the argument ignores the sense in which the very possibility of a fundamental and irreversible change across such a vast scale of time and space is threatening to us, especially when the consequences of such a change cannot be predicted with anything like a high degree of accuracy.

But this suggests an important shift in this account of the ambiguity of climate change. What we make of ambiguity is also a matter involving value judgments, and many have opted to use ambiguity as a basis for denial: if we cannot prove that climate change is a real threat, then we may safely ignore it. This is not the only possibility, however, as ambiguity itself might be perceived as a threat. Consider that, as organisms who participate in a world of flesh, we depend on our familiarity with the world. To grow food, to develop our communities, we rely on relatively steady and predictable cycles of warmth and cold, sun and rain. We never quite get what we need, since no year is ever really "normal," but the fluctuations generally stay within a certain predictable range, and modern humans have never before faced the possibility of a dramatic, unidirectional shift in the range of fluctuation itself. Perhaps even the mere possibility of climate change menaces us precisely because it forces us to be aware of our dependence on the climate even as it calls the future of that dependence into question.

We must choose and act on the basis of what we know, but what we know serves chiefly as a frame for all that we do not know—and what we do not know can easily destroy us. In the end, if we are paying attention, acknowledging the ambiguity and uncertainty of our impact on global climate may serve to bring us more sharply up against our vulnerability in its most general sense, as an irreducible aspect of our lives in the world. In short, we should be concerned about global climate change because we are mortal, because our vision and our capacity for action are limited, because all that we value can be broken or lost. If we practice the humility appropriate to our predicament then a little knowledge of dangerous things may well serve to transform our experience of daily life: even if many of the connections between cause and effect remain obscure to us, we may no longer be able to go about our lives with casual thoughtlessness—drinking coffee, turning on the lights, driving to the multiplex, or flying to conferences—as though our every action were a matter of right.

Epilogue

Merleau-Ponty's ontology of flesh is one of many possible points of entry to the investigation of human vulnerability. This first essay weaves together some of the threads of a phenomenology of environmental change, especially the primordial perception of vulnerability and the relation of the natural sciences to perception. A number of loose threads remain, however, a few of which I would like at least to mention here.

First, there is a great deal more to be said about the perception of threats to other people, especially to people who are themselves invisible to us. The basic observation here is that at the core of nearly every environmental problem lie matters of justice. For example, those who contribute the most to increasing concentrations of greenhouse gases are not the ones most vulnerable to the likely consequences of climate change. Working Group II of the IPCC notes that "the ability of human systems to adapt to and cope with climate change depends on such factors as wealth, technology, education, information, skills, infrastructure, access to resources, and management capabilities." As a consequence, developed countries could adapt to a changing climate, while the least developed countries "have lesser capacity to adapt and are more vulnerable to climate change damages, just as they are more vulnerable to other stresses" (IPCC 2001a, 8). The indifference of people in the developed world toward the potential consequences of climate change, then, might hinge in part on a tendency to regard people we cannot see as mere abstractions. The oft-cited fact that more than one billion people do not have access to safe drinking water does not do justice to the suffering of any of the individuals lumped together in that statistic.

But on what grounds could we establish our solidarity with others—not with the poor, or with humanity, or with any other abstraction, but with myriad individual others who suffer when they are wounded? The

possibility that I might experience the suffering of others, if only vicari-
ously, may be grounded in what Merleau-Ponty calls intercorporeity:

> this circle which I do not form, which forms me, this coiling over
> of the visible upon the visible, can traverse, animate, other bodies
> as well as my own. And if I was able to understand how this wave
> arises within me, how the visible which is yonder is simultane-
> ously my landscape, I can understand a fortiori that elsewhere it
> also closes over upon itself and that there are other landscapes
> besides my own. (VI 185/140–141)

But what of others I have not yet met, others who do not live "yonder,"
just over there, but live on the other side of the world in landscapes I have
never seen? It would be helpful to have some account of what might be
called "remote intercorporeity," perhaps in terms of the contiguity and
overlapping of landscapes.

Second, there is also more to be said about the misperception of
threats that would lead us either to underestimate or overestimate their
importance. Even the most extreme forms of misperception are common
in human experience. On the one hand, we are often blithely unaware of
even the most lethal threats, and most of us learn at some point that what
we do not know *can* hurt us. On the other hand, we sometimes panic
over threats that do not exist, imaginary threats based, often enough, on
nothing more than superstition and stereotype. Merleau-Ponty notes
that, in the philosophy of reflection, the possibility of such illusions is
taken to indicate a break between the real and the imaginary: the real is
real because it is coherent, and illusion is such because it is incoherent.
In response, Merleau-Ponty insists that matters are not so simple: "when
an illusion dissipates, when an appearance suddenly breaks up, it is
always for the profit of a new appearance which takes up again for its
own account the ontological function of the first . . . The dis-illusion is
the loss of one evidence only because it is the acquisition of *another evidence*." One reality breaks up only to give way to another reality, a
process through which, in Merleau-Ponty's words, "we learn to know the
fragility of the 'real'" (VI 63/41). These considerations are helpful, but it
would also be helpful to have some account of how and why we often
resist dis-illusion: we still need a phenomenology of denial as well as a
phenomenology of paranoia, and perhaps even a phenomenology of the
apocalypse.

Third, the phenomenology of denial opens up the entire domain of the unconscious and the irrational in human thought and behavior. Could it be that the secret inner structure of my own perceiving body systematically distorts perception for some purpose of its own? This goes well beyond the bounds of phenomenology as traditionally conceived, but at some point, something must be said of the evolutionary history of these bodies that we are, fashioned by the hidden armature of natural selection, motivated perhaps by the self-centered drive to survive, to reproduce, and to accumulate power.

Fourth, this darker side of human motivation feeds into the realm of politics, in the pejorative sense of the term. Here, the key observation is that many of the distortions that have been introduced into debates over environmental change are politically motivated. For those with vested interests in the status quo, widespread acknowledgment of the threat of climate change is itself a threat, since it could lead to a change in the political and economic climate that has served them so well. To prevent such a change, defenders of the status quo must strike at the weakest link in the chain: public trust in the apparatus of modern science. All it takes is to portray scientists and environmentalists as the enemies of prosperity and liberty. Of course, there are also those who, perhaps because they have a vested interest in overturning the status quo, exaggerate the severity of the threat in order to galvanize the public. There may be any number of possibilities in between but, because scientific research is a social enterprise that takes place in social and political contexts, no scientist can be wholly neutral on the political questions raised by climate research.

Notes

1. When a living hand touches a dead hand, both participate in flesh because they are both perceptible; "the difference between them is that one is entirely and only perceptible; the other, because it is still able to perceive, is not" (Cataldi 2000, 192).

2. Both activities are connected to the production of greenhouse gases. Electricity is most often produced by burning fossil fuels, which releases CO_2 and other gases connected with warming. Aside from the use of fossil fuel in agriculture generally, cattle are ruminants and so produce methane as a byproduct of digestion; methane is greenhouse gas.

3. Working Group II of the IPCC notes a number of possible benefits of climate change, including increased crop yields in some midlatitude regions, "reduced winter mortality in mid- and high-latitudes," and "reduced energy demand for space heating due to higher winter temperatures" (IPCC 2002a, 6).

REFERENCES

Cataldi, Suzanne Laba. 2000. "Embodying Perceptions of Death: Emotional Apprehension and Reversibilities of Flesh." In Fred Evans and Leonard Lawlor, eds., *Chiasms: Merleau-Ponty's Notion of Flesh.* Albany: SUNY Press, pp. 189–202.

Ihde, Don. 1997. "Whole Earth Measurements: How Many Phenomenologists Does It Take to Detect a 'Greenhouse Effect'?" *Philosophy Today* 41 (Spring), 128–134.

IPCC. 2001a. "Climate Change 2001: Impacts, Adaptation, and Vulnerability. (Summary for Policymakers)." Geneva, Switzerland: Intergovernmental Panel on Climate Change.

IPCC. 2001b. "Climate Change 2001: The Scientific Basis (Summary for Policymakers)." Geneva, Switzerland: Intergovernmental Panel on Climate Change.

2

An Inquiry into the Intercorporeal Relations Between Humans and the Earth

Kenneth Liberman

By prong I have entered these hills:
That the grass grow from my body,
That I hear the roots speaking together . . .
It is not man made world
Or made order or made grace.
Learn of the green world
What can be thy place.

—Ezra Pound

OUTLINE OF THE PROBLEM

In North America much has been made of "the wilderness experience." Popularized by the Sierra Club, Friends of the Earth, Outward Bound, and other outdoor organizations, a national yearning for primitive experience with nature has become part of American mythology. Even those citizens who remained at home were deeply touched by Sierra Club Books that convincingly proclaimed, "In wildness is the preservation of the world." Although it was presumed that these environmental groups had tapped into some fundamental and universal principle, in fact "the wilderness experience" they celebrated was deeply indebted to the cultural imagination of the western United States, which contain wild lands vast enough, and unthreatening enough (contrast the impenetrable jungles of the Amazon, southern New Zealand, etc.) to foster a benevolent encounter with the wild. The prophets of this phenomenal cult of serious campers—John Muir, Jack London, David Brower, Gary Snyder, and so on—all lived in the American West.[1]

The earth brought to you by the Sierra Club, for instance,[2] is a highly ordered, bureaucratized location filled with rules and regulations for proper wilderness orientation and etiquette. The wilderness experience we so richly appreciate is in large part cultural participation, and the intimate experience they/we are having is with our own abstractions. Earth First! offers a postmodern version of this along with a cogent critique of the anthropocentrism of the aforementioned environmental groups, but they too are replete with ethical sentiments that owe as much to the Puritans as they do to the earth, and there is no pure "natural" no matter how happy it makes them to think so. In brief, there is no unmediated encounter with nature. We know this already from Hugh Silverman, who has dismissed the notion that we can refer to an independent "nature" that stands with its own essence, apart from all cultural and conceptual practices; in a significant address, Silverman asserted, "There is no nature!"[3] Michael Zimmerman made essentially the same point at the inaugural meeting of the International Association for Environmental Philosophy when he argued, "Humans cannot discover values that inhere essentially in natural phenomena,"[4] even though there is some tendency for us to do so. Steven Vogel has offered a cogent, sustained critique of the excesses of the ideology of environmental activists in his important study, *Against* Nature. These critics suggest that the terms *nature* and *wilderness* themselves are so invested with human dualism that they could never serve as an independent source of valuation.

These criticisms constitute a controversial but serious challenge to the efforts of ecophenomenologists to describe honestly the ways that a wild, uncontrolled earth intrudes upon and interrupts our being and experience, no matter how it is culturally or philosophically formed. These ecophenomenologists respond to these astute critics with an enormous "Yes. But . . ." This "But" gains its vigor from the immediate prephilosophical experience of these ecophenomenologists with the earth. They pose the question, In addition to and beyond the cultural interpretation and linguistic regimes, is there something more out there? Ted Toadvine argues that there is and that we need to interrogate it: "The backside of nature that we have not thematized should be the principal subject matter of phenomenology."[5] More particularly, Glen Mazis argues that there is "an intercorporeity with the world that is itself a pleasure and a kind of longing for a place among the circulation of other things" (2000, 243), that is, wanting to "learn of the green world" is more than romantic sentiment and touches something basic to human existence. My thesis in this reflection is that there is an intercorporeality with the earth, that it *precedes* value, and even that it is in some way originary; and so I wish to interrogate this "enigma of the brute world" (VI 156) and explore what definiteness can be added to its description, in the hope that Liberman can somehow trump Silverman and Zimmerman's skepticism, because their skepticism is necessary but not sufficient. I want to think of our wild-ness in the light of the later Merleau-Ponty's revaluation of ontology, while retaining some of the discipline of postmodern criticism. But this deepening interrogation of our intercorporeal relations with the earth must proceed, even though in Merleau-Ponty's words (VI 39) we are not at all certain that such an interrogation is really possible:

> [*Sur-réflection*] must question the world, it must enter into the forest of references that our interrogation arouses in it, it must make it say, finally, what in its silence *it means to say*. . . . We know neither what exactly is this order and this concordance of the world to which we thus entrust ourselves, nor therefore what the enterprise will result in, nor even if it is really possible.[6]

Merleau-Ponty's doubt here is humbling, but our task here is such that we can put that humility to good use.

Can there be a direct and unmediated experience of brute being? Merleau-Ponty himself tells us, "There is a fundamental narcissism of all vision" (VI 139). Certainly, there is not any unmediated experience for reflection, but for our bodies? To the body and its perception, I believe the answer can be yes—for instance, is experiencing an earthquake, or a sunrise, primarily a cultural or linguistic experience? Merleau-Ponty has emphasized, "The world is not what I think, but what I live through" (PhP xviii), and he suggests that it is part of the job description of phenomenologists to investigate such experience: "All its efforts are concentrated upon re-achieving a direct and primitive contact with the world" (PhP vii). So, what is this "wilderness experience?" Why do people seek primitive contact with the earth? And *how* do they seek it?

THE "OBJECT" OF OUR INVESTIGATION

It is commonly said that phenomenologists investigate immanent experience, but we are not solipsists as is evidenced by our frequent cry, "To the things themselves" (PhP viii). What things are these? Although we have learned that everything cultural is derivative, Merleau-Ponty refers to a brute contact with things that have a "primordial nature." In one of his most fecund comments (and one which threatens to erase constitutional phenomenology), Merleau-Ponty insists, "Primordial nature is non-constructed, non-instituted . . . Nature is what has a sense without this sense being posited by thought" (1988, 19–20). One does not fathom this sense by means of conceptual understanding. Yet this brute contact with the earth is not nothing! Rather, it is something that makes itself felt, which means that the agency belongs to both the earth and to ourselves.

Merleau-Ponty criticizes Descartes and Kant for their overreliance on categories of understanding (1988,133–134), and he insists on a notion of a "primordial being which is not yet subject-being and not yet object-being and which in every respect baffles reflection" (ibid.). The "things" he wishes to pursue are not of the "sphere of 'pure things'" (ibid., 147), and they are not to be thought of as an in-itself. They are not a "flattened out" or "derivative objectivity" (S 110): "To posit the theoretical world to which 'pure things' become primary, is an extreme form of idealism" (Merleau-Ponty 1988, 148). His sense of phenomenological rigor clings closely to the immanent experience of "the wild Being behind the cleavage of our acquired culture" (VI 121). I am reminded of the group of traditionally oriented Aboriginal people I lived with for two years and who displayed a cynical resistance to (or lack of respect for, depending on your viewpoint) any mathematization of nature. They enjoyed ridiculing my calculations of the distances in kilometers of a number of Aboriginal sacred sites we visited. They considered absurd the confidence in my voice regarding having something objective in hand about the truth of those sites. They mused, "Oh, and how about the moon—it must be one hundred million, billion of them, mm?" As they spoke, they cackled together at what they saw as the arrogant ignorance of European praxis.[7]

Merleau-Ponty insists that there is something deeper than these limited objectivist projections and also that there is a unique sense to brute nature that can be interrogated (Mazis 2000, 224). In "Philosophy and Interrogation," Merleau-Ponty writes, "Through having 'forgotten' the flux of the natural and historical world, having reduced it to the constructions of the objectivity of the natural sciences, reason and philosophy have become incapable of understanding and so of mastering humanity's historical fate" (1988, 176–177). It is the task of phenomenological reflections, first, to teach us that the supposed "thing" in-itself is a cultural artifact, and second, to assist us in gaining that more "direct and primitive contact with the world." During his career, Merleau-Ponty never wavered from this project, and in his "Working Notes" (VI 168) he described his undertaking as "philosophy as radical reflection, as reduction to transcendental immanence." This reduction aims at giving us some access to what our consciousness does not yet know about things, so it is not a mere rehearsal of knowns. "We are interrogating our experience precisely in order to know how it opens us to what is not ourselves" (VI 159). We are inquiring into our experience with the brute earth, our own silent encounter with "brute being as revealed to us in our perceptual contact with the world" (Merleau-Ponty 1988, 166).

Nature as Event

Our inquiry, then, does not consist of changing things into their meaning (VI 108) but demands a different mode of access to things. *We begin not with thoughts but with our body's engagements with the earth*—with intercorporeal activities. "Nature as an event or an ensemble of events remains different from nature as object" (Merleau-Ponty 1988, 138). It is not really a single event because there is no unity-in-itself in the way an essence is considered to have, but there is an interconnectedness. We are told that there is "a brute unity through which the universe 'holds'" (ibid., 142). Bruce Wilshire[8] speaks frequently of a "primal coherence," with which we as bodies are *already* integrated. The coherence exists not primarily for an intellect but as "the corporeal 'preconstitution' which sustains things" (Merleau-Ponty 1988, 149). It is the body's knowing: "Now we must think of the human body (and not 'consciousness') as that which perceives nature" (ibid., 149). And the body's knowing occurs in the form of the "I can" (VI 38). The environment is revealed in terms of the possibilities of the body's "I can"; however, the agency here is not exclusively the human, it equally belongs to the earth. The landscape tells me where my legs can carry me, what is too far or too high. A breeze, or lack of breeze, collects me. It is "subjectivity as *movement*" (Toadvine 2000, 112). The earth's body engages my body, and my space is molded, which is to say that the truth of my world is presented to me, and such "things . . . are revealing as much as they are revealed" (Mazis 2000, 242). This is why Merleau-Ponty is able to say, "I feel myself looked at by things" (VI 139).

The intercorporeal situation we are describing, "when things situated around a body assert a direct power over it" (Olkowski 2000, 191), involves a being-done-to more than a doing. Perhaps this is part of the "reversibility"—we find ourselves as objects for an earth that has agency of its own. This engagement with the earth exceeds the idea of "conserving nature" or the English notion of nature preserves that also underlies the American conservation movement, for in those affairs the agency remains exclusively human, and so there is no revealing. It is not that an all-powerful mankind permits a few rhesus monkeys or leopards to subsist in some jungle "reserve" somewhere. That is a sentiment that retains solidarity with colonialism. Rather, there is a reversibility whereby the leopards chase us out or eat us, and we do not belong there. Nor is it best revealed in the sedate landscape of the French countryside, where there is nothing more to contend with than the domesticated cow. Happily, the wildness that can humble our arrogant ignorance is heartily available in the western United States' remaining untamed forests and deserts, and so it is not surprising that some contribution to the philosophy of ecology has been forthcoming from those quarters.

Why do we require such a thing as "the wilderness experience?" It is to mitigate the totalization instituted by our own culture, to free ourselves so that we make visible our full being, a being that is fathomed not by appropriating the earth but by being appropriated by it. And people *solicit* this transcendence of culture—we want to feel "penetrated" (OE 167) by something more primordial than our culture and ego. Merleau-Ponty (PhP xi) writes, "There is no inner man, man is in the world, and only in the world does he know himself." The deepest sort of knowing is summoned by this anonymity, which subsists not as knowledge but as events. Climbers climb not to conquer mountains but to have the rocks speak to them. Why do backpackers hike, and how far must they keep traveling? They need to abide with the landscape until they recollect that their culture and ego do not matter so much in the face of all these reciprocal relatings. It is not the human agency that is critical here—no one conquers anything—it is the relinquishment of human agency that is everything. This is how humans "comprehend our own obscurity" (VI 39), the principal legacy of the wilderness experience.

Engaging the Earth

Henri Bergson is cited by Merleau-Ponty, who is cited by Toadvine (2000, 107): "Instead of trying to rise above our perception of things [we] plunge into it for the purpose of deepening and widening it." This notion of *plunging* is picked up by Merleau-Ponty (VI 38–39) as a method for engaging things:

> We are catching sight of the necessity of another operation besides conversion to reflection, more fundamental than it, of a sort of *sur-réflection* [that] would not lose sight of the brute thing and the brute perception and would not finally efface them, would not cut the organic bonds . . . [of] our mute contact with the world when they are not yet things said. . . . It must plunge into the world instead of surveying it.

What is the methodology for this plunging? The earth draws us out of ourselves not just to explore the terrain in order to dominate it but to learn from our contact with it, and from the resistance it offers us, what is the meaning of our world. The friction (Kaput 2000, 169) produced by this contact is the site of our education, and we solicit such friction in order to know ourselves. Our orientation at such moments is best described as circumspective, and our gaze is an *Umsicht:* "Things attract my look, my gaze caresses things, it espouses their contours" (VI 76). In a footnote, Macquarrie and Robinson (Heidegger 1962, 98) define *Umsicht* as "looking around for a way to get something done," and Heidegger describes it as "a way of discovering what is ready-to-hand" (ibid., 159), a sort of praxis whereby the present-at-hand is retransformed into a ready-to-hand. But the sight being spoken of is not merely that of the eyes but is also of our skin and muscles. Our skin leaps out of itself to seek this contact with the flesh of the earth, and the world's flesh comes to include my body. Our work is to "interrogate it according to its own wishes" (VI 133). It is a pleasantly intense bodily interrogation, pleasant because it is the work of being human and a way to belong.

Jack London has written eloquently of how trappers and miners in the Yukon and Alaska engaged in intercorporeal contact with the cold. The risk of freezing compelled them to witness with extraordinary clarity every component of carefully organizing their survival—layering their clothes, keeping matches dry, and building fires. The men do not merely engage the earth, the earth is engaging them; they merely offer up "the resonance" that is required (VI 101). In the always wet Pacific Northwest finding dry firewood can become an obsession, and one incorporates every tool that is at hand—a yellow moss that will burn even when it is wet, knots that may be pulled out of dry-rotted, fungi drenched fallen trees, knots whose memory bears the solidified pitch that will still burn fiercely. This fire of knots provokes a further circumspective search amidst the incessant, soaking rain: our skin leaps out across the landscape and the search for knots becomes a primordial exercise. We hunt for dozens of knots to keep the family warm and safe, while the rest of the damp tree-mass on the forest floor, useless for warmth, recedes from our gaze. These things "call upon the body to become more completely the grip it has on them" (Evans 2000, 66). Our pursuit becomes a fever, and apart from an occasional intervention not at all conceptual. The relationship with the earth is intercorporeal. What is it about this intercorporeality that is so satisfying?

Merleau-Ponty queries, "We have to ask ourselves what exactly we have found with this strange adhesion of the seer and the visible?" (VI 138–139). One cannot say whether we or the landscape is in command (VI 133). We have found, "rediscovered" (VI 95), Merleau-Ponty tells us, "the being that lies before the cleavage operated by reflection, on its horizon, not outside of us and not in us, but where the two movements cross." More precisely, it not just that we have found our incarnate being, we have *lost* our obsessive selves. In place of a collection of highly refined synthetic artifacts of self-identity, we inherit an incarnate being that is more truly our real home. Merleau-Ponty names this incarnate being "flesh" (VI 140), and it is for him an ultimate notion. It is not to be known in the way that most notions are to be known. It is to be lived. And this is why environmentalists are at such a disadvantage when they try to engage in a political dialogue about the environment, for in that dialogue only what is known and available to objectivity and representedness (Heidegger 1962) is given status. As Merleau-Ponty (1988, 140) explains so astutely, "The philosophy of human representation is not false, it is superficial." Yes, the most real being of the earth is hardly more than "a phantom," although it is there nevertheless, but it is always unavailable to those engaged exclusively in dominating nature. "Flesh" is active only when we are seen as well as see, for flesh only acts in, and as, our reciprocal relations with the earth:

> I feel myself looked at by the things, my activity is equally passivity
> . . . not to see in the outside, as the others see it, the contour of a
> body one inhabits, but especially to be seen by the outside, to
> exist within it, to emigrate into it, to be seduced, captivated,
> alienated by the phantom, so that the seer and the visible recipro-
> cate one another and we no longer know which sees and which is

seen. It is this Visibility, this generality of the Sensible in itself, this anonymity innate to Myself that we have previously called flesh. (VI 139)

Merleau-Ponty is calling us to "emigrate" out of our narrow conjuring acts and, even at the risk of feeling "alienated," engage in reciprocal relations, so that we can come to collect the "anonymity" that is our heritage. Merleau-Ponty is speaking in solidarity with sentiments he expressed early in his career: "It is impossible to say that nature ends here and that man . . . starts here" (PRI 67).

I spent more than a decade leading "wilderness" backpacks, during which I provided an intimate introduction to the earth for more than 1,000 clients. I preferred week-long treks, and it was my policy never to run a trip under three days, for it takes that long for the temporality of a natural habitat to penetrate the urban temporalities that my clients would bring with them. Also, in the view of some of them I was a tyrant regarding the use of Walkmans and radios. I had to silence their notions in order to convey them to their flesh. But is it mere romantic projection to speak of a natural temporality? Surely, "time is . . . *my* relation to things" (PhP 412), and there is no basis for privileging any temporality, indigenous or otherwise, or for validating a notion of temporality that has an existence apart from me.[9]

But Mazis (2000, 161) suggests something different in his summary of Merleau-Ponty's reflections (at 1995, 161): "There is also a time inherent in nature, not imposed on it, which is inherent in things as unfolding processes, which also embraces us in our openness to the participation in the unfolding of things." There is an unfolding in the timorous way a patch of desert gentian occupies a high ridge, and a natural temporality that develops from our engagement with that place, a temporality we do not create but receive. Yet it is possible to prepare ourselves for receiving it, and we can find ways to be "woven into the further unfolding of the field" (Mazis 2000, 233). We desire to be woven into a fabric that pre-exists us but also includes us.

ECOLOGICAL RECOVERY

Each human finds her/himself caught up "proximally and for the most part" (Heidegger 1962, 180) with the totalization that "language, custom, ego and personal advantage strategies" (Synder 1980, 172) have presented to her/him. How do we shake ourselves out of this "gaze directed upon an experience reduced to its signification" (VI 120)?[10] One excellent method is to become lost, which presents one with an opportunity to regain one's bearings by recommencing from the flesh of the earth. Thomas Mann describes an occasion in *The Magic Mountain,* when Hans Castorp, fully fed up with the limited social reality of his fellow residents at the Alpine sanitarium, heads off on skis into "The Snow." Castorp solicits the landscape and gaily skies through a blizzard during white-out conditions. Thoroughly lost at last, he finds his self in its anonymous being and gains the clarity for which he has sought so long. He narrowly escapes death, finds an abandoned cabin, waits out the storm, and at dusk (when the storm clears) he finds his way on skis back to the sanitarium, where he is provided with a small late meal. As he stares into his plate, he reflects that what was so clear to him just moments before was already slipping away. The phantomlike truth of his nature is more real than it is tangible.

What methods are there for reweaving our flesh with increased input from the brute being of the earth? Low (2000, 52) recommends decentering our perceptual fields. How do we speak about this without romanticism but also without any of that arrogant objectivism, which is really just a perverted idealism, that is so prevalent among our intelligentsia? As an illustration, I grew up with a Los Angeles River that was cemented for virtually its entire course, just another concrete byway in the semiotics of southern California's cement-scape. Postmodern semioticians may well find no grounds for privileging one concretion over another; however, the earth's natural unfolding will rear up and assert itself in the flooding that will one day come hurling down the mountains surrounding the LA basin. I remember returning to Los Angeles after my first month-long Outward Bound trip. My new landscape praxis drew me to the top of whatever was there, in this case Griffith Park not far from the "Hollywood" sign and close to where I was born, and my mouth dropped open in the blazing evidence of what was there. For the first time in my life, my gaze revealed that the Los Angeles River was where the water naturally flowed in the gravity that ran from Mt. Wilson to the sea, and that Los Angeles itself was built alongside the river, instead of the river being added to LA after its establishment, as if it was just another Wilshire Boulevard, which it does indeed resemble. I had regained some reciprocal intercorporeality with my homeland. (My Aboriginal friends once asked me what my "home" water was, and on the basis of this experience I was able to reply to them.) Yes, the LA River really is *more fundamental* to earth-dwelling beings than are its malls and concrete boulevards, although its citizens hardly suspect it.

Contemporary urbanites fear brute nature, in part because nature is indeed to be feared but also because people are living where they were not born and have never actually dwelled. The prisoners who are brought to the hillsides to remove the "weeds" growing in the LA basin can hardly distinguish what belongs there from what does not, and they set to work at devastating the agave and other native species that offend their sensibilities. But I am not speaking here on behalf of the overly cultivated notions of native botanical societies. The earth itself, in this case the dry climate of the region, will in the end sort out what belongs and what does not. On its own, drought will take care of the aspidistras. The earth has a habit of making its presence felt, even though that presence will be experienced by some as alienation. It is an alienation that may be salutary, though most white Australians in the Central Desert will cling with desperation to their five-by-ten plots of green lawn. Eventually the local ecology will force its way through even the most totalized vision and institute "a generalized buckling of my landscape" (VI 119) that "opens it to the universal, precisely because it is rather an *unthought*." To be sure, there is disorientation to be experienced when "the immemorial in the present" (Merleau-Ponty 1988, 133) is faced, but the reorientation that must ensue as its sequel awaits us as an unavoidable restorative force.

There is a "pleasure we experience in establishing a spontaneous accord between the contingency of what exists and the legislation of understanding" (PRI 141). The recovery of intercorporeality need not exclude intellection altogether, although its work is primarily the work of our flesh. Once there is revealed a "brute unity through which the universe 'holds' and of which the unity of human understanding is the expression rather than the internal condition" (Merleau-Ponty 1988, 142), we can adjust our understanding in the direction of more reciprocal relations. For me, a prototype may be found in the cultural landscape of the Pitjantjatjarra of Australia's Central Desert whose conceptual world is derived from the natural landscape—their spiritual-cum-social imagination and the red desert are entwined as flesh to flesh—although *even they* defer too frequently to their cultural notions, at times prioritizing them over the very landscape from which they are considered to be derived. The "problem" of squeezing the brute being out of our everyday lives is not only a problem faced by modern urban dwellers, it is a riddle and quandary for so-called primitive humans as well. For no humans are truly primitive, and human cunning everywhere has alienated us from the garden. But the restorative potential to be derived from cultivating reciprocal relations with the earth by means of our brute contact with it is fully available, even in these late times. It is not that there will ever be a total or final solution, but we can come to learn, as a cultural praxis, to tune in more closely to what is really there and precedes us. In a fit of humility that involves surrendering some of our jealously celebrated agency, we can retain more intimacy with what in the end will best nurture our nature.

Notes

1. Even Ezra Pound was born in Idaho.

2. I was employed by the Sierra Club Foundation for the two years 1972–1973.

3. Hugh Silverman, paper presented to the International Association of Environmental Philosophy, The Pennsylvania State University, 2000.

4. Michael Zimmerman, paper presented to the International Association of Environmental Philosophy, Denver, Colorado, 1998.

5. Paper presented to the International Association of Environmental Philosophy, Eugene, Oregon, 1999.

6. The emphasis and the ellipsis belong to Merleau-Ponty. Since I am not happy with the translation "hyper-reflection," I am leaving the term "*sur-réflection*" in the original French.

7. See Liberman, *Understanding Interaction in Central Australia*. London: Routledge (1985).

8. Wilshire first barked this phrase from the audience to Hugh Silverman after Silverman's address in which he claimed that "There is no nature!" Since then, Wilshire has amplified his thinking in conversations and e-mails: "By 'primal,' I mean that 99% of the biology of the genus *Homo* was formed in harmony with periodic light and darkness, fertility and infertility, growing and dying. Nature resists or punishes when we suspend our anciently formed generative and regenerative rhythms and attempt to subvert it beneath our own recent cultural designs."

9. Here postmodern and phenomenological insights need to be merged somehow.

10. The problem for us, most of the environmental movement included, is that our experience with the wild is an experience reduced to signification.

References

Evans, Fred. 2000. "Chaosmos and Merleau-Ponty's View of Nature." *Chiasmi* 2, 63–82.

Heidegger, Martin. 1962. *Being and Time*. Trans. John Macquarrie and Edward Robinson. New York: Harper and Row. Originally published in 1927 as *Sein und Zeit* in Edmund Husserl, ed. *Jahrbuch für Philosophie und phänomenologische Forschung*, Band VIII.

Kaput, Antje. 2000. "The So-called 'Barbarian Basis of Nature' and Its Secret Logos." *Chiasmi* 2, 167–182.

Liberman, Kenneth. 1985. *Understanding Interaction in Central Australia.* London: Routledge.

Low, Douglas. 2000. *Merleau-Ponty's Last Vision.* Evanston, IL: Northwestern University Press.

Mazis, Glen. 2000. "Merleau-Ponty's Concept of Nature." *Chiasmi* 2, 223–245.

Merleau-Ponty, Maurice. 1988. *In Praise of Philosophy and Other Essays.* Trans. John Wild, James Edie, and John O'Neill. Evanston, IL: Northwestern University Press.

———. 1995. *La Nature.* Ed. Dominique Séglard. Paris: Editions du Seuil.

Olkowski, Dorothea. 2000. "A Psychoanalysis of Nature." *Chiasmi* 2, 185–204.

Toadvine, Ted. 2000. "Nature and Negation." *Chiasmi* 2, 107–117.

Vogel, Steven. 1996. *Against Nature.* Albany: State University of New York Press.

3

The Liminal World
of the Northwest Coast

Patricia M. Locke

On the Pacific Northwest Coast of North America, spanning Washington, British Columbia, and southern Alaska, there is a world of fjords, forested islands, and irregular coastline. The proximity of land to sea and sky is intense and saturated with human meaning for the Haida Indians whose culture reflects this environment.[1]

Maurice Merleau-Ponty's attention to the context in which human meaning, even perception, is possible can be brought to bear on the geography, architecture and myths of this region. In his last work, *The Visible and the Invisible,* he presents flesh and its reversibility as that context. Flesh is a *between* concept, prior to all binary oppositions like earth and sky, human and animal. The world of the Haida Indians is a fluid one, punctuated by transformations of animals into human form and back again.[2] Because of the danger and possibilities inherent in such transitions, an elaborate ritual life and articulation of architectural forms took shape. Therefore, it may be easier to grasp the notion of *flesh* when we see it expressed in this non-Cartesian yet highly developed social world.

Merleau-Ponty states, "In a sense the whole of philosophy, as Husserl says, consists in restoring a power to signify, a birth of meaning, or a wild meaning . . ." (VI 155). By wild meaning, he does not refer to an idealized primitive consciousness or a natural landscape untouched by human shaping. His notion of wildness is compatible with the high culture of the Haida people. The prereflective quality of wild meaning indicates that the subject and object have not been tamed into separate realms. Instead, they may be thought of as the convex and concave sides of the same bowl, as close as the "sea and the strand," where each defines the other. Merleau-Ponty circles around the concepts of flesh and wild being, using metaphorical language and example to approach their meanings. For instance, when he describes color as "a sort of straits between exterior horizons and interior horizons ever gaping open," he is trying to get at the way color is "a momentary crystallization of colored being or of visibility" (VI 132). Merleau-Ponty is interested in "participation in and kinship with the visible," which occurs when human perceivers understand themselves as perceived, as part of the sensuous world (VI 138).

How do we come to understand ourselves in this way? Merleau-Ponty takes as his example the field of tactility. I touch textured things with my hands, and as I do so, one hand can touch the other. I feel myself as touched and touching. My left hand holds my right one, which becomes an object in the world. My right shifts into active grasping of the now quiet left and my perceptions shift as well. I cannot feel one hand being both touched and touching at the same time; between these two moments there is a slight gap, a "tissue" or "straits" between my interior horizon and the exterior one.

When I perceive, my body is as if latent. I am caught up in feeling the texture of the object the world presents to me. If that object is part of my own body (for instance, my hand felt as soft, bony, etc.), then that object is not feeling another but is apparent as an entity of the felt world.

Merleau-Ponty states further: "Through this crisscrossing within it of the touching and the tangible, its own movements incorporate themselves into the universe they interrogate, are recorded on the same map as it; the two systems are applied upon one another . . ." (VI 133). My experience of my own body is unique: when I take your hand I do not sense it in the same way as my own. Yet when I grasp your hand firmly to shake it, aren't you responding? Who is to say which of us is held, which holding?

The tangible world in its wild being is reaching out toward the one who senses it. My skin is the limit, the straits, making possible the connection between my interior life and the world. My gestures toward the "outside" become part of that world; simultaneously, my contact with it brings it "inside" my horizon. Further, my enfleshed existence is a part of your external horizon, as an object within your view. I come to find out that I am both inside and outside, both a subject and object for myself (as in the experience of holding my own hand) but also one for another. I don't simply attribute interiority to you; I can perceive your intentions as they are acted out.

Merleau-Ponty goes farther than interpersonal relations in his claims for reversibility of the flesh. I may be more sensitive to the cues given me by other human beings, but in Merleau-Ponty's estimation inanimate objects show themselves to me as well. "The look . . . envelops, palpates, espouses the visible things. . . . As though it knew them before knowing them, it moves in its own way with its abrupt and imperious style, and yet . . . finally one cannot say if it is the look or if it is the things that command" (VI 133). They show themselves as colored, as moving, as wholes, as beings in the world that take account of my looking at them. This is somewhat difficult to swallow, since our habit is to consider a canoe or a building, for example, as a physical structure or as a site of functions, not as a companion in dwelling.

Merleau-Ponty's definition of the reversibility of the flesh is suggestive but not transparent, so we turn to the Haida people for a sense of what it is like to live in the straits. They live literally in between the domain of sea creatures and those of forest and sky. They rely for food in part on the temporally fluctuating intertidal pools. Since the Haida believe that animals were at one time people, their myths and art express transformations of creatures into one another across space and time. Fauna and flora thus not only sustain human existence, but are respected as companions who may shape shift again.

FIGURE 3.1   Human-bear carved pole detail.

Claude Lévi-Strauss did much cross-cultural analysis of Pacific Northwest peoples with American Southwest and European mythmakers. His work on transformations through masks and stories showed a necessary link between the material artifacts and the told story versions. I would like to extend this link to the transformations in winter longhouse architecture. Merleau-Ponty did not address Pacific Northwest Indian culture directly, as far as I am aware, but he was engaged with Lévi-Strauss's structural work in this area. In turn, Lévi-Strauss dedicated *The Savage Mind* (1962), to the memory of Merleau-Ponty.[3]

I will focus on the Haida tribe, who live primarily in the Queen Charlotte Islands (Haida Gwaii), though many of the characteristics I describe are true of their neighbors, the Kwakiutl, Tlingit, and Bella Bella bands as well.[4] Nineteenth-century traders, ethnographers, and missionaries followed eighteenth-century European explorers searching for the fabled Northwest Passage, each group recording the changing Indian culture. Metal tools provided the impetus to a last flourishing of architecture and decorative arts, before the dissolution of Indian communities by disease and religious conversion. Christian missionaries urged the abandonment of communal households and traditional village life, which led to a consolidation of the population in trading/mission centers.

If we look at that moment in time (1870s–1905) for which we have photographic and written information as well as artifacts, we see a "world as sharp as a knife," balanced on the thin blade of treeless land above high tide. Here a row of houses faces the ocean, hierarchically arranged with the chief's house toward the center. This massing echoes the landscape, with tall poles bristling like a forest near the line of homes. The houses display their owners' positions in a vertically stratified society by their position relative to the village chief's house and by the symbolic crest poles.

Winter houses are built of cedar planks, vertically layered and held together in grooved baseboard wall plates.[5] They have gable roofs, with beams projecting beyond the planked roofs in the unique six-beam Haida style. This opens up a spacious interior of larger dimensions than the post and beam construction of neighboring bands that rely on two beams only. There are a few legendary homes of eight beams, able to house a hundred people and to host large clan gatherings.

Each cedar plank house is rectangular, with the longitudinal axis running in the front door, through a sunken stepped-platform arrangement in the interior, and back beyond the house to latrines, mortuary houses and the forest, whose tall trees are understood as gateway to the sky.[6] On ritual occasions, a cedar rope may be stretched from the door to the sea, further emphasizing this axis and the intimate tie of house to the water, a threshold to the underworld (Swanton 1909, 178).

A latitudinal axis distinguishes the front and back within the house, repeating the intertidal/high tidal zones evident in a beach environment. The longitudinal and latitudinal axes meet at the central fireplace within the house. The house then is a crossroads, and like any liminal point, is a place of mediation of different realities.

Take the front door as an example.[7] Pacific Northwest Coast culture is known best perhaps for its "totem" poles, tall (30 feet to 50 feet high) cedar sculptures made from a single tree, which display the crest animals of particular families, tell origin stories, or commemorate important chiefs or events. Many of these poles are freestanding sculptures, but a house frontal pole is attached to the house to announce the ancestry and deeds of the inhabitants. We enter many houses through an elliptical opening carved and painted as the mouth or abdomen of an animal. As we enter, we are swallowed up or returned to the womb. In this respect, the house is perceived as an animal body. It is also a symbolic return to the mother and the ancestors whose emblems are carved on the crest pole.

Entering into a living being, a Haida is enveloped by a truly inside world in which he will be nurtured. He is not an organ of this house-as-animal-body, but his activities define its space and functions, making it a microcosm of the outside world.

When the Biblical Jonah entered the great fish, he sat there intact as indigestible matter until he was vomited out three days later.[8] By contrast, when a Haida woman enters the mouth of a whale, she acts as its lifeblood by her work and her gender. She helps establish the socially stratified interior along the horizontal and vertical dimensions. The front of the house is a place for men's hunting and fishing tools, stored ready for use. The center of the house is marked by the fireplace, for cooking by the slaves and women, and for ritual activities of the shaman.[9] The rear of the house is the domain of the chief and his immediate family, including storage of his ritual garb and most valuable artifacts. The left corner is reserved for the ritually impure menstruating women, with a simple sliding panel opening at the rear of the house for them to use.

Entering a whale also reminds Haida men and women of their clan myths and thus who they are. Whale is traditionally the food for Thunderbird, a sky deity who lives in a symbiotic relationship with the underwater creature. Whale washes ashore as a gift to the people of light, food, and bones that can be used as building materials and tools. Entering a Raven or Grizzly Bear House achieves a different effect in terms of clan identity, which is reinforced by elaborately carved and painted interior house posts.

Claude Lévi-Strauss draws an analogy between these house posts and "de vivants piliers" of Baudelaire's famous poem, "Correspondances." Bill Reid, a Pacific Northwest visual artist, summarizes this view: "correspondence is the exact translation of the indigenous term designating these sculptured poles which supported the beams of houses; poles which were less things than living beings with 'regards familiers' inasmuch as they too in days of doubt and torment, issued 'de confuses paroles' guiding the inhabitant of the house, advising and comforting him and indicating the path from his difficulties."[10] The carved house posts support the roof and actively watch over the family. This is an example of what Merleau-Ponty describes as things looking at or responding to the person viewing them. The house as companion in dwelling should be one that guides inhabitants to live in an upright way. The carved animals remind them of who they are and what their ancestors have done. Baudelaire's "forêts de symboles" is more decadent than the Haidas' imaged logs, which still hold a direct connection to the natural world outside the longhouse.

The point here is the reciprocity of seeing and being seen by elements of the surrounding field of vision, the house interior. Merleau-Ponty goes further, asserting that we see these things "in their places, where they are, according to their being which is indeed more than their being-perceived"; we see them at a specific distance. That distance is the distance of the flesh, which is at the same time "deeply consonant" with what we are looking at (VI 135). Human perceivers find themselves in the heart of the house, surrounded by and consonant with the visible by kinship *as* visible beings.

Kinship is the significant meaning of the Haida building arts, both because the longhouses shelter large groups and because the ornamental detail communicates natural relations and history. House poles display figures of husband and wife's necessarily different clans. The history of the family is bound up in stories of transformations between different states of being or between different animals. Killer Whale, for instance, is both most powerful of underwater beings and a sometime inhabitant of land, found under mountains or other prominent physical landscape features. Thus Killer Whale also reveals a latent deep connection between the sea and the mountains.

The supernatural Snag, a personification of uprooted driftwood hidden below the surface of the water ready to snag an unwary canoe, is often depicted with the fins of a killer whale, but can also be carved as a grimacing human being. These complex images express metamorphosis: one can "read" an animal as Killer Whale and by reorganizing its parts, now see supernatural Snag. The image is the same, but the perceiver manipulates the figure-ground relationship to complete it, just as he or she can feel a hand grasping or grasped. Thus, a creature in two different manifestations can be suggested. Alternately, two distinct animals can share the same space. Figures may be interlocked: Whale may be found between Thunderbird's wings, with a human face peering out its blowhole and Frog between its teeth.

The ease with which animals shift from one appearance to another or from one kind of being to another is matched by Haida visual interpretive flexibility.[11] One becomes aware of the gap between the two distinct views, parallel to Merleau-Ponty's example of the hand touching/touched. The Haidas' complex figures are as body-based as the touching hands and have an internal logic, since they often depict animals that can live in two realms, such as the amphibian frog or beaver. Thunderbird, a creature important to most Native American tribes, is said to live comfortably in human form on a high mountain until it puts on a cloak of feathers and takes to the air in search of food.

Fluidity of boundaries, marked by transformation from one distinctive shape to another, is one way of expressing the reciprocity of human beings, animals and inanimate natural entities (such as snags). The Haida crest poles are a vivid example of the active role of the perceiver in constituting the image and participating in the story. The storyteller becomes the mediator between complexly intertwined images. It isn't simply a matter of interpreting a neutral oscillating foreground figure, such as a Necker cube, against a background read as negative space. The figures themselves demand to be acknowledged as transformers.

At the same time, these vivid animal figures are human artifacts, displaying the *style* of the human/inanimate beings' reciprocity. The Haida style is basically a two-dimensional relief carving that is "wrapped" around the pole, holding closely to its shape. Christie Harris describes the effect: "A good totem pole was truly terrifying. It seemed to be a concentration of enormous tensions, as if something were trying to break out, as if a conflict were trying to resolve itself" (Harris 1992, 188). This conflict displays a human experience of the natural world, mediated by the flesh.

Haida crest poles are painted with designs that increase tension by interrogating sculptural forms. When a colored region contradicts rather than outlines a carved shape, it heightens the sense of the latency, or flesh of things that Merleau-Ponty points out. An animal's face comes out to me even while its three-dimensionality is brought into question by color. The viewer is forced at every turn to respond to the multiplicity of the images that crisscross in meaning. The sense of weaving color and shape gives the perceiver a dynamic experience of the reversibility of the flesh.

I dwell on this concept of reversibility of the flesh because it is one that is central to Merleau-Ponty's thought and because it is not simply a binary opposition that is overcome by a distinct mediator. The perceiver is actively involved in the perception of shape and color, but at the same time color is never entirely one with form. The perceiver may know him- or herself touching an object by hand or more distantly by eye, yet there remains a gap, or straits, between the touching and his or her self as touched or seen by the world. He or she is always on the verge, the border between touching and being touched, between being human and animal, but never entirely able to be aware of both at once. All objects, including his or her corporeal existence, have a thickness, a depth to them that is suggested by the textured surface he or she sees and feels. The limit of the darkness of the interior life and the perceptible exterior world is the skin.

One can consider the plank-framed structure as the "skin" of the house as animal, or as the defining outline of the house as crossroads. In either case, the Haida house is a porous field that breathes like human skin. We have noted the elliptical opening of the frontal pole, but there are less significant openings at the back or along the sides for working slaves to bring things in and out. These sliding panels are rather ad hoc doors, and do not carry the liminal crossing danger of the main entry.

That sense of threshold danger does apply to the smoke hole in the center of the roof.[12] The roof is made of wide cedar planks or bark strips held in place by stones or poles, and has a cover for the smoke hole that slides across it during rainstorms. As the pivotal position in the house as crossroads, the central smoke hole is open to the sky world. The shaman's power is concentrated at the fireplace, where he burns offerings to the dead or to the supernaturals. Here too he dances to heal diseases or expel evil spirits from the possessed (Blackman 1980, 283). In the early period of Haida culture, the shaman's body was hoisted out through the smoke hole on his death, indicating his return to the spirit world. His remains were interred with his ritual implements far from other mortuary poles, because of the residual danger and power of his bones.[13]

The shifting nature of the roof simplifies the renewal of deteriorating parts. The walls too protect against the wet weather, but are porous enough to allow the inhabitants to tell when spring comes again by a shaft of light falling in a predictable place on a wall.[14] The house as body breathes, takes in nourishment, and regenerates itself.

If we push Merleau-Ponty's view further, the house can be known as the exterior of an interior family life. The exterior shell, or skin, folds over a sense of interiority. We can experience the house from outside, noting the frontal pole carvings and the regularity of the wide planks. But once we enter through the animal mouth, we perceive the surface of the interior. That is in some way a surface; yet, it is both exterior and interior. These two concepts fold together, intertwined and dependent on each other. This gives us a sense of depth, of going within but without penetrating to absolute surfacelessness.

The dark enclosure gives a far different sense of place from the world outside, bound by the verticality of the forest on one side and the waves of the horizontal sea-border on the other. The house envelops the inhabitants, but is also a defining feature of the landscape outside. It marks off a social arena in the natural world, while incorporating natural materials and being responsive to seasonal and daily changes.

The house as body goes through a major transformation in the winter ceremonial season.[15] By the addition of painted screens and partitions at the rear of the house, it becomes a theatrical space for the reenactment of clan myths, for initiation rites and dance performances. The screen typically has an elliptical opening for the actors. Most of these screens have vanished, but a particularly beautiful one, the Rain Screen, displays the scale and style of two-dimensional form line decoration.[16]

The aspect of thickness, of flesh, is indicated by use of screens. Merleau-Ponty claims, "There is no vision without the screen: the ideas we are speaking of would not be better known to us if we had no body and no sensibility; it is then that they would be inaccessible to us" (VI 150). They are given to us as ideas only in a carnal experience. If we are trying to grasp what it is to be an enfleshed being, rather than a thinking self inside a containing body, we must acknowledge the necessity of the screen. The painted screen is analogous to the spatiality of our own bodies. Overlapping sensory systems give us, by necessity, awareness of their partial perspectives. The thick darkness of what is between our sensory perceptions and the skin that is in contact with the world is the place where enfleshed ideas resonate with us, body to body. The carnal echo of that experience is manifest in what we create. The Haida Indians make cedar longhouses that correspond to our spatial nature, showing us that, in Merleau-Ponty's words, "what is proper to the visible is . . . to be the surface of an inexhaustible depth: this is what makes it able to be open to visions other than our own" (VI 143).

Through dance and ritual, we can come to know viscerally our animal life or the life of our ancestors made present. These arts bring the temporal dimension into the spatial context of the plank house. Time is made visible in rhythmic movement. Franz Boas observed a kinesthetic relationship between the dance and the sculptural arts of the Northwest Coast Indians.[17] The aesthetically enhanced environment provides a backdrop for the sequential gestures unfolding throughout the night. In the thick air and flickering light of the feast, dancers cast deep shadows. The dances awaken the space, and do so by reconstituting those who have haunted it in the past. Time is altered when perennial heroes reappear or when animal spirits join the dance.

Dancers wearing transformation masks begin to enact the myth of Raven bringing light to the people, and dip below their robes to reemerge as another character. These masks are destroyed afterward, or hidden away, so that there is no sense of actors taking on roles. Rather, the man who dons a Raven headdress becomes Raven. Often members of other clans are invited to the winter festivities to witness the transformations taking place, the renewal of clan life.

Lest we succumb to the lure of the exotic and place the Haida world at an impossible distance from ours, we can consider the house as crossroads of social life. Like ours, Haida society admires prestige built on material wealth. That requires the circulation of goods, ostentatious display, notably in the elaborate decoration of enormous houses, and the giving of spectacular feasts. At these feasts, known as potlatches, the prestige of the host is enhanced by the amount of material goods he or she has amassed and gives away. As in Homeric host/guest friend relationships, the more the host gives, the more honor he receives. Of course, his neighboring village chief will feel compelled to respond in kind. Many of the most beautiful artifacts and trade goods were in active circulation in the old days, passed from house to house and gathering value along the way.

Potlatches are given at intervals during the construction of a house. The Haida people determine the size of a family's house not by its square footage, but by the rank of the inhabitants, and by the number of people who help erect the building. A different chief selects each cedar beam of a six-beam house, has it cut and trimmed in the forest, and hauled to the site. Potlatch gifts commensurate with their efforts are expected. Built on commission, the house poles also call for a feast of gift giving. Thus the house is a social construction, and can serve to unite kinship groups and make peace with neighboring clans.

Monster House, one of the largest buildings of the historical period, had two extra beams to support its 55-foot-square expanse. It had an 18-foot-high house post just inside the front door, a square house pit that was 27 feet in length, and a fireplace roughly 10 foot square like the smoke hole directly above it. The sunken house pit, a stepped feature of the grandest houses, had to be dug in one day (Curtis 1916, XI: 129–130). Thus the size was proportionate to the number of people who turned up to dig. Over 2,000 people contributed to the building of Monster House in 1850.[18] The prestige of a house chief is evident in the power he has to call on others to help erect the structure, and that prestige is enhanced continually by the results. Only those who can handsomely gift people who bring materials and labor attempt a grand house.

Many Haida villages are ghost towns now, abandoned to the wet climate. Poles fall to the ground and become host logs for new growth. Thus the forest crowds ever closer to the beach. Haida houses survive by reputation, given in their names: Flicker House, Ribs of Killer Whale House, Daybreak House, Eagle House, Valuable House, House of Dead Man's Head, House Climbing Up, House Where People Want to Visit, Frog House, House by Itself.

I have written this in the present tense, for the Haida world is alive primarily in story and song. We cannot underestimate the effects on the culture and building traditions of the widespread elimination of the people in the late 1800s, through diseases such as smallpox. The Christian missionaries' prohibitions against the potlatch drove it underground, and their insistence on European-style nuclear family dwellings made the great plank house obsolete. Yet the Haida clans have been steadily gaining ground in numbers and in cultivating their artistic traditions.[19] Potlatching is again a vital and creative part of their culture. It is an example of the deliberate choice made to reclaim a wild being that once could be taken for granted. Much as ballet dancers train rigorously and with forethought in order to dance in an effortless manner in performance, desire and art combine in the experience of wild being in the renewed Haida ritual. At Skidegate, BC, for example, several new totem poles have been erected in the last few years, standing as representatives of the lost villages. Village and house names are bound up with traditional cultural and natural knowledge that is specific to place.

This architecture echoes our corporeality and defines its natural surroundings. The Haida world can be an occasion for the experience of reversibility of the flesh. A genuine depth is latent in a topography shaped by the ghost towns dotting the islands. In 1905, Swanton reported that "To signify the narrow margin between life and death, and what a slight cause is required to bring about a change from one to the other, it was a saying at Masset that 'the world is as sharp as a knife,' meaning, if a man does not take care, he will fall off (i.e., end his life quickly)" (Swanton 1909, 37). If we do not take care, the fragile balance of the remaining fragments of the Haida world will be destroyed.

Restoration of stories and house names is coupled with a renewal of Haida building. The training of young Haida carvers makes the preservation of mature forests a more urgent matter, since they cannot build without 100-year-old trees. This time the indigenous island peoples of British Columbia and Alaska are more politically insistent upon their rights as sovereign peoples. Current struggles over rapid clear cutting pit the Pacific Northwest Indian bands and environmentalists against major logging companies (such as Weyerhaeuser) and the provincial government.

What Merleau-Ponty has to offer this politically charged moment is twofold. His elemental concept of flesh, with the reverberation of the world known in our bodies and echoed back again, strengthens our connection to other peoples and species. This felt commonality is a basis for protecting forest, sea, and endangered natural or cultural habitats. Merleau-Ponty states, "When I find again the actual world such as it is, under my hands, under my eyes, up against my body, I find much more than an object: a Being of which my vision is a part, a visibility older than my operations or my acts. But this does not mean that there was a fusion or coinciding of me with it" (VI 123). This common ground of Being is more fundamental than the acts of an individual perceiver. The Haida Indians show us what flesh can look like, through carving and building arts that suggest the invisible depth lying beneath the visible.

Merleau-Ponty's second contribution to an engaged commitment to the environment and to each other is in his emphasis on the shifting horizon of our individual perspectives. Simply because we are embodied beings, able to move through a landscape, the horizon of our awareness moves with us. Like the longhouse as crossroads, we carry marks of the deep past into the present moment. This past bears on the meaning that the present has for us, and insofar as we turn to look in that direction, can give us guidance toward the future.

Imagine a cedar rope extending not only spatially from the sea, through the front door and out the back of the house to the forest, but crossing this moment back in time through our parents and their parents and so on. Grasp the rope, which has the thickness of this moment within it, separating us from intellectual coincidence with those times. As Merleau-Ponty says, "the weight of the natural world is already a weight of the past. Each landscape of my life, because it is not a wandering troop of sensations or a system of ephemeral judgments but a segment of the durable flesh of the world, is qua visible, pregnant with many other visions besides my own" (VI 123). We can restore the past when we give it meaning *as* present. We can invite others, such as the Haida Indians, to share their visions with us. Their rituals and building traditions explicitly display our ability to transform ourselves, drawing on the invisibility of the past. This high culture shows us that human beings can change, and unlike other sentient beings, can know that we do so.

We stand here, on the edge of the knife, and it is our sense of ourselves as kindred with others and as individually responsible for creating meaning in our present place and time that can make a difference in what kind of future we will have. There will be a deep future to balance this past only if we act together to protect and restore natural and culturally significant places. While we may not live in the dynamic world of forested islands in the Pacific Northwest, we too can fall off of the edge of the knife.

Notes

1. The heavy rains and mild temperatures provide the optimal climate for the growth of red cedar. Virgin forests held trees 200–300 feet tall, and even today trees in the islands may have such thick trunks that two or three people with arms outstretched are needed to encircle them.

2. Claude Lévi-Strauss: "These objects—beings transformed into things, human animals, living boxes—seem as remote as possible from our own conception of art since the time of the Greeks. Yet even here one would err to suppose that a single possibility of the aesthetic life had escaped the prophets and virtuosos of the Northwest Coast." Quoted by Holm and Reid (1978, 12).

3. While teaching at the New School in New York City, during 1942–1945, Lévi-Strauss had access to the extensive holdings of the American Museum of Natural History. These include material artifacts, including totem poles, a village model, masks, clothing, and a

full length Haida canoe, as well as written and photographic materials. The size of the poles is evident: they were cut in parts because they were too long for railroad cars to transport them from the islands to New York. Several poles are still on display. The Thomas Burke Memorial Museum at University of Washington in Seattle, WA, and the Museum of Anthropology at the University of British Columbia in Vancouver, BC, also have considerable material holdings.

4. The Haida call their islands Haida Gwaii, and consider themselves a sovereign nation that has neither been defeated by nor made a treaty with Canada or the United States. The islands are situated in sailing proximity to Alaska and Vancouver Island. One abandoned Haida village, Ninstints, is a World Heritage Site.

5. Haida seasonal living arrangements included roughly built summer fishing camps, but they did not dismantle their winter homes for building materials as did their Kwakiutl neighbors. House walls were sometimes removed when the house chief died.

6. Northern Haida villages in coastal Alaska have homes that are more nearly square, but the same axes govern the space.

7. Postcontact photographs show European style doors next to the pole entrance. Like glass-paned windows, these are prestige objects without the usual meaning of a door. They are off-axis, reserving the significant place for the traditional pole entry. Windows may be aligned longitudinally, but are often so high that one cannot see through them from inside or out.

8. Book of Jonah, 1:17, 2:10.

9. Slaves were acquired through warfare or raids on neighboring tribes. They were valued for their work and as markers of prestige. During ordinary time, they slept in the house pit, in order to tend the fire, and traveled with the villagers to summer fishing camps. During the winter ceremonial period, they were displaced and did not participate in the rituals. They often crowded around the front door to watch the elaborate spectacle.

10. Claude Lévi-Strauss, in Holm and Reid, *Indian Art*, 12.

11. Analogously, contemporary American teenagers have developed the ability to interpret the rapid "morphing" of computer-generated creatures without discomfort at their incongruity.

12. It is said that Raven once wore a cloak of white feathers, which turned black with soot as he sought to escape from a feast through a smoke hole. Harris (1992), 84.

13. Margaret Blackman (1980, 290). Since the tribes were decimated by disease in the historical period, women are allowed to become chieftains and shamans so that the ritual life can continue.

14. See also George MacDonald (1992, 104). He describes their cosmological beliefs in the World as House/Box, with stars as openings in it and seasons marked by varying positions of sun shining through onto the "walls" of the world. He also characterizes the boxlike steps of the house pit as descending into the underworld. The world can be seen as a set of boxes, and our making of homes and coffins a reenactment of the larger cosmos.

15. George MacDonald (1983, 18): "The plank house reflected the Haida concepts of transformation from one realm of creation to another and of personification of inanimate

objects. It could function in the secular realm as a dwelling as well as in the spiritual realm as a ceremonial center. It was the abode of the living as well of their ancestors. …The house was the container of human social life in the same way that the universe was the container of the natural world. The logical cross-reference between the dwelling and the universe, or between culture and nature, was common to all pre-literate societies. The house structure could be comprehended by the individual, while the cosmos could not, so it helped man's system of cognition (individual as well as cultural) to impose the structure of the house, with its floor, supports, and protective roof, on the universe with its pillars and vault of heaven."

16. George T. Emmons (1916, Plate 2, Winter and Pond photo). This is a Chilkat screen, but similar to reports of Haida partitions. The central figure with the hole represents the Rain Spirit, while the small figures crouching in the border are "Raindrops Splash Up" after bouncing off the ground.

17. Bill Holm quotes Boas, and continues, "I, myself, have derived a certain physical satisfaction from the muscle activity involved in producing the characteristic line movement of this art, and there can be little doubt that this was also true for the Indian artist. To say that there may be a kinesthetic relationship between this movement and dance movement is not to say that there is any visual or spatial similarity, though there may be, but to a lesser degree. Because of the purely sensory nature of the suggested relationship, it is difficult, if not impossible, for one who has not personally participated in both activities to be aware of it" (1965, 92–93).

18. Peter Nabokov and Robert Easton, *Native American Architecture* (New York: Oxford UP, 1989), 266. This is one of the best books on this subject.

19. *Seattle Post Intelligencer*, May 2002, documents the 3,700 tribal members' renewal of building arts and carving traditions, even as the raw material (old growth cedar trees) is disappearing due to clear cutting by the lumber industry. See also continuing articles by Paul Shukovsky, *Seattle Post Intelligencer*, April 20, 2005 and following, concerning the Haida Nation's political actions against the logging companies: paulshukovsky@seattlepi.com.

References

Blackman, Margaret. 1980. "The Northern and Kaigani Haida: A Study in Photographic Ethnohistory. Ph.D. dissertation. Ohio State University, 1973. Ann Arbor, MI: UMI.

Curtis, Edward S. 1916. *The North American Indian,* vol. XI. Cambridge, MA.

Emmons, George T. 1916. "The Whale House of the Chilkat." *Anthropological Papers of the American Museum of Natural History,* vol. XIX, Part 1. NY: AMNH.

Harris, Christie. 1992. *Raven's Cry.* Vancouver: Douglas & McIntyre.

Holm, Bill. 1965. *Northwest Coast Indian Art: An Analysis of Form.* Thomas Burke Memorial Washington State Museum Monograph No. 1. Seattle: University of Washington Press.

Holm, Bill and Bill Reid. 1978. *Indian Art of the Northwest Coast, A Dialogue on Craftsmanship and Aesthetics.* Seattle: University of Washington Press.

Lévi-Strauss, Claude. 1966. *The Savage Mind.* Chicago: University of Chicago Press.

MacDonald, George. 1992. *Haida Art.* Seattle: University of Washington Press.

———.1983. *Haida Monumental Art.* Vancouver: University of British Columbia Press.

Nabokov, Peter and Robert Easton. 1989. *Native American Architecture.* New York: Oxford University Press.

Seattle Post-Intelligencer. May–June 2002. April–May 2005.

Swanton, John R. 1909. *Contributions to the Ethnology of the Haida.* Memoirs of the American Museum of Natural History, vol. VIII.

4

Borders and Boundaries

Edging into the Environment

Edward S. Casey

I

Merleau-Ponty did not concern himself much with borders and edges—not as such. He was always looking farther afield, quite literally so. His interest was always to find the greater continuity, the larger whole, the most refulgent entity or event: whether this be called the "phenomenal field," the "speaking word," or the radiant work of art. In the *Phenomenology of Perception* he says explicitly that an entity, above all the human body, is never simply "where it is, nor what it is" (PhP 197). In "Eye and Mind," he proclaims that vision has "a fundamental power of showing forth more than itself" (178).[1] The situations are different, but the point is much the same: what matters is what is more than any definition can give, any contour contain, any edge delimit. Despite all his dissents from Husserl, he shares with the latter the premise of continuism, according to which experience is never entirely disparate, never altogether fragmented: hence his early predilection for models of arc and horizon, and (later) for "folds" and "coiling over" rather than abrupt edges or strict borders. Husserl guaranteed the continuity of experience in two ways: by the structure of time-consciousness, wherein retentions and protentions stitch together any stretch of duration; and by invoking the "adumbrations" (*Abschattungen*) through which we know in advance, with great likelihood if not with certainty, how the subsquent perception of something will turn out. Whatever epistemic "disappointments" (*Enttäuschungen*) may arise in the course of experience, they will not undermine an experience from within: they will be tucked into the next experience, which will surely take account of them, given Husserl's eager espousal of cognitive optimism. Similarly, for

Merleau-Ponty any "breaks" or "divergences" (*écarts*)—a word that comes into increasing prominence in *The Visible and the Invisible*—are to be regarded as departures that will be eventually reincorporated into the pre-reflective sphere, even if not into the sphere of consciousness and its intentionality. They will be folded over and back into the ongoing substructure of experience, which will resume its course even when rudely interrupted. Such is the faith—the "perceptual faith" of which Merleau-Ponty also speaks in the same late text. Continuity is guaranteed not by adumbrations or time-consciousness but by the lived body—which subtends all experience, even the most disjointed—and eventually by *flesh,* a term that brings body and world together in a literally convoluted but ultimately consistent manner: the "flesh of the world" is a whole than which nothing can be greater and in relation to which discontinuities can only be momentary fissures within its encompassing embrace.

The depth of Merleau-Ponty's commitment to the "closely woven fabric"[2] of the continuous and the whole is nowhere more evident than in his aversion to treating the *end of things*—that area or place where a thing (or field or person or place) runs out, either by ceasing to exist, turning in a radically different direction, or simply dropping out of sight or touch. This end is the *edge,* a term I take to include perimeters, limits, and borders: that is to say, all the ways in which something comes to an abrupt and decisive termination. Each of these threatens the double premise of continuism-cum-wholism. For each offers a challenge to the idea that we can know in advance, albeit only with a high probability, what is coming next in our experience. Around every edge lurks the genuinely unknown and the truly unpredictable: what foils the most likely forecast, as on 9/11. Edges are occasions for possible violence: either they do actual violence to our expectations, or they conceal a scene of violence from our view or thought. They undermine what resides within the realm of comfortable and conventional thought. They disconnect and discomfort us. No wonder philosophers, including Merleau-Ponty (and probably you and me) don't really want to think about them. Not at all, or certainly not very much.

In a very rare reference to edges, Merleau-Ponty writes (in "The Philosopher and His Shadow") of material things as "upright, insistent, *flaying our glance with their edges,* each thing claiming an absolute presence which is not compossible with the absolute presence of the other things" (S 181).[3] Here he acknowledges the violence inherent in edges—in this case, a violence to our very look, our fleeting glance. To flay a glance, an edge must tear up the anticipations embedded in that act of looking, upsetting them by presenting something we had not anticipated at all—as often happens: I walk to the corner of the corridor on which my office is located and, suddenly, I encounter someone I have not seen for twenty years, a former colleague who has come back, unannounced, to visit the department of philosophy. I had thought I would simply walk around the same corner to pick up my mail in the department office before going to teach: instead, I encounter a person who has not only appeared unexpectedly but who has himself changed appearance radically, so much so that for a very brief moment I do not recognize him at all. Going around edges, then, even in the most mundane circumstance, is positively Heraclitean: in the proximity of edges, we must (in the words of the sardonic sage) "expect the unexpected."[4]

Apart from exceptional mentions such as the one I just cited, edges are not an important item in Merleau-Ponty's repertoire. The abruptness of an edge, the precision of a border, the delimitation of a perimeter are not phenomena to which he is characteristically attuned. I would even go so far as to say that he has a blind spot for them, seeking (and almost always finding) a tempered edge, a mellowed-out border. In short, a *boundary*, a porous band or region in which there are continual movements of transition back and forth between limits that prove to be putative or provisional only. If an edge always makes us feel somewhat uncomfortable—"edgy"— a boundary puts us more at ease. Its presence is at once embracing and open, in contrast with an edge, which emphasizes alterity and difference and which (thanks to the surprise it so characteristically yields) brings us disappointment or (for that matter) delight.

A primary instance of a boundary in the sense just mentioned is the *horizon,* which Merleau-Ponty posits as the presumptive synthesis of the phenomenal field and the correlate of my gaze (PhP 68, 70). A horizon is never a sheer border or perimeter; even when it seems to assume the form of a "horizon-line," it proves to be an arena of interchange between diverse things and places as I move toward or away from it. Always altering, it changes with my bodily movement and the environmental circumstance. As I walk toward it, it recedes with every step, showing itself to be different at every moment. Instead of flaying my glance, it invites it to move on—and on and on. The horizon is always in principle open—to new content, new structure, new possibilities. It does not act as an edge that would impede my moving or looking, or else reveal something wholly unexpected. "The sun also rises"—on the horizon. I can count on this, despite Hume's acid skepticism. For the horizon is the very place where the earth and the sky meet in patterns of deliverance, which I already know or which, even if new in exact appearance, are modifications of previous experiences of other horizons.

Beyond the passage I quoted a few moments ago, as close as Merleau-Ponty ever comes to pursuing an edge—a true border and not a boundary—is found in his discussion of "line" in "Eye and Mind." There he is struck by the power of a line to determine the identity of something: for example, in Matisse's line drawings and etchings, where the artist "put[s] into a single line both the prosaic definition (*signalement*) of the entity and the hidden (*sourde*) operation which composes in it such softness or inertia and such force as are required to constitute it as *nude*, as *face*, as *flower*" (OE 184).[5] But we must not think of line as "a positive attribute and a property of the object in itself . . . [as] the outer contour of the apple or the border between the plowed field and the meadow, considered as present in the world, such that, guided by points taken from the real world, the pencil or brush would only have to pass over them . . ." (ibid., 182). Leonardo da Vinci is quoted: "The secret of the art of drawing is to discover in each object the particular way in which a certain flexuous line, which is, so to speak, its generating axis, is directed through its whole extent."[6] The line as generating axis is a line that is no longer a positive presence, no more an entity in itself—and, by the same token, it no longer belongs to the object as its literal out-line or outer edge. For

> there are no lines visible in themselves . . . neither the contour of the apple nor the border between field and meadow is in *this* place or that . . . they are always on the near or the far side of the point we look at . . . [T]hey are indicated, implicated and even very imperiously demanded by the things, but they themselves are not things. (OE 183)[7]

Inspired by Klee and Michaux as well as Matisse, Merleau-Ponty calls for "freeing the line" (OE 183) in such a way that every line "will form an adventure, a history, a meaning" (ibid.). This adventure, which entails "a certain disequilibrium kept up within the indifference of the white paper," indeed "a certain constitutive emptiness" (ibid.), must depart from the strictures of the edge, which is always on the far end of something as its visible terminus. We can say of edges what Merleau-Ponty says of nongenerative lines: they are "the restriction, segregation, or modulation of a pre-given spatiality" (ibid., 184). An edge is the abrupt termination of a lived space that is the primary reality and that contains within itself the source of the continuity and wholeness of our experience.

Perceptual reality is indeed a "closely woven fabric," within which there is little room for the kind of definition that contour lines, including those border lines called edges, bring with them. This is all the more true for horizons, which remain ineluctably "indeterminate."[8] In effect, then, Merleau-Ponty has transformed two plausible candidates for borders— contours and horizons (which are in effect contours of the landscape)— into boundaries, which are essentially indeterminate. This is in keeping with the Merleau-Pontian commitment to a general indeterminacy of human experience:

> . . . there is in human existence a principle of indeterminacy, and this indeterminacy is not only for us, it does not stem from some imperfection of our knowledge . . . Existence is indeterminate in itself, by reason of its fundamental structure. (PhP 169)[9]

It follows that boundaries fit his ontology much more better than do edges, borders, and perimeters, each of which threatens to undo the dense texture, the "tufts" or "thickets" of meaning that are everywhere apparent to this philosopher's discerning eye.[10] And yet this same eye, for all its generous range of vision, has its own macula, as well as its own shadow—as Merleau-Ponty himself insists. [11] My suggestion is that determinate endings and distinct lines belong to Merleau-Ponty's own shadow: they are part of what he must ignore or repress in the dazzlement of his own brilliant ontology. In "the joyous realm of things and their god, the sun" (OE 186), there is no room for edges and limits, borders and perimeters. Blinded by the blazing light, I can no longer see something "as it is and where it is . . . [in] any identical, specific place."[12] Yet these same places call for limits and thrive on them, and the things that inhabit them possess edges.

II

I do not mean to suggest that borders and limits are always good things— hardly! From the current situation in the Middle East we know the dangerous and even disastrous results that can ensue from the strict enforcement of existing legal and political borders. We also know how arbitrary many border-lines are—and how often they are artifacts of human greed for property or of a tendentious politics (most conspicuous in the gerry-mandering of political districts). Their invocation may reflect a restrictive sense of the natural environment, as in the opposition to reintroducing wolves to the Greater Yellowstone region on the part of ranchers who feared attacks on their livestock. From these self-serving and ultimately self-defeating circumstances we rightly recoil, and only too gladly flee into the welcoming arms of a much more open and embracing model of the limits of place and the edges of things—into the arms of boundaries, in short. Who can resist the invitation contained in Heidegger's proclama-tion in "The Origin of the Work of Art": "A boundary is not that at which something stops but, as the Greeks recognized, the boundary is that from which something *begins its presencing*" (Heidegger 1971, 154; his italics). Given the choice, most of us would opt for a geographic, environmental, and political paradigm of free movement *across* borders, with as few restrictions as possible (except for situations in which this movement is itself manifestly harmful, as when immigrants are admitted to a country where they will in fact suffer more than in their place of origin). Else-where, I have set forth the case for thinking of place, including natural place, as calling for porous if not bleeding boundaries. (And I come from "Bleeding Kansas" after all—just a few hundreds miles to the west of St. Louis, where I first gave this chapter as a talk.)

Here I want to open a reflection on the role of borders vs. boundaries as they figure into the environment, both natural and urban. Let me start by asking, Is it always a good thing that in painting "there are no lines visible in themselves . . . [that] the border between field and meadow is [not] in *this* place or that [but] always on the near side or the far side of the point we look at . . . always between or behind whatever we fix our eyes upon"? (OE 183; his italics). Merleau-Ponty's point about art (at least modern art) is certainly valid, but does it translate straightforwardly into natural landscapes or cityscapes? Surely, discernible and stationary lines between parts of a land-scape can be constructive presences, yielding a minimal structure that helps to organize a scene before our eyes. When I looked with a friend over the Ruhr River this summer toward the fields beyond, I experienced the divi-sions between fields and between fields and forest not just as aesthetically attractive but as deeply right, even though they were unabashedly linear and would be represented as such were I to sketch or paint them. When I walked just outside Terre Haute, Indiana, last fall, I was not distressed to find myself alongside a well-managed cornfield with a quite definite edge that gave me a sense of closure and direction: I preferred to walk along the cleared edge than straight through the densely planted cornfield itself, where I'd soon feel lost and overwhelmed by the gigantic cornstalks that towered up to eight feet! So, too, losing the trail in thick woods one night in the Berkshires when there was no moon (and I had no flashlight) brought with it a very special anxiety of disorientation and a corresponding longing to be back on a straightforwardly linear trajectory! This need for, and satisfaction in, precise delimitation is not only an anthropocentric conceit. Virtually all animals and insects need and respect the limits of the biotopes and bioniches in which they live: these limits, typically traced out by leaving scents, help diverse species to coexist, to "know their place."

Edges and limits, borders and perimeters are strange entities: oppressive and restrictive in many contexts, they are comforting and orienting and even essential in others. They can be the occasion for creative action and thought: Stravinski said that his freedom as a composer "consists in moving about within the narrow frame I have assigned myself" (Stravinsky 1960, 68). In assessing their role in the natural environment, where one cannot oneself assign the limit, we need to avoid the extremes of thinking that they are either to be avoided at all costs—as if their only effect was to flay our vision or obstruct our movement—or to be subsumed into indeterminate boundaries: or (as often happens, I think) the latter because the former. They have their appropriate place, and my aim in this chapter is to figure out what this may be.

In order to do this, I shall restrict my discussion to borders and edges in contrast with boundaries, leaving for another occasion a discussion of the closely related (but finally distinct) notions of limit and perimeter.[13] A *border* is a legally or historically or cartographically recognized delineation of a place of some kind; but it is also established by bodily actions and ritualistic practices, both human and other-than-human. The place can be altogether natural and wild, but it can also be part of an officially recognized region or territory that is marked down on a map, or photographed from afar (e.g., in infrared images taken by satellite cameras). "Border" can be considered a "horizontal" concept insofar as it almost always characterizes an existing place that is itself part of, or continuous with, land. Since land is an outer layer of the earth, its demarcation by borders will be on a plane more or less perpendicular to the gravity exerted by the earth itself.

An *edge,* in contrast, is normally a vertical phenomenon, being the intersection of two planes, at least one of which is upright in comparison with the other: tilted to some significant degree from the horizontal or flat. Formally defined as a "convex dihedral angle"[14]—that is, the wide angle formed when two surfaces intersect—an edge is experienced as the region where vision is occluded or movement obstructed. Short of moving around it, we are stymied by an edge, put into a position where (unless it is transparent) we can at most *imagine* what lies beyond it or else try to *glance* around it—to catch a sense of what lies beyond it. Edges adhere mainly to material things, being their rims or contours. Unlike borders, they are nether subject to continual cultural and historical variation; nor are they the products of ritualistic activity. But they can prompt such activity, and they certainly play a part in many repetitive practices (e.g., as in the edges of relics used in rituals), just as they figure into cultural and historical practices (e.g., the coherent history of photographs of Half-Dome in Yosemite Valley from Muybridge and Watkins to Ansel Adams: a rock formation with a very pronounced edge that each of these photographers tried to capture in his own way).

It is not surprising that edges rarely figure into philosophical accounts, including Merleau-Ponty's. (And it is significant, too, that these same accounts also downplay imagining and glancing, the two primary ways in which we cope with edges in everyday life.) For edges are recalcitrant to most philosophical efforts to assimilate them; they do not fit tidily into schemes of synthesis or subsumption, dialectics or dynamics; they tend to tear the dense fabric of the perceptual world, jutting through this fabric as much as the earth (on Heidegger's assessment) juts through the world that encompasses it and interprets it.[16] This is part of their verticality: their standing up against the aggrandizing efforts of philosophical systems to draw them into their midst, to en-compass them; but it is also due to their occlusive and obstructive powers, their resistance to open vision and free movement. If borders draw *out*—that is, trace out limits of the land and of cultural space—edges draw *up*, tightening the limits of a thing in angular compression. Borders are linear or quasi-linear tracings of a laid-out land and space, while edges are intensely focused endings of compacted things short of their implacement in a more capacious environment. We need both, and we have both: most notably in the case of the natural environment, but also in certain cityscapes.

III

Where and how do borders and boundaries figure into the natural, the other-than-human world, and what are the consequences of their interplay in that world? Consider the well-known fact that "birds sing to mark out their territory."[16] They also move in groups in relation to the same sense of territory. What do these facts really mean? The situation is of some environmental urgency. It is well known that in 1972 there were approximately 7.72 million skylarks in England; by 1996, their population was down to an estimated 3.09 million. Everywhere and not just in England, one hears fewer songbirds. This is attributed to the loss of their "ecological niches or homes—hedgerows, heaths, ponds, meadows, moors and marshes—[that] have been eroded by the intensive use of agri-chemicals and pesticides which have decimated their food supply" (ibid.). A destruction of places has meant a loss of the songs that demarcated—and celebrated—these places. Place is thus a key: if its edges are eroded, then the place-specific activities that occur in its midst will no longer be supported and will drift or die away. Just as the pesticides and agri-chemicals seep into places and undermine them from below (in terms of soil erosion as well as the contamination of underground water) as well as from above (in the form of acid rain and wind-blown chemicals), so the songs that honored them will lose their point and vanish. The singers will go elsewhere—to other places, with more intact identities thanks to healthier substructures. If they can be found . . .

The fact that we are dealing with sounds and not with overtly traced lines should not mislead us: borders and boundaries are established in many ways, not just by visible marks left on stone or soil. So too the edge of Spanish Harlem near where I live is not marked by any single street or even set of blocks; rather, it is established by cultural practices, ways of talking and gesturing that no city map could ever capture. Nevertheless, there is a distinguishable place coherently called "Spanish Harlem" that has its own exactitude and its own means of measurement—no less so than do the territories staked out by birdsongs. In both cases, it is a matter of a "prespatial" implacement by means of moving bodies. Viewed from the standpoint of cartographic and geographic precision, Spanish Harlem and a skylark haven in the British countryside might seem to be degenerate cases of location in the cityscape and landscape respectively. Yet they have their own standards of precision, their own determinate forms.

In *Ideas I* Husserl distinguishes between "exact" and "morphological" essences; the latter are "intrinsically vague," as we can see in the shape designated as "umbelliform" (i.e., a shell-like structure). Many things can count as umbelliform—ranging from seashells to washbowls, dishes to watercolor palettes—since there is no one rigid model that must be replicated throughout in certain specified dimensions and proportions. Considerable variation is allowed, indeed in certain contexts (e.g., ceramics) encouraged—and still the basic umbelliform shape survives and is recognized as such. This signifies that it has its own determinacy, its own way of *staying the same* in the midst of change; of which sameness of style is one important variant. Such determinacy and sameness are compatible with considerable differences of manifestation and perception—in contrast with a criterion that would require replication of an identical pattern as a basis for seeing and designating something as continuously recognizable. (For example, I was painting along the Connecticut shoreline this August—an annual ritual I undertake with several painter friends, though usually in Maine—and I was at first struck at how different the Connecticut coast was from that of Maine: fewer boulders at the edge, no conifers growing right above the beach, a less tumultuous sea. But after painting at several locations along this coast, I began to realize that, nevertheless, there were significant commonalities such that one could say that *this* shoreline was continuous with *that* coast farther north—and that both were integral parts of what one would designate as "northeastern American Atlantic coastline." [Indeed, each shoreline was what Merleau-Ponty calls a "total part": a part in which the whole fully resides and vice versa.[17]] So here is an instance of an edge that was morphologically the *same* in and across manifest differences: it was not identically the same [that is why I was at first disappointed to find so many discrepancies], but it was still essentially the same: where "essentially" connotes sameness of coastal configuration that is exemplified in the very midst of difference.)

Here is another recent experience that points in a similar direction. Every day at about six P.M. I can see from the windows of my high-rise Manhattan apartment a congregation of birds whose identity I cannot make out because of their distance. They gather from I know not where to form a flock of some twenty to thirty to fifty birds (and sometimes, two such groups) that proceed to move together over a certain set of buildings—always the same three or four buildings. They do not descend to scavenge for food; they stay in pattern throughout a period of some forty minutes or more; eventually, they move on, still as a group, into a more distant area where I cannot discern them any more. This is doubtless a piece of ritualistic behavior, and it is enacted not by sounds (not any that I can detect from my distant aerie) but by flying in a repetitive vortical pattern. I have the sense that they are not so much demarcating, much less claiming, lasting territory, as creating (and continually recreating) a momentary place in the sky that is their own. This is done in relation to human habitation and quite specifically a set of buildings on the ground; but these seem to act as orientational anchors rather than as irreplaceable locatory references (as is signified by the fact that the birds are able and willing to move to another such scene). They are not wedded to the scene I am witnessing, yet they do re-create it daily and at much the same time, suggesting that the temporality of the birds' ritualistic motions is part of their place-making power. They are not creating castles in the air but lairs there—atmospheric places to which they can return again and again. These places have their own boundaries that are traced out by the birds' circumambulation: boundaries that are morphologically if not analytically precise.[18]

What I am saying here is not just that there is something regular and repetitive about the ritual I watch late every day but that, still more important, something *spatially specific* about it. This spatial specificity consists in a definite shape with its own boundaries—such that I can designate the outward contour traced by the flock's collective flight as a gentle vortex, a solid form that is recognizably the same day after day. (One is here reminded of Descartes's claim that space is composed of a dense series of vortices, one packed into another, world without end.) It is also specific enough to contrast with other forms I see in the same panoramic prospect from my window: most strikingly, the aggressively linear path of airplanes descending to land at nearby LaGuardia Airport (many of which arrive in New York just about the time the birds decide to do their place ballet: the teleological track of the planes standing in stark contrast with the seemingly purposeless purpose of the birds' winged movements). Yet the shape itself, being traced out differently every day, would not pass muster as a "vortex" as defined in a classical textbook on topology. Here we have, then, a study in the generation and presentation of boundaries that do not fit classical criteria yet are part of the everyday ecology of the city in which I live. They have their own coherence and their own life, even if this life is not often appreciated for what it is: a fantastic creation and recreation of a recurrent morphological shape in air as thin as it is empty. To *this* all too human bird, myself, the spectacle is altogether moving—and altogether mysterious. At the very least it shows that the definite and the indefinite— border and boundary, edge and free motion—meet and are compatible in the other-than human world. The initial opposition between these pairs of terms, as well as that between exact and morphological geometries, begins to melt away the closer we look.

IV

Other birds, seen from my same perch, fly alone and trace out even more arcane arabesques in the form of very fluid flight patterns. Certain gulls and white herons fly their own course, glide high above Morningside Heights Park (where I first spot them), then dart between or behind the tall towers close by, continuing toward the East River—out and out until they disappear from my unassisted sight. Here I can detect no regular pattern, but I have been looking only for a month now and I believe that with time I shall discern a larger topo-logic in these fluent flights. The mere fact that such birds wing it alone does not mean that they are not tracing out regions whose shapes would become evident to the close observer.

One bird I saw recently flew straight over Central Park, circling above the "Harlem Meer," the lake in the northeastern corner, then headed south along Fifth Avenue, apparently on its way to the Gauguin show at the Metropolitan Museum. That set me to thinking about Central Park itself as a most curious hybrid place: it is certainly an amalgam of the natural and the constructed—many of the original geological features (hills, large rocks, trees) having been kept even if incorporated shrewdly into the very extensive landscaping that was first undertaken in the 1860s in accordance with Olmsted and Vaux's prize-winning plan and still being modified down to this day: to the point where every natural feature is now part of some more or less cultivated landscape, while beneath the park itself is a vast underworld of drainage lines, irrigation lines, storm sewers, electric lines, gas and telephone lines, and the walls of abandoned reservoirs.

But more important for our purposes, Central Park is a paradigm case of a place that has creatively incorporated and transformed a rectilinear outer edge—it is nothing but a huge rectangle, after all, set in the midst of a relentless grid plan in the center of America's largest city. Viewed externally from above—from the perch of "survol" of which Merleau-Ponty speaks and which, ironically, is occupied only by birds, those proto-geometers—it seems to capitulate to all the baneful aspects of what Eugene Minkowski called "morbid geometrism" (1970, 277 ff).[19] Its literal edge is geometric in the most classical Euclidean sense, and it is difficult to see any redemptive virtues in a severe linearism that is reinforced by streets acting as a formal frame (110th Street on the north, 59th on the south, Fifth Avenue on the east, then Central Park West). One is confronted with this outer edge not only from without or above but from within, since at many points inside the Park one glimpses the schist perimeter walls that line the framing streets. It is precisely when contemplating such an unrelieved outer shape that one is drawn to the virtues of boundaries, as I have done myself in previous writings on place: boundaries being once again osmotic and open, places of traversal across which lived bodies move—in short, where "something begins its presencing." Proceeding in this high-spirited way, one contrasts (as I have also done) French formal gardens in their overt geometricity with English parks that attempt to be as unbounded and wild as possible—to the point where the boundary is itself literally buried in a shallow trench that cannot be seen from more than a few hundred yards: the trench being called a "ha-ha," as if to mock the idea of a strictly defined property line. (Central Park has its own version of the ha-ha in the form of burying and obscuring from view the tranverse roads that cut across Central Park from east to west at several points.[20] A tempting dualism—yet in the end just another binary as dubious as those more conceptual contrasts that Western metaphysical thought continually invents and reinvents to comfort and protect itself.

The remarkable thing about Central Park—"the genius of the place" (in Alexander Pope's resonant phrase)—is that it massively and materially deconstructs the dyad of exclusive options bequeathed by the European park tradition. It combines touches of French formalism (e.g., in the grand promenade or "Literary Walk" in the center of the Park and in the circular Rose Garden) with English wildness (in sectors marked "Forever Wild"),[21] all in the same place, by an ingenious strategy: with rare exceptions, the formality is kept at the edge, indeed *as* the edge, while the sense of countryside (a word in which we still hear "contra": *against* the temptations of geometry) flourishes within these same borders. The straight line has its place at the outer limit, while what Capability Brown called the "curvy line" is allowed to proliferate and prosper everywhere within this fierce limit. (I refer to the myriad pathways throughout the Park, some well-marked and public, others barely traced; but all winding through the space in ways that respect the local topography.) Any straight lines inside the Park's perimeters—whether transverse roads or utility lines—are literally encrypted from view.

In fact, the matter is still more complex than this and all the more philosophically interesting. The Park is not just a piece of burgeoning landscape set within a box—any more than New York City itself is nothing but a grid pattern situated between two rivers serving as strict edges. Rather than tightly containing, the very borders of the Park are perforated throughout

by incursions of several sorts: cross-streets that suddenly lose their straight-
ness once they enter the Park (e.g., at Eighty-second Street, and from the
extreme north and south ends); broad gateways, for example, at Seventy-
second Street; countless entrances for pedestrians, themselves highly varie-
gated (some just narrow passageways, some leisurely walkways that can
accommodate large groups, some opening straight onto flat land, others
scooped out of sheer rock, etc.). At certain points, Central Park seems
almost barricaded by dense outcroppings of stones and trees; at others, it is
altogether pervious and accommodating. At the northwestern corner, near
where I now live, one can enter the park in at least six different places, each
of them different, yet all within a few hundred yards of each other. In all of
these ways, and many others, the exactitude of the edge is tempered and creatively transfigured. It remains an edge, reinforced by the unremittingly perpendicular streets around it and their unrelenting traffic, the surrounding
sidewalks, and perimeter walls along most of the Park's border. But this is an
edge like no other—no other in the official lexicon of continuous straight
lines that exclude any such free variation.

What is most remarkable is that this is the case of something that is
experienced (seen, felt, known) *as an edge* yet as an edge that does not
exclude but, on the contrary, *opens itself to its own penetration.* Here is an
edge that retains the rigor of a formal border—it is unquestionably a termination: here the Park ends!—yet also displays all the mellow receptivity
of a boundary: here the Park begins! Refused is not just the choice between
French versus English park styles (Olmsted and Vaux were themselves
most influenced by the Picturesque, already a third alternative), but more
important, any forced choice between edge and interior, perimeter and
content, limit and the unlimited. For the outer edge of Central Park opens
in such a way as to lead immediately to what is inside: no sooner do I enter
the northwest corner than I find myself in the midst of rather wild under-
brush, dense copses of trees, obscure paths, hidden streams, gigantic rocks.
All of this in the center of one of the most populous and putatively civilized cities in the world! Here, indeed, we truly "edge into the environment," wherein the difference between borders and boundaries, otherwise
as sacrosanct as that between geometry and experience (and ultimately
tributary from this latter binary), dissolves under our very feet as we enter
the Park. In such an experience, it is as if elements from one of the contrasting terms were already present in the other: factors of the boundary
are present in the border, matters of the border in the boundary. As a landscape architect who has reshaped parts of Central Park has written to me,

"In many ways, Central Park is a series of edges [and] boundaries rather than a complete[ly] integrated place. Perhaps that is why it is so dangerous, because its danger comes from the city to which it is so porous, and not from nature against which it is so opaque. There is no center [here] innocent of its perimeter."[22]

This does not mean that we must give up the contrast between borders and boundaries, paths and perimeters—Central Park shows that we need both kinds of spatial limits, rigorous as well as mellow ones, to account for our full experience there—but it does show that the differences are far from absolute: that they are compenetrative presences. What Merleau-Ponty said of the archetypal differences between nature and culture could be said as well of borders and boundaries:

> . . . the distinction between the two planes (natural and cultural) is abstract: everything is cultural in us (our Lebenswelt is "subjective") (our perception is cultural-historical) and everything is natural in us (even the cultural rests on the polymorphism of the wild Being). (VI 253)

This very statement, I should add, is particularly apropos of Central Park, in which what is natural and what is contrived, what found and what cultivated, have become inseparable over time and often finally indistinguishable. So, too, what is boundary and what border have become so intertangled as to be inseparable—though still in certain respects distinguishable. They have become not just compatible with each other but act to augment each other's presence—much as the frame of a painting, though altogether rectangular, may enhance our experience of the painting itself.

V

But enough of the local landscape! We need to fly farther afield—to St. Louis. I have fond memories of being a participant in the Phenomenology Workshops led by Herbert Spiegelberg in the late 1960s. One fine summer day we decamped to the Gateway Arch, then being built. Herbert asked us, in the spirit of direct description, to write of our experience of the overtowering structure. Each of us found this difficult, for reasons we went on to discuss: issues of scale, of novelty of style, of unclear purpose, were at stake.[23] Now, decades later, the Arch has been completed and is an accepted part of the regional scene. I drove by it a year and a half ago on my way from Carbondale to the St. Louis airport, and barely batted an eye. But on further reflection I realized that the Arch raises questions closely related to those under pursuit in this chapter: What kind of opening does the Arch represent? Is it a boundary or a border? What is its relationship to history? To nature? What is its ecological significance?

Here is a structure that reaches as high as birds fly and that suggests upward movement by its very structure.[24] This structure is that of a solid hyperbolic parabaloid, and yet in experiencing it one is not primarily interested in its exact geometry—no more than one consciously thinks of the rectangular shape of Central Park when on a picnic there. One feels the soaring, and one looks not just at the Arch but through it into the distant landscape and the sky beyond. The aperture is as important as the formal structure. Also striking is the way the Arch rises directly from the earth, reminding us of Blake's engraving of Newton holding his calipers and looking at a blueprint while his two feet are as firmly planted on the unadorned ground as the two ends of the Arch are on the St. Louis earth. And one cannot help but notice the Mississippi River flowing by at the feet of the Arch. This is an entity which, despite its formal perfection, is very much rooted in the elements of earth and water below even as it links up with the air and sky above. It is a Gateway to the elements as much as it is a Gateway to the American West.

As the latter, it is embroiled in history as well as nature. It is poised at the eastern end of this Western world—at a place through which many early pioneers and settlers passed. The Arch commemorates this place and period by its very location on the border of the West. In this aspect of its identity, precision of implacement is indispensable: it could not just be located anywhere in the Middle West. By taking up a stand just *here,* it establishes itself as the herald of what it seeks to commemorate. At the same time, its symbolism of opening—of being a Gate/Way—institutes it as a boundary, as something through which much has passed (including my forebears on their way to Kansas) and continues to pass. If its status as an edge is resolutely geographical—placial, though not a matter of simple location—its status as a boundary is spatiotemporal, in short, historical. The arch must serve as both border and boundary in these senses if it is to be a fully effective monument. As with Central Park and the birds that fly near it, though now in a very different shape, these two notions of limit cannot be kept apart: here as well they enter into a complex commixture in which elements of one are present in the other and the reverse. The precision of the border rejoins the vagueness of the boundary: precision as geometrical (i.e., the shape of the solid curve) and geographical (i.e., the location on the Mississippi and in eastern Missouri), vagueness as morphological (one's sense of being enticed through an opening with an unusual torus-like shape) and historical (just which period is being commemorated? has it ended? to whom did it belong?).

But we must press on to other, more pointed questions that concern our life in the present: To what kind of life did the life that streamed through the Gateway Arch give rise? Is the very concept of gateway any longer viable today? Here I shall be employing the gateway as an opening onto issues that are ecological and technological—and that continue to bear on the border/boundary distinction. One striking fact in this context is that the pesticides and herbicides that have been used for some time now in the farmlands to which the Arch gives access spatially and historically have had a strikingly deleterious effect: these same farm lands are the very likely cause of the so-called Dead Zone in the Gulf of Mexico, that oxygen-deficient part of the Gulf that is inimical to creatures of the sea.[25] These nitrogen-loaded agri-chemicals have washed downstream from the Smoky Hill in Kansas and the Platte in Nebraska and other like waterways into the Missouri and thence the Mississippi, flowing right by the Gateway Arch itself on their way to debouchement in the Gulf, where they have collected and formed an enormous vortex in which it is difficult for fish to breathe: very different from the innocent shape that was sky-sculpted by the birds I observed over Manhattan. This is a sinister spiral that deals death to everything that enters it. Stagnant and self-perpetuating, it only gets more deadly with time as more and more chemical debris comes into it from the very Midwestern farms that were first established in the period celebrated by the Gateway Arch (i.e., the mid-nineteenth century). These farms, often laid out on a square or rectangular grid pattern (in keeping with the Land Survey Act of 1785, which ordained that counties west of Pennsylvania should be as rectilinear as possible), cannot contain their own poisons, which seep out under their legally established borders into adjoining lands, joining underground waters there in a continual runoff into adjoining creeks and streams—then into rivers, small and large, then into the Gulf. Invisible to the eye, and not even felt underfoot, this disastrous hydropharmacology ends by endangering a major region of the earth's oceanic waters. Here the precisely determined edges on the surface of the land—marked out by "boundary stones" or designated in surveyer's maps—cannot control, or even reflect, what is happening underneath them by way of deleterious seepage. What had been a virtue when confining edges are compared with a more porous model of delimitation—Husserl's as well as Heidegger's starting point—now shows its dark underside, its shadow beneath the surface of the earth. One moral to be drawn from this appalling situation is that when borders are obsessively created and maintained in legal or cartographic precision, human beings are led to neglect what is happening at a level that, invisible in itself, subtends them. Keeping borders strictly on the surface of the earth—as literally happens with "property lines"—courts disaster in the dark chthonic depths, in whose Cimmerian darkness neither borders nor boundaries can be discerned.

VI

But our concern is with ecology, and I want to end with some reflections on the larger ecological significance of the border/boundary issue. I take "ecology" to be very broad in scope, broad enough to include an ecology of mind in the spirit of Bateson and Guattari, and manifest and public enough to render places like Central Park and the Gateway Arch ecological ventures in their own right. These latter are attempts to realign our thinking and living in relation to the natural landscape, and in this regard they are to be ranged alongside the more concerted environmental experimentation undertaken at places like the Land Institute in Kansas or the Nature Institute in upstate New York. Central Park reshaped a comparatively untamed part of the island of Manhattan—filled with promontories and rocks, shanties and goats—to create a single complex region in which trees, water, earth, and humans (and birds, if no longer goats!) could coexist. After the burial mounds in Ohio and elsewhere, it can be considered America's first significant earth-work.[26] The Gateway Arch is a massive structure reminiscent of a single vault of a vast nave built right over earth and river, an "air-work" encouraging human beings to look through it to lands farther west in which the natural and the human had made their (admittedly imperfect) peace. The difference is that Central Park is an ongoing ecological experiment (parts of its are still being landscaped and reconstructed), while the Gateway Arch, now complete and with a flourishing park of its own at its base, points primarily to a past experiment in land settlement and agricultural practice. It is an ecological monument as it were, symbolic of the opportunities of settling into the Middle Western environment of an earlier era.

Everybody knows that *oikos*, the root of the first part of the word "ecology," means "home," "dwelling," "household." But we don't often reflect on the fact that every home or dwelling is what it is only because of the walls with which it is built—walls that protect and support as well as give access (by way of doors and windows) to people, light, and air. These walls are borders for the household and consist of edges throughout: windowsills, corners, and so on. Anything eco-logical in this core sense will therefore have to do with limits and not just with growth and life; a biocentric ecology—and most ecological thought has had just this focus—needs to be supplemented by a nomocentric sensitivity: where *nomos* brings connotations of distribution in space from the root verb *nemó*: "to take to pasture." As Toynbee and more recently Deleuze and Guattari stress, nomadic life is composed not of merely dispersed movements but of circular and recurrent journeys that move from preestablished place to preestablished place.[27] These places, though not demarcated by any official state apparatus and though not consisting of walls or even fences, nevertheless possess definite limits—that is, edges known to the nomads who traverse them and live in them with seasonal regularity. In short, they have their own precision, one that is very different from what the rational *logos* of the state would dictate. This amounts to a landscape morphology that cannot be captured by any formal geometry: a "dialectical landscape" in Robert Smithson's term, one that allows for change and the unexpected (e.g., in weather and in shifting populations) and not just for the stasis of settled form. Here we have ecology of distributed movement and dwelling in an open landscape, long before any Royal Science such as Euclidean geometry has intervened—ecology without the constrictive logic of such a Science. As Smithson writes apropos of Central Park in his remarkable essay, "Frederick Law Olmsted and the Dialectical Landscape":

> A park can no longer be seen as a "thing-in-itself," but rather as a process of ongoing relationships existing in a physical region— the park becomes a "thing-for-us" . . . Price, Gilpin, and Olmsted are forerunners of a dialectical materialism applied to the physical landscape. Dialectics of this type are a way of seeing things in a manifold of relations, not as isolated objects. Nature for the dialectician is *indifferent* to any formal ideal.[28]

The key phrase here is "manifold of relations," signifying the way in which the edge of something, most notably a place with ecological import, is not merely a matter of occlusion or obstruction (as we tend to believe on a first consideration of the concept) but of an open matrix of ramifying relations: those between what is inside and outside the edge to be sure, but also the myriad relations that obtain between the parts (and parts of parts) of any given ecological whole (a park or a monument, a house or a region) and in turn between these ever-proliferating parts and the whole itself. To explore ecology through the edge, far from closing down on inquiry, is on the contrary, to open up an entire domain of thought.[29] "Looking on the nature of the park, or its history and our perceptions of it," adds Smithson, "we are at first presented with an endless maze of relations and interconnections, in which nothing remains what or where it is, as a thing-in-itself, but the whole park changes like day and night, in and out, dark and light . . ." (1996, 165). A statement such as this returns us to Merleau-Ponty, for whom the surrounding world is to be regarded as *"for us* an *in-itself"* (PhP 77; his italics). Despite his lack of interest in edges per se, and even though he did not (to my knowledge) engage with the ecological science of his time, his conception of landscape is very close to that of Olmsted and Vaux—and Smithson, their most insightful recent interpreter. Had Merleau-Ponty ever come to America, I think he would have enjoyed Central Park as a remarkably complex landscape set in the midst of a city. More important, his own version of dialectical materialism—in which the lived body is the moving center of any landscape scene—would embrace the kind of ecology that is exemplified in the planning and continued creation of the Park.

VII

Let me return in closing to my three leading examples for a last look: the flight of the birds, the layout of Central Park, and the monumentality of the Gateway Arch. Each is ecological in the expansive sense on which I have just drawn. The circulating birds create a distinctive eco-zone by their sheer movements, a transparent vortical shape that is swept out by their winged flight. There are no walls here, and the transparency is not crystalline; neither is it lasting: it has to be re-created each time, not only each day in the late afternoon but by each encirclement of the congregated brethren. The morphological shape they trace out is no less impressive for being created by bodily motions alone, pure kinetics. And it remains a matter of edge, since the observer is aware of the outer limits, the boundaries, of the flight pattern even if these are, strictly speaking, invisible. Let us call this extraordinary situation *spontaneous ecology*. It is not limited to birds; any free but regular and repeated movement of bodies will do the same, for example, in the household economics of family members as they assume characteristic positions and locations within the home-place on a daily basis. But birds manage to bring forth eco-places from thin air, with no ulterior motives of power or productivity, and thus in a most spontaneous fashion.

The St. Louis Gateway Arch is at the other extreme of eco-placement. Far from spontaneous, it is dependent on high and heavy technology, so much so that it is in danger of being surpassed by better technology at any moment of its history. Regarded as a gateway, it is now all but replaced by telecommunicational networks, which (as Virilio argues) dispense with the gateways of the city, and are at once abstract and instantaneous—unlike the concrete and successive relationships at play in eco-places with material boundaries and borders.[30] The Gateway Arch, for all its bold architectural glory, gives an ambiguous message in the end, divided as it is between a modernist identity in terms of style and the commemoration of a premodern agricultural past. As a pure but physically static symbol, it cannot compete with the speedier technologies of transmission that relentlessly traverse it without looking back. This is why it ends as a *monument*—a word that connotes stasis in time as well as space—instead of being an active and changing eco-place in its own right. The Arch is frozen forever in its elegant exact shape; there is no longer any change, much less spontaneity, in the circumstance; only the river flowing by and the park below, added since my primal experience of the breathtakingly gigantic structure, provide ecological relief, thanks to the vegetation of the one and the water of the other; but the true action is elsewhere—out in the prairies, there in the past, or (if there is a present here) in the ecological disaster seething beneath the meager topsoil of these same prairies. The result is a monumentalization of ecological region and its transformation into a static site.

Lying between these two extremes is Central Park, which I have presented as a viable eco-place that is neither a matter of wholly spontaneous movements (it is too earthbound for that) nor of high technology (the highest order machine in the park is a simple telephone to call the police in distress; even the lamp posts have a nineteenth-century design). Modest in its appearance, it boasts no monumental buildings—only boathouses and restrooms. If birds are uniquely capable of creating the first kind of eco-zone and human technology (aided by an inspired architect) the second, in the case of Central Park we witness a creative commixture of the human and the other-than-human in a decidedly low-tech environment. This is why it offers a genuinely dialectical landscape composed of terms normally in tension but brought together here in a rare embrace: trees and open fields, animals and humans, paved streets and barely traced paths, public and private (a private corporation now oversees the park, even though public workers are employed to keep it clean and pleasing),[31] not to mention the many ethnicities and social classes who here commingle in a complicated and sometimes dangerous but ultimately coherent coexistence. This "democratic dialectic between the sylvan and the industrial"[32] is very nineteenth-century in origin and inspiration—a period in which the prevailing cultural axiom was "les extremes se touchent" (e.g., in the form of religion and science, spiritualism and evolution, nature and culture)—but, in Central Park, unlike the Gateway Arch, there is no monumentalizing of previous time, no obsession with the past. Instead, the inherent power of the place, its considerable ecological resources, are open to new times and new peoples in an encompassing democratic vista in which the incompossible becomes possible overnight. In contrast with the gulls' guileless gliding, this is an enormously effortful ecological project (ten million house-cart loads of earth had to be moved to reshape the Park in its first years).[33] But this is nevertheless a continually adaptive and readaptive ecological circumstance that takes on all comers and then some: all weathers, all peoples, all events. Perhaps this is because it exemplifies so consummately the Merleau-Pontian postulate cited earlier: "everything is cultural in us . . . and everything is natural in us . . ." That is certainly the case here: every bit of landscape is culturally saturated, and anything identifiably cultural (e.g., the Dutch design of the boathouse at the Harlem Meer) is ensconced in a natural setting.

But I have suggested that in Central Park there is also a marriage of the border and the boundary—the exact and the inexact, the geometric and the morphological, the limited and the undelimited—that is as rare as it is ecologically salutary. The failure to bring these particular extremes together is itself a primary failure of ecology, and I claim that the Gateway Arch, for all its architectural merit and formal verve, suffers from this very failure: its beauty as a sheer shape in effect defying its implacement on the earth and by a river, its elegant edges out of touch with the blunt boundaries of its base, its verticality flying too far free from the local landscape. Central Park—mostly flat, with no soaring structures in a city renowned for the height of its buildings, and with no trace of high modernism—is a far more successful *place* for man and beast and fowl, earth and water and air to become partners in a common ecological project that is still ongoing and from which we still have lessons to learn: lessons about the creative merging of borders and boundaries and about how to edge into the environment: how to make edgeway there. Let the birds of the air take notice—in flocks! Let human beings enter—in droves![34]

Notes

1. It follows that "this internal animation, this radiation of the visible is what the painter seeks under the name of depth, of space, of color" (OE 182).

2. "The real is a closely woven fabric" (PhP x).

3. My italics. Another reference is at PhP 13: "The question is, what makes up this significance [of the parts of a Gestalt whole], what do the words 'edge' and 'outline' mean . . . ?" It is striking that Merleau-Ponty does not go on to answer his own question.

4. The full statement is: "Unless you expect the unexpected you will never find [truth], for it is hard to discover and hard to attain." (Fragment # 18 [Diels] in the Philip Wheelwright translation in Philip Wheelwright [1968, 10]).

5. Merleau-Ponty's italics. The case of Matisse is in fact more complex, as Merleau-Ponty avers himself a page later: he "taught us to see their contours not in a 'physical-optical' way but rather as structural filaments (*des nervures*), as the axes of a corporeal system of activity and passivity. Figurative or not, the line is [here] no longer a thing or an imitation of a thing" (OE 185).

6. Cited by Merleau-Ponty from Bergson's "La vie et l'oeuvre de Ravaisson" at OE 183.

7. Merleau-Ponty's italics. He adds that such lines are "*between* or *behind* whatever we fix our eyes upon" (ibid.; my italics).

8. "The point-horizon structure can teach me what a point is only in virtue of the maintenance of a hither zone of corporeality from which to be seen, and round about it [are] indeterminate horizons which are the counterpart of this seeing" (PhP 102).

9. Cf. also PhP 6.

10. ". . . significations in tufts, thickets of proper meanings and figurative meanings" (VI 130).

11. On blind spots, see Working Note of May 1960 entitled "Blindness (*punctum caecum*) of the 'consciousness" (VI 248); see also p. 255. On the shadow, see "The Philosopher and his Shadow" (S 159–181).

12. OE 182; Merleau-Ponty italicizes the "as."

13. Roughly, a *limit* is the extremity of an action or a thing, a *non plus ultra* which functions exclusively in terms of *that which* it limits; a *perimeter* is a linear contour that fully surrounds a given artificial or natural thing: it traces out the shape of what would otherwise be a border or limit.

14. This is J. J. Gibson's formulation in *An Ecological Approach to Visual Perception*, Glossary.

15. "Earth juts through (*durchragt*) the world and world grounds itself on the early only so far as truth happens as the primal conflict between clearing and concealing" (Heidegger 1971, 55).

16. From the Translators' Introduction to Félix Guattari (2000, 7).

17. On the "total part," see VI 134: the visible and the tangible form a composite in the body such that "the two parts are total parts and yet are not superposable."

18. A friend suggests that what I describe in this last paragraph is something quite different called "tossing": a school of racing pigeons who are being trained on rooftops: they are released from coops and fly round and round: tossing. Older pigeons called "droppers" are trained to return to the coop after a signal from the trainer, who yields a long stick to guide the birds in their flight. This may well the case, but I have not yet seen any such stick and I do not have the sense that the birds return to the same rooftop. I shall have to leave the matter open for now (Christina Maile, communication of 9/15/02).

19. One is reminded of the Nazca lines whose geometricity can only be appreciated from far above, even though in the case of Central Park its regular outline is present at the periphery of one's vision most of the time, for example, by glimpsing the buildings facing the streets of the perimeter as well as the walls around the same perimeter. Even when one has no such visual reminders, the lamp posts bear the number of the nearest cross-street.

20. These transverse roads introduce a rectilinear factor inside Central Park, and their literal incorporation seems to act as a defense against their presence: as if to say that there is already enough rectilinearity around the Park, whose inner space should be kept for more curvaceous and winding paths and roads.

21. The "Forever Wild" portions were introduced in the northwest part of the Park within the last few decades; they were not part of the Olmsted and Vaux design. They are thus "more an acknowledgement of current sensibilities than of the original aesthetics of Olmsted and Vaux" (Christina Maile, communication of 9/15/02). But the original design nevertheless *allowed for* this contemporary development: that, too, is intrinsic to the genius of the place.

22. Christina Maile, e-mail communication of 9/15/02.

23. Only Edward Ballard rose to the challenge, publishing an excellent study of the experience of the Arch (Smith 1970, 187–201); reprinted in Moran and Embree (2004, II 30–42).

It is notable that one always thinks of the Gateway Arch in elevation—that is, as seen from the side—whereas Central Park is imagined in plan, that is, from above (Observation of Christina Maile in e-mail communication of 9/15/02).

24. On the formation of the Dead Zone, see Nancy Rabalais and R. E. Turner (2001, 1–36). For a discussion of this example in the context of boundaries, see Wes Jackson & Jerry Glover, "The Need for a Taxonomy of Boundaries," paper delivered at a conference on "Toward a Taxonomy of Boundaries," Matfield Green, Kansas, May 30–June 2, 2002.

26. Smithson regards Olmsted as "America's first 'earthwork artist'" (1996, 164). Smithson continues: "Central Park is a ground work of necessity and chance, a range of contrasting viewpoints that are forever fluctuating, yet solidly based in the earth" (ibid., p. 165).

27. On the regularity of nomadic life, see Arnold Toynbee (1947, 164–186), as well as Gilles Deleuze and Félix Guattari (1987), chapter 12, "Nomadology."

28. Smithson (1996, 160; his italics). He adds: "Olmsted's parks exist before they are finished, which means in fact that they are never finished; they remain carriers of the unexpected and of contradiction on all levels of human activity, be it social, political, or natural" (ibid., p. 160).

29. It can be argued that the theory of evolution as natural selection took a definitive step forward when Darwin began to take seriously the mutations that occurred *at the edges of given populations*. It was at the outer limits of these populations that Darwin detected the presence of the most innovative alterations—as if only there was significant experimentalism, freed from the cloying habitudes of the major population, possible. See Charles Darwin, *Origin of Species*.

30. "The representation of the modern city can no longer depend on the ceremonial opening of gates . . . In terms of access, telematics replaces the doorway. The sound of gates gives way to the clatter of data banks and the rites of passage of a technical culture whose progress is disguised by the immateriality of its parts and networks . . . Where once one necessarily entered the city by means of a physical gateway, now one passes through an audiovisual protocol in which the methods of audience and surveillance have transformed even the forms of public greeting and daily reception" (Paul Virilio, 1991, 13–14).

31. More exactly, the City of New York Parks and Recreation Department maintains the Park and improves the local landscaping, while restoration projects are funded by the private corporation called Central Park Conservancy. Another public/private dyad is found in the juxtaposition of wealthy residences that ring a space open to everyone. Smithson cites Paul Shepard's observation that for Olmsted "the opulent . . . should be induced to surround the park with villas, which were to be enjoyed as well as the trees by the humble folk, since they 'delight in viewing magnificent and imposing structures.' A kind of American doubletalk reconciling villas with democracy and privilege with society in general had begun" (cited by Smithson 1996, 160), from Paul Shepard (1982).

32. Smithson (1996, 162). Smithson cites Lewis Mumford in *The Brown Decades*: "When Charles Eliot Norton said of him (Olmsted), towards the close of his career, that of all American artists he stood 'first in the production of great works which answer the needs and give expression to the life of our immense and miscellaneous democracy', he did not exaggerate Olmsted's influence" (cited in Smithson [1996, 168]).

33. Smithson cites this figure (1996, 164), where he also calls Olmsted an "ecologist of the real."

34. I wish to thank Susan Bredlau, William Hamrick, Wendy Gittler, Christina Maile, Parvis Mohassel, and Henry Tylbor for helpful comments on an earlier draft.

REFERENCES

Ballard, Edward G. 1970. "The Visual Perception of Distance." In Smith, 187–201, and reprinted in Moran & Embree, II: 30–42.

Deleuze, Gilles and Félix Guattari. 1987. *A Thousand Plateaus: Capitalism and Schizophrenia.* Translated by Brian Massumi. Minneapolis: University of Minnesota Press. Originally published in 1980 as *Mille Plateaux, Capitalisme et schizophrénie.* Paris: Les Editions de Minuit.

Guattari, Félix. 2000. *The Three Ecologies.* Translated by Ian Pindar and Paul Sutton. London: Athlone Press.

Heidegger, Martin. 1971. "The Origin of the Work of Art." In *Poetry Language Thought.* Translated by Albert Hofstadter. New York: 1971. Originally published in 1950 as "Der Ursprung des Kunstwerkes" in *Holzwege.* Frankfurt Am Main: Vittorio Klostermann.

Minkowski, Eugène. 1970. *Lived Time.* Evanston: Northwestern University Press. Translated by Nancy Metzel. Originally published in 1933 as *Le Temps vécu.* Paris: Collection de l'Evolution Psychiatrique.

Moran, Dermott and Lester Embree, eds. 2004. *Phenomenology: Critical Concepts in Philosophy.* New York: Routledge.

Rabalais, Nancy and R. E. Turner. 2001. "Hypoxia in the Northern Gulf of Mexico: Description, Causes, and Change." In *2001: Coastal Hypoxia: Consequences for Living Resources and Ecosystems. Coastal and Estuarine Studies* 58, American Geophysical Union, 1-36.

Shepard, Paul. 1982. *Man in the Landscape: A Historic View of the Esthetics of Nature.* College Station: Texas A & M University Press.

Smith, F. J., ed. 1970. *Phenomenology in Perspective.* The Hague: Martinus Nijhoff.

Smithson, Robert. 1996. "Frederick Law Olmsted and the Dialectical Landscape." In *Robert Smithson: The Collected Writings.* Edited by Jack Flam. Berkeley: University of California Press.

Stravinsky, Igor. 1960. *Poetics of Music.* New York: Random House.

Toynbee, Arnold. 1947. *A Study of History.* Abridged by D. C. Somerwell. New York: Oxford University Press.

Virilio, Paul. 1991. *The Lost Dimension.* Translated by Daniel Moshenberg. New York: Semiotext(e).

Wheelwright, Philip. 1968. *Heraclitus.* New York: Atheneum Press.

5

Logos of Our Eco in the Feminine

An Approach Through Heidegger, Irigaray and Merleau-Ponty

Carol Bigwood

Preparations

Readers may well be wondering what I mean by *in the feminine.* By this term, I am not intending an ahistoric feminine principle. Neither am I restricting the meaning of feminine to the female sex. I understand "in the feminine" as a way of doing philosophy in a time when the cultural symbolic ignores and denies a feminine imaginary. In a vein similar to Irigaray's approach to philosophers, I am putting into relief feminine encoded meanings and metaphors in the work of philosophers with whom I engage. Thus with Heidegger's work, I focus on the more feminine aspect of our dwelling and building in the world earth home, which I understand to be the *techne* of cultivating. From Merleau-Ponty's descriptions of Flesh I will tease out an understanding of the body as primal ecological home. In this way, I hope to develop the notion of elemental being-in-touch, where touch is understood as empathetic, tender, and questioning. Although I do agree with some of Irigaray's misgivings about Merleau-Ponty, such as his propensity to rely on vision with its grasping nature in his descriptions of our perceptive being, I nonetheless think Merleau-Ponty's ontology can help "flesh out" her own notion of an ontology of the tangible.

By thinking on ecology as the "*logos* of our *eco,*" I am not inquiring solely after the structure or logic of the term *eco.* "*Eco*" is from the Greek "*oikos,*" meaning "home" in the sense of belonging to a household. I will understand "home" initially by following Heidegger's analysis as the place where we dwell and build in place for a time, focusing on home as a cultivating, and as a being in the earth-world-home, our human place of generative belonging. Then, with the help of Merleau-Ponty, Irigaray, and Sheets-Johnston, I will make the body more central to this discussion of our *eco*.

For an understanding of *logos*, I do not mean *logos* as in opposition to mythos, or in opposition to nature. I turn with Heidegger to the ancient Presocratic meaning of *Logos* (Heidegger, 1975b, 59–78). We have a recollection of this earlier meaning of *Logos* when we speak, for example, of the "nature" of things where we are not asking about the logic of a thing separated from its fuller being. For the pre-Socratics, the meaning of *Logos* is mergent with the meaning of *Phusis,* which is the ancient Greek word for "nature." *Phusis* is "nature" understood as the coming to be and passing away of all that is. It emphasizes nature as movement, growth and decay. Following Heidegger's analysis of Logos as the laying-out-that-gathers into a sheltering and safekeeping, I understand ecology (the *logos* of our *eco*), then, as the laying-out that gathers the *eco* where "gathering" remains an essential movement.

The following approach to eco-logy attempts to draw together ecofeminist and phenomenological thought. I am thinking alongside ecofeminists who understand women as forming a central part of environmental solutions. In coming to an understanding of our intimate relationship with the earth-world-home, they see a need to think feelingly, to pay attention to the health of our children and our own bodies, and they make use of intuitions that can occur in our simplest day-to-day experiences. They attempt to uncover the deep connections between many forms of oppression and are concerned with the effects of environmental degradation on the poor and vulnerable.

Ecofeminist philosophers often work to disrupt the mind/body dualism that contributes to the discontinuity of ourselves with nature. In my own attempt to dislodge this dualism, I pay attention to the way of writing itself. I search for thinking pathways that are poetic in their rationality, of ways of speaking that aren't cut off from my breath, and words that live in the atmosphere of my body. This search has led me to write "body papers," meaning that my bodily movements are an integral part of the meaning and creation of the essay. In a speaking context, I would deliver this paper with the full involvement of my body performing various movements and percussive effects at certain places in the paper, particularly when discussing Irigaray's work.[1] Given the written context of this paper,

I have provided cues for movement as one sees in a script so that the reader might imagine the words connected to a body in movement, rather than disconnected as in our usual texts. Words that are intended to be spoken in a call and response dialogue with a participant are italicized. In these portions of the text the reader should imagine the italicized words as accompanied by a body in full movement.

My intention is to let the body itself also speak, ensuring that the body is not just talked about but enters into the discussion. Bodily movements may imitate the meaning of words, strengthen arguments, add new connotations, and punctuate words with breath. Even in a written context, descriptions of a performative body can serve to allow the body an entrance into the discussion, remind the reader of how we are an intimate part of the animal kingdom, and how our bodily being is inextricably elemental.

DWELLING IN THE FEMININE: CULTIVATING

(My body spiraling around, and opening out with varied gestures of offering.)

To begin, I turn to Sappho for inspiration concerning logos. Why Sappho? She is a contemporary of Anaximander, he who wrote the first existent line of Western philosophy. And wasn't she a philosopher herself? Plato, 200 years after her death, still referred to her as "the tenth Muse" (Weigall 1932, 314). While the renowned poet, Homer, was known simply as "the Poet" in his day, Sappho was known as "the Poetess"(Weigall 1932, 314). She didn't follow the standard Homeric meter, but invented her own which has been described as giving Homer "a dancing step" (Miller and Robinson 1925, 69, 330-1). She lived at a time when communication was changing from an oral tradition to the written word.

When I turn to Sappho for a hint for thinking on logos in the feminine, what do I find? The only occurrence of the word logos *in the tattered remains of Sappho's poetry is accompanied by the word* sweet *(dulogoi).[2] Sweet logos?*

Sweet is the home that Heidegger describes where we dwell and build in a place for a time, where we remain in peace, sparing and preserving things from harm, letting things be free in their own nature (Heidegger 1975b, 145–161). Dwelling is our human ethos, he says (Heidegger 1977a, 233). It is the basic character of our human being at home. Dwelling is not to passively exist but to create, build, and engage. We build in two basic ways: by constructing things that do not grow and by cultivating things that grow (Heidegger 1975b, 148).

In the cultural symbolic and lived world, these two ways of building give us a surprising contrast. First of all, we immediately recognize constructing as building proper, whereas we must stretch its meaning to understand cultivating as a sort of building. While constructing demonstrates human intelligence, cultivating, particularly in the sense of taking care of the young, is shared by many animals. Constructing is making tools, and building edifices. It is masculine and idea-oriented. Cultivating is tilling the soil, growing food, tending animals and taking care of the young and vulnerable. It is feminine, and body-oriented. Constructing means money, a developed world, a technologically advanced society. Cultivating often means poverty, a not fully developed world, a preagrarian or agrarian society. Constructing implies literacy and luxury; cultivating implies illiteracy and subsistence living.

Constructing results in edifices that are very visible and often proudly displayed, and socially admired and is traditional men's work. Cultivating is the caring and tending of growing things and is traditional woman's work. Globally, cultivating is still predominately the work of women who do most of the farming, healing the sick with herbs and medicines, and taking care of the young and the home.[3]

Cultivating is essential but is often taken for granted invisible work. It also involves inconspicuous activities like weeding, keeping the fire going, carrying water and wood, and cooking and cleaning. Those who construct are often publicly honored for their lasting creations, while those who cultivate often remain invisible and the fruits of their labor, if tangible, are usually transitory. Most often, these invisible cultivators are not given access to institutional power and decision making in the allocation of funds and societal resources in their locales, yet they are the ones who work most closely with their environments and bear the brunt of environmental degradation.

The arts of cultivating and constructing, says Heidegger following the ancient Greeks, are *technai,* which means they bring forth that which does not arise from itself. For example, when a carpenter builds a table, he brings his own idea of the table into the bits of wood that he skillfully assembles. A table does not grow on its own. Cultivating brings forth in the sense of helping living beings grow to maturity, and maintaining their health. Cultivating tends generative beings, helping them to arise on their own.

It is noteworthy that tending growing beings is an other rather than subject oriented kind of building and, moreover, that cultivating's active principle is intimately involved in generative nature. I would call cultivating a *mediating techne* because the agency of cultivating is cogenerative with nature. The cultivator or nurturer never works on her own. She is not a clear agent who actively produces from her own self. Her nurturing touch is generative cooperation. She may cure the sick goat, but without the regenerative powers of the goat's own body, her medicines and care are as nothing at all. Bringing up children involves training and education yet the maturing occurs in the other. The bucket of sweet milk belongs as much to the good cow as to the milker, and the healthy crops to the land and sky as to the farmer. Because of this co-agency of cultivating, sometimes nature even takes all the credit. In cultivating there is not a clear final product of one's own making to be readily displayed like a building or monument. The final outcome may even be something as vague and ambiguous as health. In cultivating, both final outcome and agency are cogenerated by nature.

Even when the farmer plants and must *plan* where she will plant her diverse crops, her plan is cogenerative and not a blueprint in advance that is brought into the materials like a carpenter's. Her plan is born in the midst of the fields that she has come to know over time, and her planting scheme is adjusted to the current conditions of the living soil, the daily changes in the weather, the seasonal rhythms of growth and decay, the cycles of the moon, and a whole community of insects, birds and animals that live in her field. Although a good carpenter will adjust his plan to the grain of wood, his adjustments are fewer than if he were working with a living tree. Most of the cultivator's work is not even in the planting and birthing, but in the continual tending to maturity, alert for indications of stress and good health. Every stage requires a different kind of attentiveness.

In helping growth, the cultivator cannot control the process of cultivating as easily as the carpenter his constructing. If she is to be skilled in what she does, she has to remain open to the shifting opportunities and calamities intrinsic to generative beings. An ethos of receptivity and readiness governs her actions in her constant regard of the other.

Appropriate cultivating and constructing are two modes of poetic human dwelling that intertwine, working with and for each other. For example, tools are constructed to help the cultivator in his or her work. However, in these times of *Gestell* (challenging-out) as Heidegger calls it, both constructing and cultivating no longer work in accordance with nature, but as an exploitation and enframing of it.

The modern industrial farming of crops, animals and fish is not cultivating in the way we have been discussing, but "violent" agriculture that consumes more than it produces, destroys local knowledge and diversity, and is unsustainable. Shiva contrasts this violent "stealing from nature" with ecological agriculture that is referred to in India as *ahimsic krishi*, or "non-violent agriculture." *Ahimsic* that is based on compassion for all species and hence the protection of biodiversity in agriculture (Shiva 2000, 119).

An even more violent and dangerous kind of modern cultivating is the reconstructing and patenting of DNA through biotechnology. Although this new technological revolution can be used to appropriately cultivate (for example, its use in gene therapy and forensics), biotechnology under corporate control is approaching all life on the planet as though it were but assembled texts of DNA to be cut and pasted for the objectives of agribusiness with little regard for the billions-of-years-old history of creation. A new world order beyond evolution is being created where animals are engineered to serve human ends, and crops are engineered to produce their own pesticides that kill beneficial insects and to have terminator genes that render seeds sterile so that farmers cannot save them for the next season.

For biotechnology, cultivating is a matter of engineering and intellectual property rights. In other words, it is a matter of constructing food and owning the newly created blueprints of life. In this process, the living organism is no longer the unit of life, but rather the gene that can be manipulated without regard for species' barriers that have been erected over millenniums through meticulous trial and error to prevent different species from exchanging DNA. With the biotech revolution, human genes are mixed with farm animals to produce biopharmaceuticals; animal genes with insect's (for example the spider's are mixed with the goat's to produce milk that can be spun into the world's strongest thread), and both human and animal genes are routinely introduced into plant species to produce commercially desirable traits. This production oriented selection of traits can have extremely harmful biological, ecological, social and economic consequences. For example, when these transgenic animals and plants are accidentally released into the environment (as often happens in salmon farming) they transfer their genes to closely related species, thereby weakening the wild species in its ability to adapt to its environment.

The danger in these times, says Heidegger, is that we "everywhere and always" encounter only ourselves and our own products (1977b, 27). Irigaray agrees but ties this modern emphasis on ourselves as fabricators and constructors to an economy of the same where humanity and culture is based on the model of man alone, and where "instrument and product" are substituted for "germination, birth and growth" (1984, 100). But neither male nor female, she says, can manifest nor experience the totality of humanity, for each gender possesses only one part of human reality. Female and male corporeal morphology are not the same and therefore it follows that their way of experiencing the sensible is not the same (Irigaray 1996, 37).[4]

(Participant reads while I squat and slowly uncurl, coming to a full and straight standing position. I struggle with locked arms. I balance on my right foot and then on my left. I rest, touching the ground with my hands. I enact full bodily ripples by contracting and releasing my pelvis.)

> "To return to ourselves as living beings who are engendered and not fabricated," says Irigaray, "is a vital and ethical need of paramount importance" (1996, 14). In the history of Western culture, "man" has represented humanity as the one, and "woman" as body to his head. In our culture, nature is the perceived adversary, and our human natural identity is relegated to the "instincts" as a "font of inclinations to be tamed" (Irigaray 2001, 90). An engendered culture, based on the recognition that humanity is born of two complementary genders that form an "elementary social community," would be a culture that cooperates with fecundity. Instead of "destroying the vitality of the soil, and the fertility of the great cosmic rhythms," it would be a culture that is faithful to fecundity (Irigaray 1984, 100). Irigaray calls for a culture of sensibility that cultivates psychophysically "through a reawakening of the senses and recognition of the pregiven body and cosmic universe" "which gives and renews life"(1984, 100). It would be a culture that remembers

(I repeat)	remembers
(Participant)	and pays back
(I repeat)	pays back
(Participant)	its debt
(I repeat)	its debt
(Participant)	to the body
(I repeat)	to the body

(Participant)   *and nature.*
(I repeat)   *and nature.*

An engendered human culture, says Irigaray, would be founded upon and respectful of difference, and is one that would embody an ecological intelligence indebted to life. I do not think that with her assertion of "two complementary genders," Irigaray is presuming a fixed binary heterosexuality. Irigaray's concern is to understand sexual difference beyond the sexual neutralization of simple gender "equality" and beyond the traditional economy of difference where "woman" denotes deviance from a male norm.[5]

In this section of my paper, I have been understanding the ecology (the *logos* of our *eco*) as a laying out that gathers the home, and I have been emphasizing the aspect of our dwelling called cultivating that tends growth. Cultivating is an intercorporeal empathy that is attuned to fluctuating moods and manners of living plants and creatures that grow and decay. It pays attention to change and may utilize a cosmic empathy that is attuned to planetary influences, the moon and stars, and to seasonal currents of weather. Cultivating builds by holding the home together and maintaining health. The skilled cultivator, true to her art, accomplishes a "fidelity to growth" (Irigaray 1996, 38) through an ecological intelligence, and an organic sensitivity to the subtle multidimensional realities of living beings. Cultivating is accomplished through an elemental being in touch that is both active and passive. It is "an aroused passivity" and an "attentive activity" (Irigaray 2001, 91).

In our most local homes, cultivating includes nurturing, "the psychosocial maintenance work" "that women of most races are socialized to do," and holds "the underbelly of social life" in community and home (Salleh 1992, 198). Every art of cultivating would seem to involve some kind of nurturing. Nurturing is the glue that holds compossibilities together, that provides for gatherings, that shelters and safekeeps us, and all we cultivate, in our localities.

These often invisible human arts that bring us directly to generative being and recall body and nature are crucial for understanding our human being in a healthier way, and for our very survival. However, at this point in history when our dwelling has become more urban than rural, constructing appears to be our dominant form of building. Moreover, with the advent of the biotechnology revolution, constructing seems to obscure and erase the meaning of cultivating, giving us a false sense of fabricating our selves. It is as though the world and all living beings were ours to undo and remake as we see fit and in accordance with our calculations, ignoring our web of relations with the biological world.

In the next section of this essay, I would like to turn to Merleau-Ponty in order to develop further an understanding of cultivating. This time I want to focus more on the body of the cultivator. Cultivating is a fidelity to growth, responding to the generativity of the living world with attuned questioning touch. In tending plants, animals, her family, and other people, the skilled nurturer has a familiarity with what Merleau-Ponty calls "feel[ing] the world" in one's body (VI 118). She attends from within to a "dehiscence that opens to itself and opens us upon it" (VI 1968, 117). I would like to sketch out this attuned self of questioning touch, this embodied self in an intelligent feeling relation with the living world.

There are many possible readings of any thinker and every thought is a being on the way. I am not interested in marking the disagreements between, for example, between Merleau-Ponty and Irigaray, but rather in reading Merleau-Ponty for Irigaray and Irigaray for Merleau-Ponty. By reading Merleau-Ponty in the feminine, he will take us to touch and touching, and to Flesh as carnal, empathetic and tender.

The following description of a relational self is in keeping with an ecofeminist understanding of self. I work within a neighborhood of such varied ecofeminists as Salleh, Kheel, Cheney, Plant, and Starhawk. It is also in the vein of the deep ecologists' relational model of self in contrast to the rational, atomistic rights-bound self. Like Kheel, however, I want to stress our "felt sense of connection through concrete loving actions" (Kheel 1990, 137). As she says, we must be "wary of a holistic philosophy that transcends the realm of individual beings. Our deep, holistic awareness of the interconnectedness of all of life must be a lived awareness that we experience in relation to *particular* beings *as well as* the larger whole" (Kheel 1990, 137).

In attempting to give voice to what Salleh calls "the repressed feminine nurturant side of our culture," it is important to pay particular attention to the problems of the relational model of self for women (1992, 203). The danger of this model is that it may reinforce women's traditional role as self-sacrificing care givers where a woman's own self remains undeveloped. Donner, for example, argues that autonomy, rationality, and strongly bounded selves are essential for self-healing and survival, and that ecofeminists who devalue autonomy and rationality in favor of interconnectedness are neglecting to think on those women in abusive relations who need the ability to rationally scrutinize their relations (Donner 1997, 382ff).

Although I would agree that these three traditional categories of autonomy, rationality, and strongly bounded are important for self-healing, I still think empathy and nurturing are just as important. I will try to describe a relational model of self that works the space *between* traditional dichotomies of self such as self/other, mind/body, culture/nature, and active/passive within which women are relegated as the inferior term. Working this space *between* might give a conception of self that may allow for female subjectivity and thereby transform both opposing terms. To retain these three traditional philosophic categories of self, I would reinterpret them in an embodied way. Thus, I can accept the need for "autonomy" understood as a healthy standing in the earth-world-home through a sense of belonging; and "rationality" as long as it is also carnal and empathetic. "Strongly bounded" I would reinterpret as having inner folds and being porous, in the sense that we are strongly bounded by our breathing membrane, our porous skin.

Such transformations in the categories that define self also affect the meaning of self-healing. It suggests that healing, one of the arts of cultivating, is never fully from ourselves but is a cogenerative touching in depth that works in the midst of the mystery and self-reticence that we are.

Flesh in the Feminine

As Elizabeth Grosz says, Merleau-Ponty's work is useful for feminists because the notion of Being as Flesh places degrees and ambiguous shifting layers in the relation of self to world, refusing "the terrain and founding presuppositions of dualisms" (1999, 149). Merleau-Ponty wants us to understand self and world, not as though they were two positive terms externally connected by tissues of flesh, but more radically as themselves given by their dynamic chiasmic intertwining. He uses the metaphors of quivering tissues on tissues, intercalated leaves, lace-works and the ever shifting rhythmic currents of water that give sea and beach to help describe this dynamic generativity he calls "Flesh."

Flesh is neither matter nor psychic, but a kind of "element" like earth, air, fire, or water which all of us share. It is the "tissue that lines, sustains and nourishes everything animate and inanimate" (VI 132). It is the condition of their interaction and intermingling. Flesh is the element by means of which our own consciousness arises and our sensory palpations of the world take place. It is "an anonymity innate to Myself," "a generality of the Sensible in itself" (VI 76, 138). Even that internal sense of cohesion with myself that appears to separate myself from things is already enfleshed, already "of" the world and engaged in an elemental alliance with sensory existence.

The relation between my self and world, says Merleau-Ponty, "is not one of immediate or frontal contradiction" (VI 76). "The world neither surrounds, nor is surrounded by my body" but rather there is a "reciprocal insertion and intertwining of one in the other" (VI 137). Between I and the things of the world, we can catch sight of a prior "complicity," an underlying "kinship," "pre-established harmony," or "secret" and "natal bond" that every sentient self has with the world (VI 32, 76, 138, 133, 220). When we perceive, "the things attract my look, my gaze caresses the things" as though I already knew them (VI 76, 133). My carnal situation is one of "flesh offered to flesh" (VI 131, n. 1). A chiasmic "embrace" takes place between the flesh of my body and the flesh of the world, before reflection (VI 271). This embrace is a simultaneous integration and differentiation, for Flesh as Being is a divergence from itself.

We could understand this ontological description by turning to touch. Every touch, every perception, says Merleau-Ponty, communicates an "an identity, difference and divergence" (VI 135–136). When I perceive "a sort of dehiscence opens my body in two" for when I am perceiving, touching with my exploratory movements, I am also touched by what I touch (VI 123). We are not sentient without being sensible and touched by things.

Given this Merleau-Pontian description of the embodied self, the core of our identity is not a separate unified still point of our being, but is already dynamically open in many directions, belonging to the pulsating flesh of the world as the flesh of the world belongs to us. Autonomy understood as enfleshed emphasizes the *belonging* in our standing. We are primordially at home not as atomistic, calculative thinkers, scrutinizing which relationships to accept and reject, but as questioning touch, as flesh attuned to others, and to the flesh of the world wherein we find kinship and belonging. This tender open flesh of self attests to the deep harm abuse can cause, but it is also the ground from which we may slowly recover to come in touch with ourselves. We heal as we find ourselves *at home* with ourselves. Healthy standing is not guarded solipsism. We may well retreat from others to heal, but no matter how solitary we become we are caught up in a heartbeat not of our making, and an embrace where, as

Merleau-Ponty says, our hold on the world is already held (VI 266). No matter how reduced our horizons have had to become in order to survive, we are elementally open to the sounds of wind and rain, the warmth of sunshine, the rhythms of our own breath and heartbeat and these may even help heal our wounds. Our self is never separate for we exist as Merleau-Ponty says " in the interrogative mode" (VI 113).

Touch, says Merleau-Ponty, is always "a palpation in depth," encountering resistance and latency (VI 128). The thing is always encountered as having more of itself to explore and as harboring an "immense latent content of the past, the future, and the elsewhere which it announces and which it conceals" (VI 114). "Because of depth," says Merleau-Ponty, "things have flesh . . . a resistance which is . . . their openness" (VI 219). We feel a thing as a field hiding most of itself, both temporally and spatially, and this essential explorability, this depth and horizon of our embodied being, lets our relation to the world be one of openness.

The self-reticence of the flesh of the world is not just what is yet to be touched, but is the condition of touching and thus what is untouchable by principle. Everything comes to pass," says Merleau-Ponty, "as though . . . the access to the world were but the other face of a withdrawal and this retreat . . . another expression of my natural power to enter into it. The world is what I perceive but as soon as we examine and express its absolute proximity, it also becomes, inexplicably, irremediable distance" (VI 8). "Distance both separates and joins" (Apelbaum 1988, 12). "Recognition of the distance between us and the world initiates a return to ourselves" (Apelbaum 1988, 12). Every touch gives us to ourselves as dynamic beings in depth.

The self-reticence of things pulls us and we so drawn announce our own identity as one of depth and pulls. We are not fully the source of our intentions, and "intentions are not just a movement toward things" but, as Glen Mazis says, are "equally lateral intertwinings and traverse currents" (1990, 262). Our being is not coincident with itself, which is the basis for the traditional isolation of the epistemological subject, but is as Merleau-Ponty says, "non-coincident," a being "by porosity," "pregnancy" and "divergence" (VI 149, 204). The cohesion of my self with self is "silent" and "blind," and never a complete coincidence, which is not a deficiency, but a source of our openness and healing (VI 204).

Merleau-Ponty will understand self-reflection after the model of the reflection of the hand touching by the hand touched (VI 204). In this hand trick, he wants us to feel how the roles are reversible but not completely, for there is an overlapping, like that between the convex and the concave. The touching-touched paradigm excited Merleau-Ponty when he first read it in Husserl. He uses Husserl's example of the right hand touching the left in *The Phenomenology of Perception*, and then in his later writings often turns to the more complicated example of the right hand touching a thing while the left hand is touching the right. He uses this experiential experiment to illustrate chiasmic embrace, to illustrate reversibility, or rather reversibility "almost."

(I touch my left hand with my right hand. Then I touch an object with my right hand and feel my right hand with my left)

I found myself doing a lot of this with myself and my friends. I don't find an easy switching about of subject and object between my right and left hand. I am distracted by the sensitivity of touch and the rhythm required to touch. When my left hand interrupts my right hand's touching of a thing, I do not now locate my subjectivity in my left hand but in that patch of sensitive skin beneath it where I am being tickled. "I" am a tickled me, not in the fingers of my right or left hand, but caught up in a third term: the tenderness of tickling, the sensitivity of flesh. Isn't it this tenderness of the membrane that makes Flesh work as a concept so that it is not insensitive dead meat?

If I try to *ignore* the tickling and concentrate instead on my fingers, my exploratory movements in each hand are not differentiated enough to be reversible. Both hands now become one through the rhythm of their touching. If I try to make my right hand moves at a different rate than my left so as to better distinguish its touching, I find it difficult, and the polyrhythms and punctuations preoccupy me more than the texture of the thing under my right hand.

If I *still* the movements of both hands, then it is as though I were feeling the pulse of my right hand with my left. My right hand's stilled touching of the table is not so much touching now but through the pressure of the table against me I am given to feel my own body's pulse. Both hands become one again, feeling an invisible, almost intangible pulse. In this experience of touching, the rhythm and sensitivity of touch preoccupy me. If I want to feel my hand as itself *sensible*, as thingly, as Merleau-Ponty wants, than I feel it best through the simple *felt weight* of my arm.

(I move into a thinker's pose, scratching my chin)
    I'm wondering with Maxine Sheets-Johnstone why such an uncommon lived experience *becomes his central experiential paradigm (1999, 304).*

(Participant, while I enact each of the movements she mentions)

She wants to take us to everyday lived experiences of moving and touching such as striding, standing, sexing, chewing, and breathing, for example (Sheets-Johnstone, 1990, 4).

(I move into a thinker's pose scratching my head and then touch participant)

I'm wondering with Irigaray why the prime example of touching is not touching another.

(Participant, while I curl up, uncurl, show the shape of a building with my hands, then entwine my hands around each other.)

She understands "touching on" as a site of communication that awakens the other to an exchange, a respectful intersubjective place that asks for silence, organizes a possible dwelling, shelters, and allows for cohabiting.

(I move into thinker's pose and then put my hands together as if in prayer)

I'm wondering with Irigaray, if self-touching, then why not one hand touching the other as those joined in prayer?

(Participant while I rest in this pose and then touch the ground)

This is a touching "more intimate than that of one hand taking hold of the other," a gesture often reserved for women, and one that "evokes, doubles, the touching of the lips silently applied to one another" (Irigaray 1984, 161).

   Irigaray cultivates a "mediate ontology," where the tangible "is the matter and memory for all the sensible" (1984, 164).

(I repeat, remaining in a squat, touching the ground)

a mediate ontology where the tangible is the matter and memory for all the sensible.

(Participant while I turn around right and left with head down and arms outspread like a bird)

a mediate ontology where the tangible is the matter and memory for all the sensible. She focuses on the invisible tangible—that self-touching that cannot be seen like that between the lip and lip, the eyelid and eye, and the fetus and mother. She wants to focus on "a touching without grasping,"

(I repeat turning sideways and enacting full bodily ripples)

a touching without grasping.

(Participant)   *a touching without grasping. She wants to focus on the "mucous of the carnal" (Irigaray 1984, 162).*

(I repeat, slowing down my movements and regaining my breath)
   the mucous of the carnal.
(Participant)   *the "mucous of the carnal." Mucous is an unthought of*
   philosophy. It is neither solid nor liquid. It is not stable but expands.
   The mucous is a threshold that is always half-open, like the threshold of
   the lips. The lips are "strangers to dichotomy and oppositions." The lips
   are "the prototype of the crossroads between" (Irigaray 1984 18).
   Mucous takes us to sexuality and speech,
(I repeat, while drumming softly on my body)
   sexuality and speech.
(Participant)   *sexuality and speech, to the threshold of the female sex*
   that gives access to the mucous, to the act of love where communion
   takes place through the most intimate mucous membranes.
(I beat a rhythm on my body and deliver the following words in time
with the rhythm. I repeat the following sentence a few times.)
   Irigaray says, "Our body itself carries those measures which lead to a
   respect for each person and for the relationship between" (2001, 90).

OUR INTELLIGENT ANIMAL BODIES:
THE SELF AND PROPRIOCEPTION

(I keep my hands moving, imitating the text where I can. I crouch down
when discussing the natural history of consciousness.)

I have been describing the flesh of home and the flesh of our perceptive bodies by emphasizing tactility. I now want to turn more specifically
to the sensitivity and rhythm of flesh. With regard to cultivating, I am still
understanding it in the context of the earth world home as a dynamic and
empathetic place, but now paying more attention to the relationship of
our felt bodies with consciousness. I hope to develop the Merleau-Pontian
preconceptual role of our earthy animal bodies in the last section by
describing our ecological being as a proprioceptive touching without
grasping.

Our human being, the embodied self, for Merleau-Ponty, is dynamic
or in movement. He would agree with Sheets-Johnstone that we exist as a
self-knowing in motion. "Absolute primacy of movement," he says in his
working notes (VI 230). We exist as "a sea of processes" (VI 232). The
flesh of myself and the flesh of the world vibrate, quiver, and buzz, for
every perception is by principle in movement (VI 7, 8, 231). The sensible

world is the ensemble of our bodily routes. The continual adjustment of our bodies in its self-moving, he says, "gives our life the form of generality and prolongs our personal acts into stable dispositions" (VI 146). Each body has a species specific range of movement possibilities, a repertoire of I cans.[6]

For Sheets-Johnstone, the body is also intrinsically dynamic. She wants to show how consciousness developed through a primal tactility. Perception coevolved with thought. Thus thinking itself is radically rooted in the body. Through her work I want to focus on our invisible, internal sense of movement, which is called proprioception, rather than on external visible, movement. In this way, I hope to think further on Irigaray's "touching without grasping" mentioned in the last section of this paper.

Proprioception is a kind of sixth sense that has been neglected by thinkers of the body. Our organs of perception give us sight, smell, taste, hearing, and touch, but all are undergirded by proprioception, by an internal sense of being moved. As Sheets-Johnstone notes, Merleau-Ponty mostly ignores this felt body or tactile kinesthetic body, but hints of it when he speaks of the body as "massive presence" and "massive sentiment" (VI 149, 134) (cited in 1999, 305). Our felt living body touches and moves as a whole when we read or run, as well as when we feel hesitation, joy, disgust, or confusion (Sheets-Johnstone 1999, 313). "Any I can is undergirded proprioceptively by a sense of agency" (Sheets-Johnstone 1999, 71). The felt orientation of our body through movement and touch puts into relief our openness as a *developing* openness based on a developing tactile-kinesthetic body.

Sheets-Johnstone explores how consciousness develops through this self-knowing in motion both ontogeneticly and phylogeneticly. She describes how as babies, we first learn to move ourselves and come to know ourselves, not by looking and seeing, but by attending to our bodily feelings of movement, and how all creatures, even bacterium have a responsivity, or a "sensitivity" in service of movement.[7]

In a chapter of her book, *The Primacy of Movement*, entitled "A Natural History of Consciousness," Sheets-Johnstone[8] explains how[9] every creature is sensitive to motion through organelles that are present from protozoa to mammals. Every animal has an internal sense of movement, sensing itself moving and when it is still. Ninety percent of animal species are invertebrates, creatures like sponges and coral as well as invertebrates that have articulable body parts attached to an exoskeleton, like lobsters, mites, segmented worms, spiders, and a host of insects. All invertebrates are sensitive in that they have external sensilla of various kinds: hairs, exoskeletal plates, cilia, spines, and slits that make possible an awareness in the double sense of the terrain outside and the bodily stresses occurring inside. Even a bacterium has a chemically mediated tactile discrimination of bodies apart from or outside of its body

A sedentary hydrozoan polyp has tentacles bearing cilia that are sensitive to vibrations in the surrounding water. A locust's face is covered with hairs that respond to wind direction and help it fly. Spiders have hairs that when bent inform them of the disposition of their body relative to their web, and even more sensitive are the slit sensilla, located on their walking legs.

When Merleau-Ponty says we must "start at the joints, where the multiple *entries* of the world cross" and that the "generality of my body and the ideas are already encrusted in its joints," I think of invertebrates like lobsters who literally have "meaning at their joints" for this is where they feel themselves move (VI 260, 114, 115).

We, too, have propioceptors in our joints, as well as in our connective tissues. I understand proprioception in the vein of Irigaray's thought as a mucous of the carnal. Like mucous, our internal sense of moving is a self-touching that cannot be seen and it is a touching without grasp. It brings us to touch and movement not in the sense of ourselves as encased by visible skin that defines the outside of our bodies, but to our most intimate interiority, to the invisible tangible of self-touching. Proprioception is the intimacy of flesh that brings us to our orifices, our connective tissues, our joints, and bones. It is our felt weight and bodily sense of orientation. It is a receptivity that is "more passive than passive, yet active," and a threshold of the passage between inside and outside (Irigaray 1984, 161).

Proprioception, which orients us like a spider in its web, recalls the body and nature for its speaks more than any other sense of the long history of textured cohabitation we share with all animals, and the pregnancies of diverse styles of being (Irigaray 1996, 121). It recalls "the gift" of *responsivity* "that comes from the living world and our body," for proprioceptively endowed creatures are always in touch with something outside themselves.[10] Proprioception attests to our continuity with all animate life and our intricate, sensitive belonging. All creatures bend and adjust to the tangible inconsistencies of their immediate elemental home. We all respond to the topological and textual irregularities, the moisture, temperature, the currents of air and water that may shift in strength from moment to moment. We all first come to understand ourselves and the world through the rhythms of movement and sensitivity of touch.

The fact that we are conscious does not separate us from animals, for all animals are self-moving and self-*knowing* in their moving. Sheets-Johnstone understands responsivity or animation as the generative source of consciousness. We have to understand consciousness, she says, neither as matter or spirit, but as a dimension of animate beings that in their multiple and complex ways are engaged in the world (1999, 60).

Proprioception is the quiet orientation of ourselves at rest and in motion, the subtle feeling of our joints, the weight of our bones, the forgotten sense that underlies our every movement. It gives us our flesh not only as "interanimal," but as empathetic, for self-knowing through motion is at the same time self-*feeling* in motion (VI 172) (Sheets-Johnstone 1999, 84, n. 16). For us, movement may make reference to the physical sensation or it may describe an aspect of our emotional life.

Merleau-Ponty hints of the flesh of our world as empathetic. We have to "think of affection, pleasure, desire, love, Eros," he says, not as positives or negatives but as "*differentiations* of one sole and *massive* adhesion to being which is flesh (eventually as laceworks)" (VI 270). He speaks of Flesh as "all that feels itself in me" and calls empathy a "quasi-reflection" (VI 255, 245). When we move, he says, there is a "sort of reflectedness," a "knowing by sentiment" (VI 249). Mazis, taking up these hints, tells us to think of "gestalt" as a "charged, dehiscent, and affective flow," and "affective meaning" as that pulsing that makes space an alive space of inhabitation (1990, 265, 257).

Understanding our human nature as self-knowing, self-feeling beings in depth recalls the history of intertwinings of our ancestral bodies and our continuity with all life forms. Proprioception makes sense to me of Irigaray's statement that "the tangible is the matter and memory for all the sensible." Our self-moving, self-knowing, self-feeling being did not come on the scene all at once, but coevolved with layers on layers of earlier rhythms and densities of traditions. Flesh has a deep historicity, billions of years old.

Our primal home is where we touch and are touched. We human animals suffer contact to an astonishing degree. Our skin, which is like an external nervous system, is almost completely naked (Montagu 1978, 2). As babies, coddling and rhythmic cradling is essential for healthy psychophysical development. Through this sensitivity we thrive in our vulnerability as animals of touch. Even within the womb, the fetus is already intimately embraced by the supporting walls of the uterus, and pulsed by the vibrations of its mother's heart, half the tempo of its own.

Rhythmic touching is a paradigm of nurturance, a healing force in itself. In being visited by the touching of another, my breathing tissue is nourished, and made expansive (Apelbaum 1988, 64). Touch is "a greeting born with a potential for transmission," "an event of interpenetration" (Apelbaum 1988, 79, 65).

Cultivators are skilled in touching. Touch is not the most gross of our perceptive abilities, but a most subtle ability that makes use of intelligent feeling. The human touch can gentle animals, encourage plants to grow, bring comfort, relax stressed muscles, heal soft tissues, and realign bones. Those skilled in various holistic arts of subtle touch therapies can diagnose and change the flow of cranial rhythms, or make subtle distinctions between qualities of pulses that have diagnostic significance. We humans who have made such arts of responsivity are profoundly gifted animals with profound response-abilities, indebted to the ancestral rhythms of the earth home from whence all life has its origin.

Epilogue: Pregnancy and the Earth-world-home

As the mother's body allows generativity of others within herself, so our earth-world home is a place of generative belonging for all that grows. Our earth-world home is a greeting place *capable of welcoming* what asks for entry. It is a fecund, inconsistent, fluctuating place and we, responsive from inside and out, are of it, engaged in an intimate generative chiasm of Flesh. In a working note, Merleau-Ponty says that the pregnancy of Flesh is firstly "the power to break forth" (VI 208). It is dehiscence, the fecund bursting of seeds from pods, and the fullness of blooms.

This understanding of fecundity seems to me a one sided description, ignoring the quiet gathering holding of pregnancy. To understand the pregnancy of our home with regard to the sensitivity and rhythms of flesh that I have been emphasizing in this paper, I turn to the ancient Greek goddess, Aphrodite, worshiped by Sappho, whose own reputation became entwined with that of the divinity.

Aphrodite is a carnal divinity of love associated with the sweetness, fragrance, and bright colors of fruits and flowers, particularly apples and roses. She is Being and sexuality in one breath. Aphrodite is a limnel goddess, crossing boundaries like Hermes, god of communication, with whom she is associated. She is the rose of dawn and dusk. Her star rises between day and night. She is an ancient sea and bird goddess associated with fecund sparrows and the beautiful swan. Her influence is psychophysical through mood. She is known as kind and tender, fond of children, sheltering all that flourishes and flowers.

Pregnancy understood with Aphrodite is not so much perpetual growth, or continual dehiscence as Merleau-Ponty would have it. She would take us to the tenderness and sweetness of fecundity.

(Participant)	*Sweet is the logos*
(I give drum call on my body and repeat)	
	sweet is the logos
(Participant)	*of our home*
(I repeat)	*of our home*
(Participant)	*that lies in kinship with all living things.*
(I repeat)	*that lies in the kinship with all living things.*
(Participant)	*Sweet the air. Sweet water.*
	Tender the flame by which a fire is born.
	Sweet the breathing soil.
	Sweet is the mystery of fecundity, the unreachable, untouchable that
	Sappho describes as a sweet apple. An apple that "reddens on a high branch / high on the highest branch and the apple pickers forgot— / no, not forgot: were unable to reach" (Fragment 105a, Carson 2002, 215).
	Tender the smile from the old and frail, the very old holding the hand of the very young, the chirp of cricket, the weed in crack, the wind soft on our cheek.
	Sweet the irresistible embrace, the elemental event of sentience effected across vibrating flesh. Sweet the beauty of the chiasmic entwining, whose style is inherently graceful, soft and multifarious like tissues fluttering.[10]
	Tender the sensitivity of our flesh, the rhythms of our movements, the elemental caresses that relate us to polyps sensitive to vibrations.
	Sweet is the love of our home that seeps back into the place where we dwell. Sweet the saving power, the carnal poiesis that reveals us as near dwellers in all our relations.
	Tender the embrace so intimate that where one part hurts, the rest feels pain.

Sweet-bitter is love.[11] *Sweet the cultivation of compassion.*

Notes

1. I delivered the first version of this paper with full bodily movements at the International Merleau-Ponty Circle, 2002. My essay, "Standing and Stooping to Tiny Flowers: An Ecofemnomenological Response to Arne Naess" (*Environmental Philosophy* 1, Number 2 (Fall) 2004), 28–45, is a "body" paper that discusses the ideas of cultivating and proprioception in the context of Arne Naess's philosophy.

2. The word is *dulogoi* from Fragment 73. Carson translates it as "sweetworded" (2002, 147).

3. "It is estimated that women farmers grow at least 59% of the world's food, perhaps as much as 80%" (Warren 1997, 8). Moreover, "[a]ccording to World Health Organization figures, [women] still provide 95% of the world's health care needs" (Kheel 1989, 96).

4. Irigaray sees a psychophysiological basis for this difference. She links the fact that the male must fabricate from without while she generates internally with man's relationship with techne where we are led us to believe that the human can be understood from without (2001, 68–76). Merleau-Ponty understands sex as "an eluctable dimension outside of which nothing human can abide since nothing which is human is entirely incorporeal" (RC 130).

5. Irigaray often seems to conflate the meaning of sex and gender as she does here. These historically mediated categories have complex shifting and even conflicting usages among Anglo-American and European feminists and queer theorists. From the perspective of sexual difference feminists, the sex/gender distinction is not helpful because it reessentializes sex.

Whether Irigaray appears to advocate lesbianism or heterosexuality, her approach is always strategic in service of this broader endeavor. She is a lover of creative difference beyond the stale binaries of man/woman, and hetero/homo. We should also keep in mind that Irigaray provided one of the first critiques of normative phallocentric heterosexuality and describes lesbian desire on a continuum with female desire.

Irigaray's envisioning of a radical *enfleshing* of men and women emphasizes the preconceptual role of our earthy animal bodies in our sexuality. It indicates what I would call an "eco-gender" theory. In much current gender theory, the emphasis is on construction (and deconstruction) and not cultivation. Thus, I find most gender theory language alien to the lived experience of sexual love and the organic ongoing process of gender identity, and that gender categories fail to capture the rich variations of many people's sexual lives. As a ecofeminist, I think gender theory should brings us radically closer to nature (but one that does not revert to traditional biologism and naturalism). Before defining myself as a woman, I would understand my sexual being as that of a female human primate, a sensuous animal of scents and secretions, movement and sentiment.

6. See also when Merleau-Ponty says, "to elucidate Wahrnehmen and Sich bewegen," show that no wahrnehmen, perceives except on condition of being a self in movement" and

"[s]how that the movement is carnal" (VI 257).

7. In the case of bacteria, they are not sensitive to movement and shape, but to the chemical composition of their environment, but through this sensitivity, they will move toward or away.

8. Although the tactile ability to discriminate bodies other than oneself is not the same as proprioceptive ability to discriminate aspects of oneself as animate form, tactility, says Sheets-Johnstone, is a vital dimension of the proprioceptive ability (Sheets-Johnstone 1999, 60).

9. Grace is from the Greek word, *chiares*. The cognates of *charis* derive from a common Indo-European root, *gher,* meaning pleasure.

10. See Sappho, fragment 130 in Carson (2003, 265).

References

Apelbaum, David. 1988. *The Interpenetrating Reality. Bringing the Body to Touch.* American University Studies series V. Philosophy 44. New York: Peter Lang.

Carson, Anne, trans. 2003. *If Not, Winter. Fragments of Sappho.* New York: Alfred A. Knoff.

Donner, Wendy. 1997. "Self and Community in Environmental Ethics," in Daren J. Warren, ed., *Ecofeminism Women Culture Nature.* Bloomington and Indianapolis: Indiana University Press, pp. 375–389.

Heidegger, Martin. 1975a. *Early Greek Thinking.* Translated by David Farrell Krell and Frank A. Capuzzi. New York: Harper & Row, Publishers, pp. 13–58.

———. 1975b. "Building Dwelling Thinking." Translated with an Introduction by Albert Hofstadter. *Poetry Language Thought.* New York: Harper & Row, Publishers.

———. 1977a. "Letter on Humanism." Edited and translated, with an Introduction, by David Farrell Krell. *Basic Writings.* New York: Harper & Row, Publishers, pp. 189-242.

———. 1977b. "The Question Concerning Technology." Translated with an Introduction by William Lovitt. *The Question Concerning Technology and other Essays.* New York: Garland Publishing, pp. 3–35. Originally published as "Die Frage nach der Technik," in *Die Technik und die Kehre.* 1962. Pfullingen: Günther Neske. Reprinted in *Vorträge und Aufsätze.* 1954. Pfullingen: Günther Neske.

Irigaray, Luce. 1984. *An Ethics of Sexual Difference.* Translated by Carolyn Burke and Gillian C. Gill. Ithaca, New York: Cornell University Press.

———. 1996. *I love to you.* Sketch of a Possible Felicity in History. New York: Routledge.

———. 2001. *To Be Two.* Translated by Monique Rhodes and Marco F. Cocito-Monroe. New York: Routledge.

Grosz, Elixabeth, 1999. "Merleau-Ponty and Irigaray in the Flesh," in Dorothea and James

Morley, eds., *Merleau-Ponty Interiority and Exteriority Psychic Life and the World.* New York: State University of New York Press, pp. 147–166.

Kheel, Marti. 1989. "From Healing Herbs to Deadly Drugs: Western Medicine's War Against the Natural World," in Judith Plant, ed., *Healing the Wounds The Promise of Ecofeminism.* Toronto: Between the Lines, pp. 96–114.

————. 1990. "Ecofeminism and Deep Ecology: Reflections on Identity and Difference." In Irene Diamond and Gloria Feman Orenstein, eds., *Reweaving the World The Emergence of Ecofeminism.* San Francisco: The Sierra Club, pp. 128–137.

Mazis, Glen. 1990. "Merleau-Ponty, Inhabitation and the Emotions," in Henry Pietersma, ed., *Merleau-Ponty Critical Essays 1989.* Boston: Center for Advanced Research in Phenomenology, pp. 251–268.

Montagu, Ashley. 1978. *Touching. The Human Significance of Skin.* New York: Harper & Row, Publishers.

Salleh, Ariel. 1992. "Ecofeminism/Deep Ecology Debate: A Reply to Patriarchal Reason." *Environmental Ethics* 14 (Fall), 195–214.

Sheets-Johnstone, Maxine. 1999. *The Primacy of Movement.* Advances in Consciousness Research. 14. Philadelphia: John Benjamins Publishing Company.

Shiva, Vandana. 2000. *Stolen Harvest: The Hijacking of the Global Food Supply.* Cambridge MA: South End Press.

Warren, Karen J. 1997. "Taking Empirical Data Seriously" An Ecofeminist Philosophical Perspective" in Daren J. Warren, ed. *Ecofeminism Women Culture Nature.* Bloomington and Indianapolis: Indiana University Press, pp. 3-20.

Weigall, Arthur. 1932. *Sappho of Lesbos Her Life and Times.* New York: Frederick A. Stokes Company.

6

Umwelt and Nature
in Merleau-Ponty's Ontology

Duane H. Davis

TRANSCENDENTAL REFLECTION EXPLAINED

Merleau-Ponty begins his reflections in *The Visible and the Invisible* with the remark that "we see the things themselves, the world is what we see . . ." (173).[1] Now most every philosopher thought that he or she was accounting for experience. Rationalists acknowledged the senses, empiricists acknowledged reason, and so on. None of these people were idiots, dreamers, or mad, contrary to what philosophers often claim about one another along the way to explaining their own idiocies, dreams, and lunacies. Philosophy is a matter of style and emphasis.

However, as Merleau-Ponty notes, while we might all agree to that obvious banality that we experience a world, we might still completely disagree about the "we" that experiences the world, what this "world" is, and what kind of relationship the "experience" may be (VI 173). As soon as we acknowledge that there *is* experience, replete with the requisite mysteries of experiencer, experienced, and experience, we have some interesting problems to confront. And the picture gets more complicated when we introduce terms like *environment* and *nature* in the context of our relationship with and within the world. These are not needless complications to obfuscate the obvious. So to say that we must attend to nature and environment implies that we address our own condition for life.

There are three closely related terms that I will use here: *transcendental*, *transcendentalism*, and *transcendence*. Initially, these terms may sound very similar to us, however their meanings will be seen to diverge throughout the essay. Without insulting the reader with an antiphilo-sophical didactic definition of these terms, it is undoubtedly necessary to begin attending to their divergence straightaway in order to be as clear as is possible.

I propose to look at the question of transcendental reflection on nature and the environment. I shall use the term *transcendental* in a sense inspired by Kant and other German Idealists—asking after the conditions for the possibility of our experience of nature. I think that it is necessary to cautiously adopt a transcendental approach to the questions at hand, though I am arguing for a less idealistic standpoint.[2] For I also want to recognize the risks that accompany a transcendental approach. One of the tenets of a phenomenological inquiry has been to disclose the conditions for the possibility of experience—an intentional relation obtains among experiencer, experienced, and experience—although phenomenologists have disagreed about what these exact conditions may be, the best means for disclosing them, and the limits of the inquiry. A fuller understanding of proper or authentic transcendental reflection will emerge as we contrast the transcendental styles of phenomenological inquiry in Husserl, Heidegger, and Merleau-Ponty.

Without abandoning a *transcendental* posture altogether, I want to see how Merleau-Ponty avoids two errors of *transcendentalism*. I want to examine two forms of transcendentalism in Thoreau and Heidegger. I shall always use the term *transcendentalism* in a pejorative sense—as a transcendental approach that has lost its way. Transcendentalism is an inauthentic style of transcendental reflection. The two forms of transcendentalism examined here each adopt a transcendental approach to understanding nature. Both Thoreau and Heidegger are creative offshoots of German Idealism—it is their inspiration, while they do the dance of avoiding certain kinds of foundational thought endemic to that movement. Both Thoreau and Heidegger are sensitive thinkers and writers who provide powerful descriptions of nature and of the environment. And both are championed by environmentalists for their styles of thinking. Nevertheless, however valuable their work may be, I think that both Thoreau and Heidegger succumb to a transcendentalism of one sort or another. Each goes too far in determining our relations to nature and the environment, portraying humans as too familiar or too estranged from nature. Of course, they were not just simply wrong—it is never that easy, since Thoreau and Heidegger were not idiots, dreamers, or lunatics. And though I think that Merleau-Ponty was moving in a more promising direction at the end of his career, his own transcendental reflection is not without its contradictions, reverie, and fantasy.

Indeed, there is a risk in any transcendental approach to understanding nature. This has to do with the very *transcendence* disclosed in our transcendental inquiry. I shall use *transcendence* to connote an existential structure—a surpassing characteristic of our existence in the world. Transcendental philosophy discloses our transcendence as the condition of our experience of nature. The risk of any transcendental approach to nature is that is takes advantage of our ability to surpass what we are in order to understand our engagement within nature. The transcendental approach to nature risks transcendentalism when it misconstrues and even reconstrues its own transcendence. I think the promise and peril of transcendental reflections on environment and nature emerge when we pose the question of what it means to be at home in nature. Our environmental actions and policies reflect how we conceive of being at home.

Two Transcendentalisms

The American transcendentalists, transcendental German Idealism's bastard offspring, offer what American philosophers like to describe as a "robust" account of experience. And while Emerson or Thoreau may not have provided the rigorous theoretical analysis characteristic of their German forefathers, they certainly did reflect on the source of our experience of nature; and they provided rich descriptions of lived experience in the process.

Emerson explained that the relation of American transcendentalism to the transcendental thought of German Idealism was merely a matter of what the transcendental "light" illuminated.

> The light is always identical in its composition, but it falls on a great variety of objects, and by so falling is first revealed to us, not in its own form, for it is formless, but in theirs; in like manner, thought only appears in the objects it classifies. (Emerson 1965, 98)[3]

Interestingly, this difference in the objects revealed was to account for the emphasis of the rather romantic naturalism characteristic of American transcendentalism as opposed to its German roots. (So there must be something quite unique about nature here in America. . . .) At any rate, Thoreau thought that it was essential to forsake the hustle and bustle of human civilization and get back to nature.

> Fishermen, hunters, woodchoppers, and others, spending their lives in the fields and woods, in a peculiar sense a part of Nature themselves, are often in a more favorable mood for observing her, in the intervals of their pursuits, than philosophers or poets even, who approach her with expectation. (Thoreau 1977, 457)

Academics want something from nature—they are unsatisfied with just appreciating it for what it is. By contrast, Thoreau's noble experiment near Walden Pond produced a variety of beautiful observations on the relation of human beings to nature. Thoreau began to revere nature in such a way that he never could have until he had spent his time in the woods. This time also began to indicate to him his own profound connection with the wild animals he observed—aspects of his existence he usually repressed or denied outright in civilized society.

> Once or twice, however, while I lived at the pond, I found myself ranging the woods, like a half-starved hound, with a strange abandonment, seeking some kind of venison which I might devour, and no morsel could have been too savage for me. . . . I found in myself, and still find, an instinct toward a higher, or, as it is named, spiritual life, as do most men, and another toward a primitive rank and savage one, and I reverence them both. (Thoreau 1977, 456–457)

As disappointing as it may be to some of us that in two years in the woods he only felt this way "once or twice," it is significant that he did, and that he recorded it in unabashedly positive terms. We are animals, subject to drives, instincts, and savagery. We live together in such a way that makes us sick when we repress or deny our animality altogether, as Rousseau, Nietzsche, and countless psychoanalytic thinkers also convincingly note.

Thoreau makes it clear that nature is beautiful, a force of propriety that has its own *telos*, one that is greater than human design and to which we would be wise to demur. Human cleverness and industry are great things to be sure, but nothing compared with the power of nature. He often tries to make his point by stressing the affinity of humans to nature. "No domain of nature is quite closed to man at all times," Thoreau remarks in his essay, *A Winter Walk* (Thoreau 1977, 71). Nature is open to us, and we belong in nature.

> In these wild scenes, men stand about in the scenery, or move deliberately and heavily, having sacrificed the sprightliness and vivacity of towns to the dumb sobriety of nature. He does not make the scenery less wild, more than the jays and muskrats, but stands there as a part of it. . . . (Thoreau 1977, 72–73)

Note both the divergence and the near convergence when Thoreau says in his *A Natural History of Massachusetts* that, "Next to Nature, it seems as if man's actions were the most natural, they so gently accord with her" (Thoreau 1977, 46). We are just slightly less natural than nature.

As we will see later, I think that this divergence is crucial; and in principle this is a *virtue* of his account rather than a liability. And one could provide much evidence for the fact that Thoreau maintains the distinction between humans and other natural beings. Nonetheless, this is not the main emphasis in his work. Instead, Thoreau is clearly guided by a romantic optimism regarding nature. For the most part, he stresses the ideality of nature in *divine* terms. Nature is innocent, omnipresent, immortal, omnipotent, omniscient, beneficent, and above all, good.

> The indescribable innocence and beneficence of Nature—of sun and wind and rain, of summer and winter—such health, such cheer, they afford forever! and such sympathy have they ever with our race, that all Nature would be affected, and the sun's brightness fade, and the winds would sigh humanely, and the clouds rain tears, and the woods shed their leaves and put on mourning in midsummer, if any man should ever for a just cause grieve. Shall I not have intelligence with the earth? Am I not partly leaves and vegetable mould myself? (Thoreau 1977, 389)

This is a truly remarkable passage! The same strokes of Thoreau's pen proclaim both the personified divinity of nature *and* the affinity of human beings to it as both mind and matter. His transcendental inquiry understands the environment as the boundary of experience that is blissfully informed with meaning by a transcendental nature-as-provider. It is the optimistic and zealous faith in this plan that is the problem—and there is no small irony in the pejorative connotation of the term Thoreau and Emerson embraced to describe themselves—it really is a *transcendental-ism*. Their transcendental inquiry goes too far in its reverie for nature. This is *transcendentalism* because its optimism results from a misunderstanding of transcendence, as we shall see later on in the essay. For now, we see that Thoreau's transcendentalism betrays a nostalgic or even mystical return to nature-as-provider—more union than transcendence.

Thoreau's transcendental optimism is as pernicious as Marcel correctly said any optimism was in *Homo Viator*—a debilitating condition that discourages engaged, responsible judgment and action.[4] When Thoreau claims that nature would weep with us if humans should grieve unjustly, does this mean that the suffering that we experience is *justified*? This is the worst sort of rationalization that poses as reason, and is an insult to those it is meant to comfort. Thoreau downplays the conflicts and struggles to the death manifest in every aspect of nature because he plays up the transcendental order of nature. We can and must explain these phenomena without explaining them away.

There is a strong existential element in Heidegger's thought. Heidegger's interest in lived experience is demonstrated in the following moving description of the sea in his analysis of a passage from Sophocles' *Antigone* in *Einführung der Metaphysik*.

> The first strophe names the sea and the earth, each of them overpowering (*deinon*) in its way. It does not speak of them in the manner of us moderns who experience them as mere geographical phenomena and then, as though as an afterthought, brush them over with a few faint and fleeting emotions. Here "sea" is said as though for the first time; the poet speaks of the wintry waves that the sea creates as it unceasingly tears open its own depths and unceasingly flings itself into them. (Heidegger 1958, 117–118/153)

His point is that the sea is not the sea bereft of the torment and the fear and so on. But note how this power requires us to objectify and appropriate the sea. One wonders if Heidegger did a lot of sailing—(or U-boating)? *That* sea on *that* day becomes an emblem in the same way the earth becomes condensation and concealment in opposition to the rarefaction and opening of the heavens in his fourfold.[5] Heidegger describes the fourfold—earth, heavens, gods, and humans—as what is disclosed in his later transcendental thought. By the time one arrives at the provocative essay, "Time and Being," Heidegger has admitted that he is no longer interested in the Being of beings, but in "*Being qua Being*" (cf. 1972, 24). In Heidegger's later thought it is clearly the case that, like Kant, and to a lesser degree Husserl, before him, Heidegger is more enamored of the conditions for the possibility of experience than he is concerned with experience itself. This transcendental approach goes too far in privileging the transcendental conditions, and is thus a new form of transcendentalism.

Indeed, Heidegger's work is infected with a vicious strain of transcendentalism. Such powerful passages seem to emerge in spite of his theoretical account, not as a result of it. But this is hardly the only example of this sort of transcendentalism. Let us turn our attention briefly to his early work to show the particular misunderstanding of transcendence in Heidegger's transcendentalism.

Heidegger's account of the environment (*Umwelt*) in *Sein und Zeit* is an existential and phenomenological account. Heidegger is making great progress from the idealistic transcendental posture of Husserl's position. Heidegger does a fine job of accounting for the objective attitude of the way we approach the world in our everydayness (present-at-hand). And he also accounts for the way that we see the world in its instrumentality (ready-to-hand). Surely there is more to our experience of the world than the objectivity of things and their usefulness—even all things taken together. That is why Heidegger says we need to look through the everyday guise of the environment to see the world in its ownmost being, as it is given. It shines forth—a *flash* of the world.

It is through the environment that nature is discovered and encountered. But he stresses that the *Um-* in *Umwelt* is less the surrounding horizon of our experience of nature, than the condition for the possibility of it. The significance of environment is not primarily spatial, but transcendental "structure" ([Heidegger 1963, 66/94). That is, even though Heidegger goes to the trouble of acknowledging that spatiality "belongs to" every environment, it is a structure fundamentally—in the sense that ontology is fundamental. And nature is described as the "limiting case of possible entities" (Heidegger 1963, 66/93–94). So Heidegger's account of environment in *Sein und Zeit* is that which discloses nature as objective, instrumental, or transcendental, is a new manner of transcendentalism. There is a rich, authentic experience of nature that is not accounted for in these three options. Perhaps it is not as clear or one-sided as I make it out to be here. There is a brief and cryptic—and promising—reference to "the Nature . . . which assails us and enthralls us as landscape" (Heidegger 1963, 70/100).[6] Nonetheless, an authentic experience of nature seems to elude the possibilities Heidegger sketches out for us in his work.[7]

In his 1949 work, *The Pathway*, Heidegger reminisces about his boyhood playing along a path near the Black Forest. His descriptions indicate that the way gathered by the path—a pathway that speaks to those who can listen carefully. It is a rich, authenticating experience directly tied to nature and our attitude toward it.

> The message of the pathway is now very clear. Does the soul speak? Does the world speak? Does God speak?
> All speak abandonment into the same. Abandonment does not take. Abandonment gives. It gives the inexhaustible power of the simple. The message makes us at home in a long descent. (Heidegger 1967, 91)[8]

This is a beautiful and, I think, profound passage. At first, Heidegger poignantly appeals to concrete lived experience. But then, as usual, the move is toward the transcendental as more significant. The significance of *that* pathway on *that* day becomes the gift of abandonment—which turns out to be cached out in terms of the fourfold, "the structure of all structures."

There are passages in his 1929–1930 lectures, *The Fundamental Concepts of Metaphysics*, where Heidegger says animals are "world-poor" with respect to humans. And later this is reiterated in *Einführung in die Metaphysik,* where he claims "animals have no world and no environment" (Heidegger 1958, 34). In that same work, where Heidegger cites the chorus in Antigone, he dwells upon the strangeness (*Unheimlichkeit*) of man. This is the strangeness from nature that we are—there is nothing stranger in all of nature—the concern we have about our own existence. The ability to make a world is that which makes us different from animals—and even different from ourselves. We are the beings who can never be fully at home in nature, which is why our existence becomes an issue for us. In this work, Heidegger's use of *phusis* or nature is inconsistent.[9] Heidegger sometimes speaks of a "darkening of spirit" in our age in the West (*Abendland*). I assume that this decadence is related to a technological enframing of nature. Again, the concrete experience of nature is reduced to a transcendental condition for the Western postindustrial malaise.

I have heard that when Heidegger was shown a photo of the earth taken from space, he thought that it was horrific. If the whole earth could be objectified, appropriated in a single human perspective, it confirmed his worst fears that it was vulnerable to destruction. Perhaps it is too late for even a god to save us now.

As I hope will become clear later, I think that this vulnerability is essential to nature. We are not only vulnerable to one another in nature, but nature is vulnerable as well. We could destroy the earth—perhaps that is what we are doing. But this same openness allows for us to care for it.

Heidegger's *Umwelt* is meant to be the existentially rich understanding of where one dwells. When one hears the incantation of "earth, gods, sky, mortals," as the manner in which the world is disclosed, it all sounds very nice. But I think that Heidegger's *Umwelt* is not very rich. It is a transcendentalism since it goes too far in its transcendental reflection in such a way that is preoccupied more with the conditions for the possibility of experience than with the experience of nature.

Transcendence: The Nature of Being at Home, and Being at Home in Nature

Camus, Sartre, and Merleau-Ponty were not the best of friends in the end, but I want to import at least one point from Camus' and Sartre's work into this Merleau-Pontyan framework with the justification of their existentialist alliance: the *absurdity* of the human condition. Surely we must own up to the absurdity of our existence. We yearn for some ultimate meaning for our lives. But we must resist the urge to *presuppose* this meaning and *create* it instead. The transcendentalisms described above risk discounting the value of our lives by reducing our lives into terms of some transcendental notion of nature. Transcendental reflection on nature recognizes our engagement within nature—as both Thoreau and Heidegger do at their best moments. But authentic transcendental reflection does not cheapen our engagement by appealing to a provider of meaning, as Thoreau did at times, nor by becoming preoccupied with the conditions for the possibility of the engagement, as Heidegger did at times. Unlike these transcendentalisms, authentic transcendental reflection on nature is an account of *nature as lived*. We must attend to the structure of value as well as to the value of structure—simultaneously. We must interrogate nature from within.

Merleau-Ponty's turn to ontology was at the same time a turning toward nature. We can see this from his courses at the *Collège de France* in 1956–1957, 1957–1958, and 1959–1960. In the first course, Merleau-Ponty examined variations in the concept of nature from the history of philosophy as well as modern science's idea of nature. In the second course, Merleau-Ponty turns his attention immediately to the ontological stances assumed or implied by selected scientific understandings of nature. Here he is in dialogue with biologists and cognitivists. And in the last course on nature, Merleau-Ponty revisits his earlier material while engaged in dialogue with psychoanalysis and evolution-theorists. Once again, he is examining the various conceptions and preconceptions made by a variety of sciences regarding nature.

Merleau-Ponty's emerging ontological project in *The Visible and the Invisible* was an interrogation of nature. And it is being worked through alongside these courses—one reason why the work that those working on transcribing and translating those notes and manuscripts is so important for understanding the promise of Merleau-Ponty's later work. Renaud Barbaras (1991) has done some very important work about Merleau-Ponty's investigations into various movements in sciences that calls explicit attention to this course material. Barbaras reminds us that Merleau-Ponty's departure from the idealistic foundationalism associated with transcendental phenomenology is accomplished in his critical engagement with the sciences of his day. Though I strongly disagree with part of Barbaras's important and innovative approach, there is no doubt that Merleau-Ponty is showing that the *praxis* of scientists is not ancillary to the grounding of their sciences—which is important since "no complete reduction is possible." After all, Merleau-Ponty's own approach to phenomenology was through the science of psychology.

Merleau-Ponty's ontological project was in no way a "fundamental ontology." He explicitly states that he wants to avoid any "top-heavy thought," which would risk a transcendentalism of the sort Heidegger at least flirts with from time to time.

But how can Merleau-Ponty's own ontological reflections on nature avoid this? This is to brush up against the enormous question as to how Merleau-Ponty's ontology differs from Heidegger's. Perhaps we will find only one small part of the complex answer to that question along our way to offering a critique of the two aforementioned transcendentalisms.

During his 1958–1959 course, *la Philosophie aujourd'hui* (*Philosophy Today*), Merleau-Ponty offers many brilliant insights into Heidegger's thought as it developed throughout a wide range of his texts. In a section bearing the title, *l'Être et Grund* (Being and Ground), Merleau-Ponty addresses the problem of essence in the context of the traditional problem of the one and the many.

> [There is, with essences,] the problem of generality (why are there many pebbles, many organisms, many humans, etc.)—that which in each case makes a pebble be a pebble. It counts for naught that this is its essence, *because it is necessary that it take part in existence.* (NC 107; my emphasis)

Merleau-Ponty goes on to say that these essences do their work from within. These essences, with respect to the many things that they typify, stand in the same relation as Being is to *physis* (NC 107). So, according to Merleau-Ponty, Being is *in* nature—no doubt as the invisible is *in* the visible.

Merleau-Ponty then interestingly turns our attention to Heidegger's analysis of the poem by Angelius Silesius about a rose in *Satz vom Grund*.

> The rose is without why
> It blooms because it blooms
> It is not troubled about itself
> Asks nothing
> Nor desires to be seen. (NC 107)

Merleau-Ponty goes on to say that for Heidegger, there exists in the rose a "continuous auto-creation" (the essence of the rose) that does *not* involve any demand. It just gives.

Yet Merleau-Ponty will do something different in his own ontology. We need only consider the many examples of the reversibility of the flesh to see this difference. In Merleau-Ponty's ontology, the relation of Being to nature is less stable and always incomplete. Consider the following working note from March, 1959: "Becoming-nature of man which is the becoming-man of nature—the world is a field, and as such it is always open" (VI 239/185).

This field is no monolithic unity, it is situated transcendence, divergence, a spread of difference. And it may surprise some when I say that Merleau-Ponty thought of this field as a radicalization of *intentionality*.

Clearly, Merleau-Ponty offers a strong critique of intentionality in many of the working notes to *The Visible and the Invisible* as part of his critique of a philosophy based on consciousness. One such note is from January 1960.

> The structure of the visual field, with its near-bys, its far-offs, its horizon, is indispensable for there to be transcendence.... And the intentional analysis that tries to compose the field with intentional threads does not see that the threads are emanations and idealizations of *one* fabric, *differentiations* of the fabric. (VI 284/231)

Later, in April 1960, Merleau-Ponty continues his attack on the limitations of the consciousness-based intentional framework. He makes it clear that the immersion in a Being-in-transcendence cannot be reduced to "perspectives" of consciousness (VI 297/243). That is, we are engaged within a world of flesh, not thoughts (VI 297/243): "This reciprocal intentional reference marks the limit of the intentional analytic: the point where it becomes a philosophy of transcendence" (VI 297–298/244).

Yet the matter is much more complicated than an abject dismissal of phenomenology and intentionality. I think that Merleau-Ponty is in the process of transforming intentionality—transforming phenomenology yet again. For his first excursions into phenomenology had already significantly transformed it. And when we see here two aspects of this latest radicalization of Husserlian phenomenology, we will also be in a better position to appreciate Merleau-Ponty's divergence from Heidegger—which is why we embarked on this road.

First, the ontological account of transcendence is sometimes explicitly described as a new form of intentionality: "It is necessary to take up again and develop the *latent intentionality* which is the intentionality within Being" (VI 297–298/244). And earlier, Merleau-Ponty had described the tendency of "wild" perception to imperceptibly forget its own status as it is so caught up in the world. What is forgotten here, and that toward which Merleau-Ponty directs our attention, is a *latent intentionality* which, once recovered, changes the traditional phenomenological account (VI 266–267/213). Merleau-Ponty tells us that this is tantamount to "rediscovering silence" (VI 266–267/213). What this *latent intentionality* provides is a differentiating field of Being to facilitate traditional acts of consciousness.

Furthermore, the most radical emphasis of differentiation and transcendence in Merleau-Ponty's ontology is *écart* [divergence]. And in a still unpublished working note from 1958, Merleau-Ponty said that "*écart* = intentionality."[10]

Second, this latent intentionality is *not* a departure from transcendental thought, though it is a radicalization of the entire transcendental posture of inquiry. It is, in one sense, a transcendental condition of transcendence. But is important to remember that this is *not* a formal ground. It is the silence that nurtures speech and intrudes within speech, an aspect of speech without which speech would not be speech. Ordinarily, we do not focus on this silence. It is our normal *Gestalt* to focus on the sense of the articulated phonemes punctuating the silence, as if the articulations began or ended in anything other than silence—as if articulation escaped silence. But silence and speech are of the same flesh. Our silence differentiates every utterance.[11]

So, given these two points, I remain unpersuaded by those accounts that claim that Merleau-Ponty's ontology is a complete abandonment of transcendental phenomenology; but only because, as we have seen, it is transcendental (in a new way), and it is phenomenological (in a new way).

Now we can apply all of this back to distinguish Merleau-Ponty's ontological account from Heidegger's on the problem of essences in nature.

Merleau-Ponty had written that "the world is a *field,* and as such it is always open" (VI 239/185). This is the field where transcendence, reversibility, occurs. This is the field where "becoming-nature-of-man is becoming-man-of-nature" (VI 239/185). And the latency of this intentional field holds the world open by *disrupting* it. This is always a *specific* demand, like a ontological normal force, one that leads Merleau-Ponty to describe paintings watching patrons in a museum and trees watching people in a forest. Contra Heidegger, nature not only gives, it takes as well.

Man-becoming-nature *is* nature-becoming-man, *and it is not.* This reversible relation is never complete because the disruptive latent intentionality keeps the field unstable, open to change. The kind of transcendental reflection we have done here are the first steps to disclosing the nature of being-at-home. We need only conclude by considering the implications of these reflections for understanding our being-at-home in nature.

Thoreau's account describes humans as, for the most part, a little too much at home in nature, due to his *transcendentalism.* Nature as divine foreclosed the contingency of the natural in terms of its *telos.* Heidegger's account described humans as, for the most part, a little too *unheimlich,* not quite enough at home in nature. This is due to the abstraction of his account of nature. Heidegger's *transcendentalism* allows for the field of differentiation to become hypsostatized as nature becomes de-natured, portrayed as giving without any questions, making no demands.

We are at home in nature insofar as we suffer its fate. We eat the fish from the river where the toxic benzene slick once flowed. We develop asthma as we breathe the air we continue to foul. But nature itself presents a threat that we try to resist through our Modern quest to master and possess it. We build against the threats of nature because we are also not at home there. Another way of showing this complex intentional relation is that we redefine ourselves and nature as we live there. The redefining presents a threat and provides a home—thus it calls for respect. Perhaps we can more wisely choose actions and policies that respect nature as threat and home, as origin and product.

What I have elsewhere called reversible subjectivity, a virtual focus of experience and responsibility, is and is not at home in nature.[12] Being at home requires construction, and it leads to calloused, dirty hands. Being at home is a struggle within our environment to define and redefine our relation to Nature. But it gives us a good place to be, for awhile.

> The river was wide and its noisy little waves reflected the light. On the other bank lay meadows which farther on merged into bushes behind which, at a great distance, one could see bright avenues of fruit trees leading to green hills.
>
> Pleased by this sight, I lay down and, stopping my ears to the dread sound of sobs, I thought: Here I could be content. For here it is secluded and beautiful. It won't take much courage to live here. One will have to struggle here as anywhere else, but at least one won't have to do it with graceful movements. That won't be necessary. For there are only mountains and a wide river and I have sense enough to regard them as inanimate. Yes, when I totter alone up the steep path through the meadows in the evening I will be no more forsaken than the mountains, except that I will feel it. But I think that this, too, will pass. (Kafka 1982, 24–25)

Notes

1. I would like to thank Glen Helman of Wabash College for conversations that were instrumental in the development of this essay, and especially for a friendship that continues to be influential in my philosophical development.

2. I hope that it will be obvious and clear that I am not endorsing Kant's definition of nature as that which can be ordered, nor am I endorsing the claims he made about the purity and certainty of the knowledge he claimed resulted from his transcendental idealism. Kant was keen to establish a pure epistemological and metaphysical foundation that I reject out of hand. And it goes without saying that I am not attributing a common conception of nature to all of the German Idealists. Finally, following some phenomenologists, especially Merleau-Ponty, I want to argue that it is possible and necessary to adopt a transcendental posture—attending to the conditions of the possibility of experiencing nature without forsaking our engagement within the environment.

3. I am citing Emerson's essay, "The Transcendentalists."

4. It is vitally important to Marcel to distinguish faith from optimism. Faith, for Marcel, is something like the positive transcendental reflection I am advocating in secularized form. If it helps, think of it as akin to what Merleau-Ponty calls "perceptual faith" in *The Visible and the Invisible*. Optimism, like pessimism, according to Marcel, gets in the way of our ability to lay claim to our own lives.

5. For an outstanding explanatory discussion of Heidegger's fourfold, cf. Kockelmans (1985, 94 ff). The stated purpose in this work is exegesis. It remains one of the finest works on the later Heidegger. Kockelmans directs the reader to the texts for further study as well as to important secondary works.

6. I am indebted to Richard Polt for suggesting this passage as an exception to my reading. I am further indebted to him for many fine discussions of Heidegger. My indebtedness to his philosophical erudition and expertise is exceeded by my indebtedness to him in friendship.

7. This cannot be established here, but I will give just enough information in a tendentious way so that all can agree with me and read on in good conscience.

8. *Der Zuspruch des Feldweges ist jetzt ganz deutlich. Spricht die Seele? Spricht die Welt? Spricht Gott? Alles spricht den Verzicht in das Selbe. Der Verzicht nimmt nicht. Der Verzicht gibt. Er gibt die unerschöpfliche Kraft des Einfachen. Der Zuspruch macht heimisch in einer langen Herkunft.*

9. Again, I am indebted to Richard Polt for this observation. He directs us to Schoenbohm (2001) in Polt and Fried (2001). Schoenbohm points out that sometimes Heidegger seems to equate nature with beings as a whole, and sometimes he seems to equate nature with Being.

10. Maurice Merleau-Ponty, notes and manuscripts deposited at the *Bibliothèque nationale* in Paris. Since 1997, when Mme. Merleau-Ponty kindly granted me access to the manuscripts, they have been reorganized and microfilmed. My citations from that visit in 1997 are to the original boxes, folders, and page numbers. This note is from 1958, Box III, 53b. Also, in the same folder in Box III, cf. Lefort's enumeration of 22 notes on Wild Being and ontology, 1957–1958, p. 14: "to make a theory of the folding as *logos*—of the tissue of the world folded as intentionality."

11. Cf. Bernard Dauenhauer's important book, *Silence* [Indiana University Press, Bloomington, 1980]. Dauenhauer offers a thoroughgoing account of silence and indirect language, and is especially valuable in understanding these aspects of the philosophies of Kierkegaard and Merleau-Ponty.

12. I have begun to work out a transformation of subjectivity informed by Merleau-Ponty's notion of reversibility in my *Reversible Subjectivity: The Problem of Transcendence and Language*.

References

Barbaras, Renaud. 1991. *De l'être du phénomène*. Grenoble: Editions J. Million.

Davis, Duane H. 1990. "Reversible Subjectivity: The Problem of Transcendence and Language," in Martin C. Dillon, ed. *Merleau-Ponty* Vivant. Albany: State University of New York Press, pp. 31–45.

Emerson, Ralph Waldo [R.E. Spiller (ed.)]. 1965. *Selected Essays, Lectures, and Poems of Ralph Waldo Emerson*. New York: Washington Square Press.

Heidegger, Martin. 1958. *Einführung der Metaphysik*. Tübingen: Max Niemeyer Verlag. Translated into English by Ralph Manheim under the title *Introduction to Metaphysics*. 1959. New Haven: Yale University Press.

———. 1963. *Sein und Zeit*. Tübingen: Max Niemeyer Verlag. Translated into English by John MacQuarrie and Edward Robinson under the title *Being and Time*. New York: Harper and Row, 1962, p. 94.

———. 1967. *Der Feldweg*, in: *Listening / Current Studies in Dialog*, Spring, vol. 2, no. 2.

———. 1972. *On Time and Being*. Translated by Joan Stambaugh. New York: Harper Torchbooks. Originally published as *Zur Sache des Denkens*. 1969. Tübingen: Max Niemeyer Verlag.

Kafka, Franz. 1982. *Descriptions of a Struggle and Other Stories*. New York: Penguin Books.

Kockelmans, Joseph J. 1985. *On The Truth of Being*. Bloomington: Indiana University Press.

Polt, Richard and Gregory Fried, eds. 2001. *A Companion to Heidegger's Introduction to Metaphysics*. New Haven: Yale University Press.

Schoenbohm, Susan. 2001. "Heidegger's Interpretation of *Physis*," in Polt and Fried, pp. 143–60.

Thoreau, Henry David. 1977. *The Portable Thoreau*. Edited by Carl Bode. New York: Penguin Books.

7

Merleau-Ponty, Ecology, and Biosemiotics

Maurita Harney

INTRODUCTION

In his *Phenomenology of Perception*, Merleau-Ponty shifts the locus of intentionality from Husserlian consciousness to the body-subject. With this shift, Merleau-Ponty effectively shakes off the legacy of the Cartesian-derived dualisms, most notably the oppositions of mind and matter, of subject and object, of culture and nature, and of human versus natural reality. This move to embodied intentionality means that intentionality is no longer the "mark of the mental" in Brentano's words (1874, 1973), but must now be seen as somehow grounded in biological processes—processes that are shared by human and nonhuman organisms alike. In dissolving the dualism that marks humans off from other living things, Merleau-Ponty effectively paves the way for a philosophical ecology. His later transition from "the body" to "flesh of the world" in *The Visible and the Invisible* marks a further move in this direction, reinforcing the idea that intentionality can now be generalized to all living organisms, and through this to the whole of nature. In this way, Merleau-Ponty sets the scene for a philosophical ecology—something that he did not fully develop himself, but which now presents itself as an important project for scholars like those represented in this collection.

If we are to develop a philosophical ecology from Merleau-Ponty's insights relating to the idea of an embodied subject "intervolved with" a world, then we must reject explanations that reduce embodied action to a set of processes conceptualized in terms of the "objectivist-scientific" attitude. The case of the phantom limb shows the insufficiency of approaches which presume ultimately a view of the human subject as a duality of mind and body; the discussion of embodied action within a world shows the inadequacy of approaches which divide humans from

133

the rest of nature. This means that we need to reject the restrictive Cartesian-derived dyadic ontology that is responsible for this perspective and its shortcomings. It prompts the suggestion that we should look instead at a richer ontology if we are to develop a philosophical ecology. In this respect, the field of inquiry known as biosemiotics might offer some insights.

Biosemiotics is premised on the idea that all living organisms engage in processes of signification and communication by means of signs. Its founding inspiration is the theory of signs and of sign processes, known as semiotics, developed by American philosopher, Charles Sanders Peirce (1839-1914). For Peirce, the sign is to be analyzed as the triadic relation of a *sign vehicle* (sometimes called a *representamen*), which stands to somebody or some context (the *interpretant*) for some *object*. So, a footprint can be a sign vehicle which stands for something—an animal which has passed by. However, it can only function as a sign if it is interpreted as such—in this case, by someone observing that footprint as a sign. Without an *interpretant* the footprint is just a physical mark along with any other in the sand.

Peirce claimed that "the universe is perfused by signs, if not entirely composed of them" (CP 5.448n), thereby indicating that the locus of meaning in the case of the sign is not the human mind, but rather processes in nature.[1] In biosemiotics, the focus of pioneering work was ethology, or communicative behavior in animals, but more recent developments have extended semiotic inquiry to the entire life sphere. Indeed Peirce himself suggested that a plant's interaction with sunlight might be understood as semiosis: "Thus, if a sunflower, in turning towards the sun, becomes by that act fully capable, without further condition, of reproducing a sunflower which turns in precisely corresponding ways towards the sun, and of doing so with the same reproductive power, the sunflower would become a Representamen of the sun . . ." (CP 2.274).

Along with Peirce's theory of signs, a key concept in the development of biosemiotics is the notion of the *Umwelt,* a term coined by Estonian born Jakob von Uexkull to describe the organism's environment or setting. However, this is not the "mere" environment that an outsider might observe; rather, it is the environment as perceived and experienced by the organism. Organism and environment are engaged in a meaningful relationship, not a mechanistic one. In biosemiotics, this ecological relationship is articulated in terms of the sign processes whereby meanings are communicated in nature: "In the biosemiotic conception, the life sphere is permeated by sign processes (*semiosis*) and signification. Whatever an organism senses also means something to it—food, escape, sexual reproduction, etc., and all organisms are thus born into a *semiosphere*, i.e., a world of meaning and communication: sounds, odours, movements, colors, electric fields, waves of any kind, chemical signals, touch, etc." (Hoffmeyer 1998a, 82).

The notion of *Umwelt* provides a convenient starting point for connecting Merleau-Ponty's ecological insights with biosemiotics. Merleau-Ponty was aware of, and indeed influenced by, the ideas of von Uexkull, and makes explicit use of this notion in his later works (SC 159; RC 94–95; NC).[2] This notion clearly resonates with Merleau-Ponty's description of an organism's *attunement* to its environment in *Phenomenology of Perception* (75) and his characterization of the relationship between organism and environment as one of reciprocity.

Because of the shared acceptance of the notion of *Umwelt*, it is perhaps not surprising to find that there a several themes or 'theses' that are common to Merleau-Ponty and to biosemiotics. First, there is a shared belief in the insufficiency of a dyadic ontology as a basis for a philosophical ecology, and the suggestion, more fully articulated in biosemiotics than in Merleau-Ponty, that a triadic framework is required. A second point of similarity is the view that meaning is generated from biological processes rather than a product of the human mind. Embodied intentionality means that intentionality is not a "mark of the mental" but a feature of all biological processes. A significant contribution can be made by biosemiotics in offering a theory of biology that incorporates the dimension of meaning by virtue of the key notion of the sign as a triadic unity. It is, at the same time, a theory of communication which can amplify a third point of connection with Merleau-Ponty, namely the view that ecological relations are communicative relations of reciprocity. Here, again, the triadic framework of the sign is operative in ensuring a nonreductionist account of the meaningful relationship between an organism and its environment.

I wish to explore these points of similarity in more detail, bearing in mind that the path by which they are reached, and the context within which they are elaborated are significantly different—in the case of Merleau-Ponty, they follow from the methodological standpoint of the embodied first-person perspective, whereas in biosemiotics they are a consequence of Peirce's theory of signs and its application to biological processes.

My aim is to show how biosemiotics might augment the insights of Merleau-Ponty when it comes to developing a philosophical ecology from the first-person standpoint of the embodied subject. The semiotic paradigm, when applied to the study of biological processes, serves as an alternative framework to what Merleau-Ponty would call the "objectivist-scientific" framework for viewing these processes. It replaces the discredited dyadic framework with a triadic one for articulating a theory of biological processes as meaningful processes of communication.

THE INSUFFICIENCY OF A DYADIC ONTOLOGY ("A THIRD TERM IS NEEDED . . .")

In his *Phenomenology of Perception*, Merleau-Ponty establishes the uniqueness of the body's role as the subject of perception. This uniqueness is borne of a particular perspective on the body—what Merleau-Ponty terms *le corps propre*—the subjectivized or *phenomenal* body as I experience it, which contrasts with *le corps objectif*, the objectified body or the body as studied by science, that is, from the "objectivist-scientific" perspective. This latter perspective finds expression in those philosophical approaches that Merleau-Ponty seeks to discredit, namely empiricism, which seeks explanations of embodied action in terms of causal determinants, and intellectualism, which offers explanations in terms of mental representations and which ultimately requires the postulation of a disembodied mind.

The case of the phantom limb demonstrates the shortcomings of these two approaches. The causal explanations of empiricists are unsuccessful: Physiological factors alone cannot account for the condition—anaesthesia does not remove it, so there must be some dependence on psychological factors. But psychological factors cannot be the sole cause either, because severing the nerves to the brain does remove the condition, indicating that physiological factors play some part in the explanation. Intellectualist accounts, which attempt to explain the experience in terms of a "refusal" to accept mutilation, also contain an element of truth, but fail to be fully adequate as an explanation because they presume a deliberate act of decision originating ultimately in a disembodied mind.

Both empiricism and intellectualism, although superficially opposed, stem from the same "objectivist-scientific" perspective, which in turn is a product of a restrictive Cartesian ontology—one that conceptualizes the human subject as a dualism of mind and body and, as a consequence of this, separates humans from the rest of nature.

It is important to note, however, that Merleau-Ponty does not repudiate scientific approaches as false—it is rather the insufficiency of these approaches to account for our experience as embodied subjects in the world that prompts his criticism. Merleau-Ponty speculates that there is a need for a "middle term" between the 'in-itself' and the 'for-itself' if we are to adequately explain the phantom limb phenomenon:

> The phantom limb is not the mere outcome of objective causality; no more is it a *cogitatio*. It could be a mixture of the two only if we could find a way of linking the "psychic" and the "physiological"… to each other to form an articulate whole, and to contrive some meeting-point for them: if the third person processes and the personal acts could be integrated into a common middle term. (PhP 77)

Dillon (1988, 35–50) traces epistemological problems like these to an underlying ontological dualism—in Dillon's formulation, a dualism of immanence (the sphere of interiority or conscious life) and transcendence (the sphere of exteriority or independently existing things). He says:

> that middle term is exactly what is required. No epistemology can succeed in mediating what an antecedently adopted ontology has defined as mutually exclusive . . . the paradox of immanence and transcendence requires a middle term, an "element," a "general manner of being" whose being does not preclude, but rather invites, being seen, being grasped. . . . (Dillon 1988, 36)

For Dillon, the epistemological problem of mediating between immanence and transcendence is generated by an underlying ontological dualism: "An ontology that defines immanence as a radical negation of transcendence cannot be coupled with an epistemology that defines knowledge in terms of a mediation between them" (Dillon 1988, 37). The need for a richer ontology is also indicated in Merleau-Ponty's discussion of the experience of bodily space: "As far as spatiality is concerned . . . one's own body is the third term, always tacitly understood, in the figure-background structure . . ." (PhP 101).[3]

Biosemiotics can make an important contribution to a philosophical ecology by way of a theoretical framework that replaces the inadequate dualistic one that Merleau-Ponty seeks to reject. It is provided by Peirce's notion of the sign which is said to be irreducibly triadic.[4] Suppose, looking at the horizon, I see smoke and I take this as a sign that there is a fire in the vicinity. Here, the relation between the *sign vehicle* (smoke) and its *object* (fire) is mediated by a third term, the *interpretant* (my thought of the fire).[5] The sign relation here cannot be reduced to two dyadic, causal relations, one between *object* and *sign*, and the other between *sign* and *interpretant*. The first of these ("fire causes smoke") tells us nothing about the smoke as *meaning* or *signifying* something. The second reduces the role of the sign to something that is only dyadically or causally related to the interpretant ("smoke causes my thought of fire"), but this is insufficient to convey the idea that signs are vehicles of *signification* or meaning: Signs are meaningful not because they act causally on us like environmental stimuli, but because they are taken by us to *mean* something.

As with Merleau-Ponty, this is not to deny that causal relations exist in the physical world for example, the physical, causal relation between fire and smoke. This dyadic relation is acknowledged and is said to constitute the "ground" of the sign. The "ground" of the sign becomes for Peirce the basis for another threefold classification of signs. An *iconic* sign stands for its object by virtue of some similarity or likeness: for example, a map, a picture, a drawing. An *indexical* sign stands for its object by means of an existential or causal relationship, for example, smoke; a weather vane; a thermometer; footprints; animal droppings. A *symbolic* sign stands for its object by virtue of convention, habit, or rule, for example, a life-saver flag; the word *cat*. All language is symbolic.

In biosemiotics, these classifications relating to ground play an important role in the analysis of signs that are part of nature. Plants exhibit primarily indexical signs, for example a plant's interaction with sunlight. Animals display both indexical and iconic signs. For example, the footprint of a bear exhibits both a relation of similarity (iconic), as well as a causal (indexical) relation to the animal's paw that left the imprint. Humans exhibit all three, the symbolic signs being constituted primarily by language (Sebeok 1991, 104).

The fact that we do not repudiate the causal relation between fire and smoke, but rather acknowledge it as the *ground* of the sign, shows how we can still admit the validity of external causal relations, or of what Merleau-Ponty would call the "objectivist-scientific" standpoint. However, as a basis for a philosophical ecology, this standpoint is inadequate. This stance and its commitment to an underlying dyadic ontology must be rejected as being insufficient to the task of constructing an acceptable account of the meaningful relationship between an organism and its environment as captured by the notion of *Umwelt*.

BODILY INTENTIONALITY:
MEANING IS NOT TIED TO MENTALITY

The emphasis given to the unique role of the body in Merleau-Ponty's philosophy of perception is not to be regarded as a way of privileging the human subject, and thereby a commitment to a dualism of humans *versus* nature. On the contrary, *le corps propre* as embodied subject serves to establish a methodological standpoint that ultimately yields a continuity between humans and nonhuman organisms, and where it is the similarities between humans and other animals and living things rather than the differences that are emphasized.

The idea of biologically based intentionality is well demonstrated in the notion of the customary or habitual body which Merleau-Ponty introduces in response to the problem of the phantom limb. The problem is to explain the "ambivalent presence" (PhP 81) of the amputated limb. As we have seen, reductionist explanations are inadequate to account for this phenomenon. Instead, Merleau-Ponty proposes a distinction which is only possible if we adopt the perspective of *le corps propre*. This is the distinction between two modes of experiencing embodiment—the habitual body and the nonhabitual body. The habitual body is the body as I have become accustomed to it—the body that moves around the world, encounters objects, or anticipates movements and resistances. It is purposive movement but there are no conscious acts of deliberation. The nonhabitual body is the mutilated body which I have now, and which has not yet become "habituated." The experience of the phantom limb is the persistence of the habitual body, which maintains its practical involvement in the world (PhP 81–82).

Habituation can be explained as a kind of "stored intentionality" that manifests itself as "skillful coping" (Dreyfus 1996, 34) in the world. It is a way of explaining how we engage in undeliberated skills or actions in making our way around the world. Merleau-Ponty calls it "motor significance" indicating that the habitual actions are meaningful and not mere reflex movements, while at the same time suggesting that the significance is biologically "embedded." It is "the grasping of a significance, but it is the motor grasping of a motor significance" (PhP 143) and not the result of mental representations. His examples of the woman with a tall feather in her hat negotiating doorways, the blind man's use of his stick, the experienced driver's ability to negotiate small parking spaces, and so on (ibid.) serve to affirm that our relationship to our environment is meaningful, but meaning itself can be "embodied" or incorporated into our bodies as a result of habit.

For Merleau-Ponty, meaning is biologically based. It is not a product of mentality. So too, with biosemiotics. The key notion of the sign is not tied to a theory of mind, but to a theory of nature. For Peirce, signs are not produced as a result of human agency or mentality. In an important sense, signs have an *autonomy*. Semiosis, or the generation of interpretants, is not the work of an interpreter be it human or otherwise, but rather the work of the sign itself. Cognition is one instance of this, but it is not the source of semiosis.[6] As Joseph Ransdell puts it: "semiosis . . . (is) always due to the agency of the sign itself, rather than to the agency of an interpreter, human or otherwise . . ." (Ransdell 1992, 2). So, meanings are not bestowed or created by the human mind, an interpreter's interpretation being "primarily a *perception* or *observation* of the meaning exhibited by the sign itself . . ." (ibid.).

Subsequent writers have avoided the mentalistic overtones of "interpretant" by speaking instead of a "system of interpretance" (Lemke 1999, 1). The autonomy thesis states that interpretants (or systems of interpretance) are generated by signs themselves, not by human agents (Ransdell 1992, 6). The interpretant can be embedded in habit: for example it is habit that mediates subsequent recognition of the relation between representamen and object. However, it is the sign that generates the interpretant and not vice versa.

Peirce's thesis of the autonomy of signs provides a semiotic equivalent to Merleau-Ponty's notion of the habitual body and associated notions of "stored intentionality." The autonomy of signs means we can identify semiotic processes operating diachronically or genealogically between successive generations of species. As Sharov puts it (1999, 2), producing offspring is a form of communication to future generations. Hoffmeyer's studies in evolutionary biology show how the organism's internal organisation can be seen to represent "a kind of 'frozen past' against which the (organism) measures present situations to decide for its further actions" (1998b, 5). The genome is an essential part of that "frozen past": "The sign vehicle might for instance be the genome, the object might be the ontogenetic trajectory whereas the interpretant would be hidden in the cytoskeletal architecture of the fertilised egg (or the growing embryo)" (Hoffmeyer 1998b, 5; see also Hoffmeyer and Emmeche 1991).

RECIPROCITY AS A CHARACTER OF ECOLOGICAL RELATIONS

Signs are vehicles of communication. In offering us a theory of biology, biosemiotics is, at the same time, offering us a theory of communication. Biological processes are semiotic or sign processes, and by that fact are communication processes. They involve the exchange of meanings through the use of signs. However signs, as we have seen, are not tied to a theory of mind. They are part of nature.

Ethology (the study of animal behavior) provides a rich resource base for the semiotician when it comes to exploring the processes of communication in nature. The pheromone emission of insects, dances of bees, and mating rituals are all ways in which organisms communicate with one another using signs. These examples which involve the use of signs to communicate messages between members of species are said to be *exosemiotic*. Signs that communicate messages can sometimes be internal to an organism—for example, the camouflage of butterflies, the song of birds, and threat behavior in baboons. These sign processes form the subject matter of *endosemiotics,* another subbranch of this field of inquiry (Hoffmeyer 1997b).

Endosemiotic (or "internal") processes are operative at the cellular and subcellular (molecular) levels. An individual cell comprises millions of 'receptors' capable of recognizing specific signal molecules in the cell environment. These receptors "function as communication channels through which our cells, tissues and organs are persistently communicating with each other all around the body" (Hoffmeyer 1997b).

But these processes are not to be understood in terms of conventional information theory that reduces communication to a dyadic model of 'signal and response' or the transfer of information between sender and receiver. This reductionist model omits the important dimension of meaning. A semiotic approach requires instead that, at all levels, communication as meaningful exchange must be understood in terms of a triadic framework. The textbook vocabulary of microbiology is highly suggestive of a semiotic model of biological processes—cells are described as "recognizing," "interpreting," "selecting," "sending messages," and so forth. What is significant about this language is the implication that biological communication consists not just in mere signaling, but in a reciprocal exchange of meanings. For this reason, biosemiotics can be seen to offer a theory of communication that is appropriate to, and might further illuminate, Merleau-Ponty's view of the organism's *Umwelt*. For Merleau-Ponty, the relationship between organism and environment is more like a reciprocal, communicative interaction than the mechanical action-reaction of a subject impinging on an inert, passive world.

For Merleau-Ponty, the body is not just the passive recipient of stimuli from an external world. Rather, it is *attuned* to the world. Even perception in the case of a minor reflex action is intentional or meaningful, and this means that "reflex actions are never themselves blind processes: they adjust themselves to a 'direction' of the situation, and express our orientation towards a 'behavioural setting,' just as much as the action of the 'geographical setting' on us" (PhP 79). *Attunement* or the idea of an orientation to a setting is a biological phenomenon that is common to human and nonhuman organisms in their interaction with their environment.

The attunement of the organism to the world is reciprocated by the action of the world (the "geographical setting") on us. The world or environment is not something inert, passive, something waiting to be acted on. The world as correlate of my actions presents itself as somehow receptive, or configured to receive, or *afford* those actions. Merleau-Ponty describes a tailor who has the lost the capacity for identifying parts of his body by pointing to them, but he nonetheless retains "concrete" perceptual abilities—he can continue to cut cloth, sew, and so on. For such a person, the world is "the piece of leather to be cut up; it is the lining 'to be sewn' . . ." (PhP 106).

The idea that the world enters into a kind of communicative or reciprocal relation with the perceiver is a case of what ecological psychologist James Gibson (1977) calls *affordance*. It means that the world that we operate in is not neutral with respect to our actions, but is in some way complementary to those actions. There is a kind of "fit" between the action and its object—for example, between cutting up cloth and cloth-to-be-cut-up, between catching a tennis ball and the ball as something-for-catching. As described by Hubert Dreyfus: ". . . the characteristics of the human world, e.g., what affords walking on, squeezing through, reaching, etc. are correlative to our bodily capacities and acquired skills"

(1996, 3). This idea of a reciprocity between the action (or the potential for action) and its correlate in the world is further developed in Merleau-Ponty's later work, *The Visible and the Invisible*. Here Merleau-Ponty reminds us of the reciprocity in perceiving and touching—that the perceiver is also the perceived and that to touch is also to be touched. The point here is that intentionality becomes 'globalized' to the world of which I am part: ". . . I am experiencing the world; yet when I attend closely to the carnal nature of this phenomenon, I recognise that I can just as well say that I am being experienced by the world" (Abram 1996, 100 n).

Conclusion

As with Merleau-Ponty's philosophy, an important lesson from biosemiotics is confirmation that meaning or significance need not be tied to a theory of mind or cognition. The world or nature has the capacity to generate meanings in the form of signs, just as for Merleau-Ponty, it is the world (and not minds) which generates meaning in the form of "affording" the lining-to-be-sewn, the tennis-ball-to-be-caught, and so forth. As with Merleau-Ponty, there is no repudiation, either implicit or explicit, of established scientific laws. However, in neither the semiotic approach nor that of Merleau-Ponty can meaning or significance be reduced to sets of causal events in the physical world. This is so in the case of semiotics, because the process of semiosis (the generation of signs) can only be understood triadically and therefore nonreductively. "What we should learn from this analysis of intentionality, subjectivity, and self-awareness is not that these phenomena are forever beyond the horizon of science. Rather we should learn that the key to scientific understanding of the mental is embodied existence and not the fictitious idea of disembodied symbolic organisation which appeals to the aritmocentric minds of traditional scientists" (Hoffmeyer 1996, 2).

In the case of Merleau-Ponty, meaning expressed as intentionality is liberated from "the mental" and becomes instead a property of biological rather than mental processes. By this means, intentionality comes to be generalised to the natural world including all living things as a distinctive characteristic of the interactions that occur within nature. But "biological processes" here cannot mean processes explicable by reductionist "objectivist-scientific" approaches. Biosemiotics provides a fruitful alternative to the latter, rejecting the restrictive dyadic ontology which gives rise to reductionist explanations, and suggesting instead that these processes can be explained in terms of communicative sign processes, understood as a triadic unity rather than as a dyadic relationship.

In *The Visible and the Invisible* (130–155), Merleau-Ponty suggests that nature might be conceptualized as language. However, this is not to reduce nature to a human convention. Rather, it is to ground language "in the visible, tangible, audible world" (Abram 1996, 95) in much the same way that Peirce's signs are grounded in the processes of nature at a multiplicity of levels. Abram states Merleau-Ponty's position thus: ". . . if the sensible world itself is the deep body of language, then this language can no longer be conceived as a power that resides within the human species, at least no more than it adheres to the roar of a waterfall, or even to the wind in the leaves. If language is born of our carnal *participation* in a world that already *speaks to us* at the most immediate level of sensory experience, then language does not belong to humankind but to the sensible world of which we are but a part" (1996, 95). A broader conception of nature as a communication system consisting of sign-processes or semiosis seems to be not too far removed from this vision.

NOTES

1. This marks an important difference between Peirce's semiotics and Saussure's *semiologie*: The Peircean sign is natural; the Saussurean sign is a product of human convention, namely, language.

2. Hansen (2005, 251–253) discusses this notion in some detail, claiming that Merleau-Ponty "appropriates" this notion in his second and third lecture of *La Nature, Notes, Cours du Collège de France*. The influence of von Uexkull (1864–1944) on Merleau-Ponty is also discussed by Carbone (2004).

3. I wish to thank Sue Cataldi for drawing my attention to this point.

4. This distinguishes Peircean semiotics from Saussure's structuralism or *semiologie*. For Saussure, signs are binary and hence dyadic.

5. This is just one instance of an interpretant. As we will see below there is no implied commitment to a theory of mind in this account.

6. The primacy of the natural sign over linguistic signs, and the consequent detachment of semiosis from a theory of cognition are important respects in which Peircean semiotics must be distanced from the *semiologie* of Saussure. For Saussure, the study of signs is subsumed within the study of human cognition; for Peirce the relation is reversed—human cognition is a subbranch of semiotics.

REFERENCES

Abram, David. 1996. "Merleau-Ponty and the Voice of the Earth," in David Macauley, ed. *Minding Nature: The Philosophers of Ecology.* New York and London: The Guildford Press, 82–101.

Brentano, Franz. 1973. *Psychology from an Empirical Standpoint.* Translated by A. C. Rancurello, D. B. Terrell, and L. L. McAlister. London: Routledge & Kegan Paul. Originally published as *Psychologie vom empirischen Standpunkt.* 1874. Leipzig: Duncke & Humblot.

Carbone, Mauro. 2004. *The Thinking of the Sensible: Merleau-Ponty's A-Philosophy* Evanston: Northwestern University Press.

Dillon, M.C. 1998. *Merleau-Ponty's Ontology.* Bloomington & Indianapolis: Indiana University Press.

Dreyfus, Hubert L. 1996. "The Current Relevance of Merleau-Ponty's Phenomenology of Embodiment," *The Electronic Journal of Philosophy.* Spring 1996: http://www.phil.indiana.dreyfus.1996.spring.html, accessed 19 September 1996.

Emmeche, C. 1991. "A semiotical reflection on biology, living signs and artificial life" *Biology and Philosophy* 6: 325–340.

Gibson, James. 1977. "The theory of affordances," in Robert Shaw and John Bransford, eds. *Perceiving, Acting, Knowing: Toward an Ecological Psychology.* Hillsdale NJ: Lawrence Erlbaum, pp. 67–82.

Hansen, Mark B. N. 2005. "The embryology of the (in)visible," in Taylor Carman and Mark B. N. Hansen, eds. *The Cambridge Companion to Merleau-Ponty.* Cambridge, New York: Cambridge University Press, 231–264.

Hoffmeyer, Jesper. 1996. "Evolutionary Intentionality." Electronic version: *http://www.molbio.ku.dk/MolBioPages/Jesper/Intentionality.html,* accessed 1 May 1998.

———. 1997a. "Biosemiotics: Towards a New Synthesis in Biology." Electronic version: *http://www.molbio.ku.dk/MolBioPages/Jesper/Semio-Emergence.html,* accessed 10 April 2002.

———. 1997b. "Semiotic Emergence" in *Revue de la pensée d'aujourd'hui,* vol. 25–27, no. 6. Electronic version: http://www.ento.vt.edu/~sharov/biosem/hoffmeyer.html, accessed 4 June 2002.

———. 1998a. "Biosemiotics," in P. Bouissac (ed.), *Encyclopaedia of Semiotics.* New York: Oxford University Press, pp. 82–85. Electronic version: http://www.zbi.ee/ ~uexkull/biosemiotics/jespintr.htm, accessed 16 April 2002.

———. 1998b. "The Unfolding Semiosphere" *http://www.molbio.ku.dk/MolBioPages/abk/PersonalPages/Jesper/Unfolding.html.* accessed 5 June 2002.

Hoffmeyer, J. and Emmeche, C. 1991. "Code-duality and the semiotics of nature" in Myrdene Anderson and Floyd Merrell (eds.), *On Semiotic Modeling.* Berlin and New York: Mouton de Gruyter, pp. 117–166. Electronic version: *http://alf.nbi.dk/~emmeche/coPubl/91.JHCE/codedual.html,* accessed 22 April 2002.

Lemke, Jay L. 1999. "Opening Up Closure: Semiotics Across Scales." Paper for *Closure: Emergent Organisations and their Dynamics,* University of Ghent, Belgium, May 1999: http://academic.brooklyn.cuny.edu./education/jlemke/papers/gent.htm, accessed 12 April 2002

Merleau-Ponty, Maurice. 1995. *La Nature, Notes, Cours du Collège de France.* Edited by Dominique Séglard. Paris: Seuil, 1995. Translated by Robert Vallier as *Nature: Course Notes from the Collège de France* (Evanston: Northwestern University Press, 2003).

Peirce, Charles Sanders. 1931–1958. *Collected Papers of Charles Sanders Peirce.* Vols. 1–6 edited by Charles Hartshorne and Paul Weiss, 1931–1935; vols 7 and 8 edited by A. W. Burks, 1958. Cambridge, Mass.: Belknap Press. In accordance with convention, this work is referred to by the abbreviation, *CP* followed by numbers representing volume and paragraph respectively.

Ransdell, Joseph. 1992. "Teleology and Autonomy of the Semiotic Process," in Michel Balat and Jean Deladalle-Rhodes, eds. *Signs and Humanity/L'Homme et ses signes,* vol.1. Berlin: Mouton de Gruyter. Electronic version: http://www.door.net/arisbe/menu/library/aboutcsp/ransdell/autonomy.htm, accessed: 10 April 2002

Sebeok, Thomas. 1991. *A Sign Is Just a Sign.* Bloomington: Indiana University Press.

Sharov, A. A. 1997. "Towards the semiotic paradigm in biology." Electronic version dated 10 June 1997: http://www.ento.vt.edu/~sharov/biosem/txt/tosemiot.html, accessed 4 June 2002. This is a short version of the paper: Sharov, A. A. 1998. "From Cybernetics to Semiotics in Biology" *Semiotica* 120: 403–419.

PART TWO

Embodiment, Sociality, and
Ecological Values

8

Earth in Eclipse

David Abram

> There *is* another world, but it is *in* this one.
>
> —Paul Eluard

Merleau-Ponty's writings enact a steadily renewed resuscitation of wonder at the exuberant mystery of the real. He worked tirelessly to draw philosophy to a sense of astonishment at the wild-flowering weirdness of the world in which we find ourselves before abstract reflection weaves its spell on our senses. Further, he sought to awaken reflective reason to its own *genesis* in the world of untamed perception, and to ensure that philosophy and the sciences would begin to frequent that dimension of direct, nondiscursive experience—testing their conclusions against the irrefutable eloquence that things display when we meet them in the flesh, taking guidance from the specific ways such elemental encounters always resist, in some manner, the formulas we use to explain them. By such a practice, reflective reason would stay awake to its derivative nature as an outgrowth or expression of that elemental world, and so—rather than strive for mastery—would hold itself *in service to* the very world that it seeks to fathom and articulate.

It was Merleau-Ponty's view that unless philosophy and science remember themselves to our felt, sensorial participation with the rest of the real—and until the sciences begin to respect this experiential dimension not only as their source but as their ever-present touchstone—then the several sciences (and the myriad technologies to which they give rise) cannot help but lead humanity deeper into an oblivion that wreaks havoc on the very wellsprings of culture—indeed on the animate Earth itself.

In his later writings, the *invisible* became Merleau-Ponty's term for the ostensibly immaterial sphere of thought and ideality: his final, unfinished book displays afresh his conviction that this invisible realm remains entwined with the whole of the "visible," dependent—in a sense—upon the whole of the earthly sensuous. Regardless of how rarefied and refined our reflections might be, no human insight ever wholly succeeds in comprehending the world from outside; no idea, for Merleau-Ponty, ever breaks entirely free from the carnal influence of Earth's gravity.

While he focused his attentions on a particular form of invisibility—the invisible space of mind, or mental process—the half-century since Merleau-Ponty's death witnessed a remarkable multiplication of invisible dimensions, a proliferation of unseen worlds and virtual realities. Those same decades, moreover, saw a dramatic increase in the fragmentation and destruction of wild ecosystems, in the rate of species' extinctions, in the destabilization of climatic and other planetary cycles. It is perhaps worth pondering how Merleau-Ponty would respond to this situation, were he alive today. In the pages that follow, however, I engage a much simpler question: How might a writer deeply informed by Merleau-Ponty's investigations begin to address (in a manner accessible not only to philosophers and scientists, but to curious persons of any background) the fragmentation of human experience, and of nature, at the start of the twenty-first century.

DISSOLVING DISTANCE

As a fresh millennium dawns around us, a new and vital skill is waiting to be born in the human organism, a new talent called for by the curious situation in which much of humankind now finds itself. We may call it the skill of "navigating between worlds."

The last hundred years have been marked by an explosion of experiential domains, an abrupt expansion in the number of apparently autonomous realms with which people are forced to familiarize themselves. There has been an astonishing proliferation of separable realities, many of them mutually exclusive, that contemporary persons are increasingly compelled to engage in, or at least to acknowledge and acquaint themselves with. Each realm has its particular topology, its landmarks, its common denizens whom one comes to know better the more one participates in that domain. Many of these realms hold a powerful attraction for those who visit them and, complicating matters, many of these experiential dimensions seem to claim for themselves a sort of hegemony, surreptitiously asserting their priority over all other dimensions. Some of these spaces have been disclosed by the questing character of the human mind and imagination. Others have been made accessible to us through the probings of science, often in tandem with particular technological developments. Still others have been created by technologies operating more or less on their own. All of them now beckon to us.

Among the most efficacious of such worlds are those various experiential realms so recently opened by the electronic and digital media. Over a century ago, the invention of the telegraph and, soon after, the telephone, made evident that geographical distance—the very sense of near and far that determines our bodily sense of place—was no longer an absolute constraint. I, or at least my voice, could now make itself present somewhere else on the planet, as a friend across the continent could now make her thoughts heard over here, where I sit speaking to her. Our voice, and our ears, now found themselves wandering in a strange, auditory realm, often crackling with static, that reposed outside of our ordinary, sensuous reality—a new experiential dimension wherein earthly distance and depth seemed to exert very little influence.

Another instance of this distance-less dimension was rapidly embodied in the radio, which brought into our home news of daily events happening far beyond the horizon of our everyday landscape—even as those very events were still unfolding! And then the *television* began to capture our gaze, its flickering glow in the living room replacing the glowing flames around which the family had traditionally gathered each evening. Through its screen, those events happening elsewhere became *visible* as well as *audible* realities. Other lands, other countries and cultures suddenly became much more real to us, both in their strangeness and their familiarity. We could no longer ignore them; they increasingly became a part of our lives, just as real as the spiders spinning their webs in the grasses outside, or perhaps—it seemed—even more real. But the television brought other worlds as well: the storied worlds of serials and soap operas whose characters became as familiar to many people as their own families. Or perhaps even more familiar.

In the final decade of the twentieth century another, more expansive, pasture opened up before us: the apparently fathomless labyrinth of cyberspace—a realm far more versatile and participatory than that inaugurated by either the radio or the television. Through the Internet and the World Wide Web we seem to have dissolved terrestrial distance entirely, or rather, to have disclosed an alternative terrain wherein we can at last step free of our bodies and journey wherever we wish, as rapidly as we wish, to dialogue and consult with other bodiless minds about whatever we wish. Or to wander, alone, in a quiet zone of virtual amusements. Instantaneous access to anywhere, real or imagined, is now available for collective engagement or for solitary retreat. Cyberspace, of course, is hardly a single space, but rather an ever-ramifying manifold of possible worlds to be explored, an expanding multiplicity of virtual realities.

THE ALLURE OF TRANSCENDENCE

New as it seems, our fascination with the bodiless spaces made accessible to us by the digital revolution is only the latest example of our ever-expanding engagement with worlds hidden behind, beyond, or beneath the space in which we are corporeally immersed. One of the most ancient of such other worlds, and perhaps the first to exert a steady pull on our attention, was the dimension of pure mathematical truths, the rarefied realm of numbers (both simple and complex) and the apparently unchanging relations between those numbers. Like great seagoing explorers setting out toward continents suspected but as yet unknown, mathematicians have continually discovered, explored and charted various aspects of this alluring world, yet its lineaments, mysteriously, seem inexhaustible. The mathematical domain of number and proportion has long been assumed to be a separate, and purer, realm than this very changeable world in which we breathe and hunger and waste away—at least since the number-wizard Pythagoras promulgated his mystical teachings in the city of Crotona some two and a half millennia ago—and the vast majority of contemporary mathematicians still adhere to this other-worldly assumption.

Pythagoras's faith that the realm of numbers was a higher world, untainted by the uncertainty and flux of mortal, earthly life, profoundly affected the thinking of the great Athenian philosopher, Plato, teaching his own students at the end of the fifth century B.C.E., and through Plato's writings this faith has influenced the whole trajectory of European civilization. In Plato's teachings, it was not just numbers and mathematical relations that had their source beyond the sensuous world, but also the essential form of such notions as *truth, justice,* and *beauty;* the ideal form of each such notion enjoyed the purity of an eternal and transcendent existence outside of all bodily apprehension. Plato, that is, expanded Pythagoras' heaven of pure numbers and proportions to include, as well, the pure and eternal "ideas" that lend their influence and guidance to human life. Indeed, according to several of the dialogues written by Plato for the students of his academy, *every* sensible thing—every entity that we directly experience with our senses—is but a secondary likeness of some archetypal form, or ideal, that alone truly exists. True and genuine existence belongs only to such ideal forms; the sensuous, earthly world, with its ceaseless changes, its shifting cycles of generation and decay—of coming to be and of passing away—is but an ephemeral facsimile of that more eternal dimension of pure, bodiless forms that, alone, genuinely exist. That dimension cannot be perceived by the body or the bodily senses: the reasoning intellect, alone, is able to apprehend that realm. According to Plato, the reasoning soul, or mind, can never be fully at home in this bodily world; its true source, and home, is in that bodiless realm of pure ideas to which the rational mind secretly longs to return. Genuine reality, for Plato, is elsewhere.

As the intellectual culture of ancient Greece mingled with other cultures in the Mediterranean region, including the monotheistic culture of ancient Israel, and as Pythagoras's and Plato's theories came in contact with the new religious impulses stirring on the edges of Hebraic culture, Plato's eternal realm of pure forms—ostensibly the true home of the intellect—inspired and offered the model for a new notion of eternity: the Christian Heaven, or afterlife. And as this new belief was given shape by the early Christian fathers, this eternity beyond the stars became the dwelling place not so much of the questing intellect as of the faithful and pious soul.

Today, the Heaven of Christian belief, together with the various Heavens proper to other religious traditions, continues to exert a remarkable influence on much of contemporary civilization. Even avowed atheists find their lives and their thoughts impacted by the collective belief in a heavenly realm presumed to exist radically outside of, or beyond, the palpable physicality of our carnal existence. Variously conceived as "the afterlife" or as "the dwelling place of God and his minions," such realms are still assumed, by many, to be both the ultimate source of the sensuous world around us and the ultimate end and destiny of our apparent existence. Indeed, such transcendent realms still possess, for many of us, a clear primacy over the earthly world.

THE SUPERSMALL AND THE ULTRAVAST

The ancient fascination with numbers was not only formative for the emergence of Christian notions of Heaven; the mathematics it gave rise to also opened the way for the development of the secular sciences, and hence for the emergence of a host of abstract and increasingly other-worldly dimensions disclosed to us by those sciences. One such realm powerfully impacting our lives today is the supersmall dimension revealed by high-energy physics: the subatomic world of *protons* and *neutrons,* of *gluons* and *mesons,* and the mythical *quarks* of which they are composed, a world of *electrons* and *neutrinos* and perhaps, underneath all these, the vibrating one-dimensional loops, or *superstrings,* that give rise to all such particles and their manifold interactions. Although very few of us have any clear apprehension of the subatomic world, or of the inscrutable particles that comprise it, we are continually assured by the physics community that this arcane realm is the ultimate source, or fundament, of all that we *do* apprehend: according to most contemporary physicists, the visible, tangible world glimpsed by our unaided senses is not at all fundamental, but is entirely composed and structured by events unfolding at scales far beneath the threshold of our everyday awareness.

And yet physicists are not the only band of scientists inviting us to look askance at the world that we directly experience. According to a majority of researchers in the neurosciences, the perceptual world that enfolds us—the world of oak trees and grasshoppers and children racing through the spray of a fire hydrant on a sweltering summer afternoon—is largely an illusion. Here, too, at the scale of our direct sensory experience, we must learn to recognize a dimension that is much more primary than our apparent experience; the realm of neurons firing and of neurotrans-mitters washing across neuronal synapses, of neural networks that interact with other neural networks, a ceaselessly ramifying web of patterns within patterns that continually generates—out of the endless array of photons cascading through our retinas and the sound waves splashing against our eardrums and the gradients of chemical molecules wafting past our nasal ganglia—the more-or-less coherent appearance of the surrounding world that we are aware of at any moment. Although we have absolutely no intuitive apprehension of these events unfolding within the brain, our colleagues in the neurological sciences insist that such events provide the hidden infrastructure of all our perceptions. They insist that this realm of neural networks and synaptic interactions must be carefully studied and understood if we really wish to know what is going on—that is, if we wish to truly understand just *why* the surrounding world appears to us as it does.

Meanwhile, in another set of laboratories, another group of intrepid researchers—molecular biologists tinkering with processes unfolding deep within the nuclei of our cells—have precipitated a collective suspicion that the real and unifying truth of things, at least for organic entities like ourselves, is to be found in the complexly coded structure of our chromosomes. After the discovery of the double-helix structure of deoxyribonucleic acid, or DNA, molecular biology has become the dominant field within the life sciences, with a majority of its practitioners attempting to isolate the specific sequences of DNA that compose particular genes, and to discern the manner in which these genes are transcribed, by multiple chemical reactions, to generate the host of proteins that compose both the living tissues of any organism and the manifold enzymes that catalyze its metabolism. In giant, massively funded science initiatives like the Human Genome Project, researchers race to map the entirety of the human genome, while other researchers puzzle out the intricate epigenetic pathways whereby networks of genes interact to give rise to particular proclivities, dispositions, and behaviors. Numerous high-profit corporations devoted to the burgeoning technology of genetic manipulation and modification are busy isolating or synthesizing the genes that ostensibly "code" for desirable traits, eagerly transplanting them into various plants and domestic animals in order to increase, presumably for human benefit, the productive yield of these organisms. Anyone even glancingly aware of these activities begins to suspect that the microscopic world of gene sequences and genetic interactions somehow determines our lives and our experiences. The ultimate source of our personality—of our habits, our appetites, our yearnings, and our decisions—would seem to be thoroughly hidden from our ordinary awareness, tucked inside the nuclei of our cells.

We are often assured that such scientific worlds are entirely continuous with one another—that the subatomic world of protons and quarks is nested within the molecular world that makes up our DNA, that the DNA in turn codes, among other things, for the neurons and neuronal patterns that weave our experience. In truth, however, these worlds do not so easily cohere, for the arcane language that enfolds each of these dimensions is largely closed to the others. Many of those who speak the language of the brain sciences believe that their discipline holds the key to all that we experience, yet an analogous conviction may be found among many who speak the very different discourse of molecular biology and the genome, as do those other experts who traffic in the lingo of particle physics. It may be useful to assume that there are multiple keys to the hidden truth of the world, each key unlocking its own realm; yet the precise relation between these unseen realms—or the precise way to *understand* the relation between these realities—remains mysterious.

Our access to many of these hidden dimensions was, of course, made possible by the invention of the microscope and its rapid evolution—from the simple optical instruments initially used by Anton Van Leeuwenhoek in the late 1600s to reveal the bacterial world, on up to the scanning-tunneling microscope and the atomic force microscope, which today enable us to examine, visually, the exact structure of a DNA molecule. While Van Leeuwenhoek's microscopes revealed a dimension one hundred times smaller than the resolution of the human eye, today's powerful instruments bring us into visual contact with entities fully a *million* times smaller than our unaided eyes can perceive!

One of the more unnerving jolts to our experience of the world around us (and, consequently, to our experience of ourselves) occurred at the dawn of the modern era, when Nicolaus Copernicus offered a wealth of evidence for his theory—later verified by Galileo—that the fiery Sun, rather than the Earth, lay at the center of the visible universe. What a dizzying disclosure! The revelation that our Earth revolves around the Sun, rather than the other way around, ran entirely contrary to the evidence of the unaided senses, and it precipitated a profound schism between the sensing body and the reflective, thinking intellect. Suddenly, even the most obvious testimony of our senses, which daily reveals the dynamic movement of the sun arcing across the sky and the unmoving Earth beneath our feet, had been dramatically undermined. Henceforth a new, modern distrust of the senses, and of the apparent world revealed by the bodily senses, began to spread throughout Europe. It is clarifying to recognize that Descartes's audacious philosophical move, cleanly severing the thinking mind from the body—separating the world into two, independent orders: that of *res cogitans* (thinking stuff), or mind, and that of *res extensa* (extended stuff), or matter—was largely motivated by this new and very disturbing state of affairs. For in order to maintain the Copernican worldview, the thinking mind had to hold itself entirely aloof, and apart, from the sensing body. Whether or not Descartes's ploy was ultimately justifiable, his conceptual unshackling of the cogitating mind from the body's world freed the modern intellect to explore not only the super-small realms of cells, atoms, and quarks, but also the ultravast spaces of starclusters and galaxies.

And here as well, our access to the mind-shattering vastness of galactic space was made possible by technological instrumentation, in this case by the invention and development of the optical telescope. It was a simple telescope that enabled Galileo to closely observe the other planets and their moons, and so to verify the Copernican theory. Only later did astronomers, using more complex telescopes, recognize what Giordano Bruno had dared to envision in the sixteenth century (at the cost of his life)—that the myriad stars in the night sky are indeed *other suns*. And only in 1923 did Edwin Hubble demonstrate that those stars are clustered into galaxies, and that most of those galaxies lie far beyond our own local galaxy, the Milky Way. Today, an orbiting telescope that bears his name reveals not just hundreds, or thousands, but *billions* of galaxies. We have heard that these galaxies appear to be moving away from one another, and many of us have accepted, intellectually, the strange proposition that the universe is expanding. We have accepted, as well, the assumption of most astronomers and astrophysicists that our universe flared into existence in a primordial "Big Bang" (our most up to date version of the biblical *creatio ex nihilo*). We've come to believe, quite matter-of-factly, in such logic-twisting phenomena as "black holes," and in the rather confounding notion that, when looking up at a particular star in the night sky, we are in truth looking *backward in time* many thousands, or even millions, of years. Today, several of our most interesting and visionary astrophysicists and cosmologists suggest that this expanding universe of hundreds of billions of galaxies is in truth only one of an uncountable plenitude of actually existing universes . . .

AN OUTRAGEOUS PROLIFERATION OF WORLDS

Thus, vying for our attention, today, are a host of divergent and weirdly discontinuous worlds. There is the almost impossibly small world of gluons and mesons and quarks, but also the infinitely vast cosmological field strewn with uncountable galaxies and galactic clusters. We may be drawn to penetrate the electrochemical reality of neuronal interactions that moves behind our psychological life, or perhaps to ponder and participate in the complexly coded universe of genetic reality that lies at the root of all our proclivities and propensities, apparently determining so much of our behavior. Our desire may be stirred, today, not only by the religious heavens that many believe will supersede this world, or by the mathematical heaven of pure number and proportion toward which so many reasoning intellects still aspire, but also by the digital heaven of cyberspace, that steadily ramifying labyrinth wherein we may daily divest ourselves of our bodies and their cumbersome constraints in order to dialog with other disembodied persons who've logged on in other places, or perhaps to try on other, virtual bodies in order to explore other, wholly virtual, spaces.

This *proliferation of worlds*—this multiplication of realms both religious and secular, supersmall and ultravast, collective and solitary—is not likely to slow down in the coming decades. The accelerating pace of technological development seems to ensure that the proliferation of spaces will continue to snowball. What *is* unclear, however, is whether the human mind can maintain its coherence while engaged in such a plural and discontinuous array, or *disarray,* of cognitive worlds. And if so, how?

Today, many persons rely on a kind of Alice in Wonderland strategy, taking one kind of cookie to shrink themselves down, and another to make them grow larger—popping one kind of pill to deal with the mass of digital information they must navigate at their desk jobs, another to deal with their cranky children at home, and still another to withstand the daily onslaught of sadness and hype to which they subject themselves whenever they turn on the news.

> "The government of Nigeria today executed three members of the Ogoni tribe, including a world-famous poet, for protesting drilling by the Shell Oil Company on their ancestral lands . . ." "Mothers! Are your little ones getting the most out of their sleep? Researchers have shown that children under the age of ten have a harder time sleeping than they used to! Try 'SedaKind™', the patented sedative for children, now available in five flavors!" "Astro-physicists are scrambling to account for the evidence, published this week in *Science,* that the universe is several billion years younger than had been assumed . . ." "An earthquake in Kashmir has left many tens of thousands dead—but first, a message about your hair. . . !"

And so we tumble from one world to another, and from there to yet another, with no real translation between them: we slide straight from the horror of emaciated refugees running from the latest spate of ethnic cleansing to a bright and sparkly commercial for toothpaste. Turning off the television we may practice taichi for twenty minutes, tuning ourselves to the Tao, then go online to buy stocks in a genetech firm whose patented process for inducing cancer in lab mice promises huge short-term returns. The discontinuity—indeed, the sheer incommensurability—between many of the experiential worlds through which we careen on any given day, or which intersect the periphery of our awareness as we go about our business, entails a spreading fragmentation within our selves, like a crack steadily spreading through a china platter. We become increasingly multiple, without any clear way of translating between the divergent selves engendered by these different worlds; we seek to draw our coherence from whatever world we happen to be engaged by at any moment. Or else we become numb, ensuring that no encounter moves us more than any other encounter, that no phenomenon impinges upon us more than any other, maintaining our coherence at the cost of our sensitivity and vitality.

How, then, can we find a way to move, to navigate between worlds, without increasingly forfeiting our integrity, without consigning our minds and our lives ever more deeply to a kind of discombobulant confusion? Airplanes glide head-on into skyscrapers, to which the U.S. president responds by asking citizens to keep shopping; he declares war on an uninvolved country and authorizes the CIA to start spying on environmentalists. Adolescent students strain, during the week, to make sense of evolutionary biology while being taught, on the weekend, that God designed the animals all at once; one unsuspecting eighth-grader posts a smiling photo of himself to an online acquaintance, and within weeks he's receiving huge amounts of money (from countless people he's never met) in exchange for stripping naked in front of his webcam every evening. South of the equator, indigenous, tribal communities that have long flourished without any notion of private property are abruptly plunged into the thick of modernity by the arrival of a television in their midst, or by the distribution of gifts by corporations eager to mine their ancestral lands. Such stark instances, for which there exist no maps to help negotiate between discontinuous realities, mirror a disarray becoming more familiar to each of us.

When it does not immediately threaten our way of life, the proliferation of experiential worlds can also, of course, be deliciously exhilarating — a wild ride that regularly spurs us into an alert and improvisational responsiveness akin, perhaps, to that known by white-water kayakers, or by jazz musicians. Can it be, then, that we must accept and adapt ourselves to this ongoing state of dispossession and estrangement? Is it possible that such ceaseless realignment must now become our home—that it is time to welcome the steady slippage from one world into another, from one set of landmarks into another strangely different set, and from thence into yet another, exchanging horizons and atmospheres like we now change clothes—becoming aficionados of the discontinuous and the fragmentary?

It is a tempting dream, but an impossible one. For in the complete absence of any compass, without a basic intuition of how these divergent universes nevertheless connect to one another—without a dependable way of balancing between realms—the exhilaration of steadily sailing from one wave-tossed medium into another cannot help but exhaust itself, giving way, in the end, to desperation, or to a numbed-out detachment void of all feeling.

But how, then, *are* we to find some equilibrium as we skid from realm to realm? How to orient ourselves within this deepening proliferation of cognitive worlds? Perhaps by paying attention to the patterns that play across these different realms, seeking subtle correlations, sniffing the air for strangely familiar scents, striving to discern—hidden within this exploding matrix—the faint traces of a forgotten coherence. Perhaps by listening more closely we might glean certain clues to the way these diverse worlds conjoin: for indeed certain rhythms do seem to echo between various of these worlds, particular textures and tastes tug at the fringes of our awareness, reminding us of something . . .

Only by such a process of attention can we begin to discern the curious commonalities that are shared among various of these discontinuous dimensions. Only through such careful noticing are we brought to suspect that there may be a particular realm wherein all these common patterns cohere—that among this profusion of worlds there is a unique world that has left its trace on all the others. A singular domain, indeed, that is the secret source, and ground, of all these other kingdoms; a remarkable realm that resides at the heart of all these others.

Yet how could this be? These experiential terrains seem far too incongruous, too incompossible, for them to be rooted in a common source. And how weirdly multiple and complex that source-world would have to be! If all these alien styles sprout out of the same land, how outrageously fecund and enigmatic would be that place!

Still, what a boon it would be to discover a specific scape that lies at the heart of all these others. For if there *is* such a secret world among all these—if there *is* a particular experiential realm that provides the soil and support for all these others—then that primordial zone would somehow contain, within its fertile topology, a kind gateway onto each of these other landscapes. And by making our home in that curious zone, we would have ready access to all those other realms—and could venture into them at will, exploring their lineaments and becoming acquainted with their denizens without, however, forfeiting all sense of orientation. We'd know that any world we explore remains rooted in that mysterious terrain where we daily reside, and so we could wander off into any of these other spaces without thereby losing our bearings; it would suffice simply to step back over a single threshold to find again our common ground.

But surely it would be common knowledge, by now, if there were (among all these diverse domains) a unique world that somehow opened directly onto all these others! Surely it would be a truth taught to us all by our parents and professors as we gradually grew up into this dizzying situation! So we would expect . . . *unless:* unless the one realm that secretly holds the seeds of all these others has, traditionally, been the *most* disparaged and despised world of all—unless it is a place our elders prefer to ignore, the one dimension our scientific institutions all habitually overlook and forget. If, that is, this particular domain has conventionally been construed as the most derivative and drab dimension of all—the only realm consistently vilified by our traditions—then perhaps our inability to notice this world and take it seriously (and our reluctance to acknowledge its unruly magic), can be more readily understood.

THE BLOOD AND THE SAP

The taken-for-granted world of which I speak is, of course, none other than the world we directly experience with our unaided senses—the realm of scents, tastes, and textures in which we are sensorially immersed. Long derided by our religious traditions as a fallen and sinful dimension, continually marginalized by scientific discourse as a secondary, derivative, and hence ultimately inconsequential zone—how shall we characterize the the sensuous world? It is the inexhaustible field of our unmediated experience, the very realm in which you now sit or recline, feeling the weight of your limbs as they settle within the chair, or the rough texture of the ground as it presses up against your flesh. It is the domain of smells wafting in from the kitchen, this field of rippling and raucous sounds, of shifting shapes and of colors: the smudged white surface of the ceiling overhead, or the rumpled gray of the gathering clouds outside the window, their shadows sliding slowly across the road and the bending grasses.

This, in other words, is the *body's* world—that elemental terrain of contact wherein your tongue searches out a stray piece of lettuce stuck between your teeth, a fleshly zone animated by the thrumming ache within your skull and the claustrophobic feel of the shoes around your feet. Yet the sensuous field is animated by so much more than your own body; it is steadily fed by the body of the apple tree and of the old oak with its roots stretching deep into the soil, and the swollen bodies of the clouds overhead, and the warm, asphalt skin of the street, and the humming bulk of the refrigerator in the next room. This living, carnal field seems to breathe with your own moods, yet it's influenced, as well, by the rhythm of the rain now starting to pound on the roof, and by the dark scent of newly drenched leaves and grass and soil that drifts through the house when you swing open the front door. Shall we step out under those pelting drops to rescue the morning newspaper? Or perhaps that's too timid for a hot day—haven't we done enough reading? Why not toss this book into the corner, pry off our shoes and charge out under the trees to stomp and splash in the gathering puddles?

Why not, indeed? Let's do it! Since this —*this!*—is the very world we most need to remember!—this undulating Earth that we inhabit with our animal bodies. This place of thirst and of cool water, this realm where we nurse our most palpable wounds, where we wince at our mistakes, and wipe our tears, and sleepily make love in the old orchard while bird-pecked apples loll on the grass all around us—this world pulsing with our blood and the sap of pinon pines and junipers, awake with the staring eyes of owls and sleepy with the sighs of alley cats, this is the realm in which *we most deeply live.*

Sadly, it is also the world we have most thoroughly forsaken.

Of course, we have not *entirely* lost touch with this place, where the moon slides in and out of the clouds, and the trees send down their thirsty roots, our nostrils flaring at the moistness of the night breeze. Our flesh calls us back to this earthly place whenever we are injured or sick, when-ever we need to wash the dishes by hand, or clean out the overflowing roof-gutters, or simply to empty our bladders and bowels on the toilet. Whenever we stumble and hurt ourselves (scraping our knee or tearing the skin on our arm); when one of our tools breaks or one of our technologies breaks down, we must turn our attentions, if only for a moment, to the bothersome constraints of this gravity-laden Earth that grips our bodies. Yet we'll linger only as long as we must; we know well that this messy world, with its stains and pockmarks and pimples, is not our destined kingdom. As soon we've bandaged our knee, or repaired the dishwasher, or wiped our bottom, we turn our attentions back toward those other, more compelling worlds. We turn back toward the computer screen, or toward the next page of our latest book on how to survive in the digital economy, or toward the churning sounds of a favorite audio disk pulsing out of our high-fidelity speakers; we dial our colleagues on the cell phone to ask if they can join us at next week's conference on the most recent gene-splicing techniques; or perhaps we plunge our attention back into our meditations on the transcendental unity hidden behind the experienced world. It never occurs to us that the most profound unity may reside in the very depths of the experienced world itself, in the unfolding web of interdependent relations that ceaselessly draws the apparently disparate presences of the sensuous cosmos, ourselves included, into subtle communion with one another.

The enveloping Earth—this richly variant world alive with the swaying limbs of trees and the raucous honking of geese—is, of course, the very context in which the human body and nervous system took their current form. Our senses, that is, have coevolved with the diverse textures, shapes, and sounds of the earthly sensuous: our eyes have evolved in subtle interaction with other eyes, and our ears are attuned by their very structure to the howling of wolves and the thrumming of crickets. Whether floating, for aeons, as the single-celled entities that were our earliest biotic ancestors, or swimming in huge schools through the depths of the oceans, whether crawling on the land as amphibians, or racing beneath the grasses as small mammals, or swinging from branch to branch as primates, our bodies have continually formed themselves in delicate reciprocity with the manifold forms of the animate Earth. Our nervous systems are thoroughly informed by the particular gravity of this sphere, by the way the sun's light filters down through the sky, and by the cyclical tug of Earth's moon. In a very palpable sense we are fashioned of this Earth, our attentive bodies coevolved in rich and intimate rapport with the other bodies—animals, plants, mountains, rivers—that compose the shifting flesh of this breathing world.

Hence it is the animate, more-than-human terrain—this earthly cosmos that carnally enfolds us—that has lent us our particular proclivities and gifts, our specific styles of behavior. The structure of our senses, our modes of perception, our unique habits of thought and contemplation, have all been profoundly informed by the mysterious character of the earthly world in which we still find ourselves. The sensuous terrain—the material Earth as it meets our senses—thus provides the inescapable template for our experience of every other world we devise or discover. Whether we are plugging into cyberspace or simply synapsing ourselves to the page of a new novel, whether we are mathematically exploring the submicroscopic realm of vibrating, ten-dimensional strings or pondering the ultravast tissue of galaxies revealed by a new generation of radio-telescopes, we cannot help but interpret whatever we glimpse of these worlds according to predilections derived from *the one world in which we uninterruptedly live*—this bodily place, this palpable Earth where we still breathe and burp and make love. Our intuitions regarding the lineaments of Heaven are inevitably shaped by those sensuous experiences that seem to correspond with such a place of equanimity and ease (luminous clouds drifting in the celestial blue, or a ray of sunlight that suddenly pours through a rent in those clouds and spills itself across a green hillside) and hence our religious heavens inevitably borrow their imagined structure from the evocative structures of this earthly cosmos. The way we envision the workings of DNA and the complex interactions between genes is similarly influenced by our encounter with the way things unfold at the scale of our most direct, unmediated experience of the sensuous Earth around us. How could it be otherwise? It is our age-old encounter with the world at *this* scale that has provided the very organs by which we see and peer through all our microscopes and telescopes, that has fashioned the complex hands and keen eyes that now design our computer models!

Our comprehension of neuronal structures within the brain, and our surmises regarding the way those structures interact, is profoundly limited by the fact that those neurons did not evolve in isolation from the senses in their ongoing intercourse with the world. The human brain, that is, did not evolve in order to analyze itself—rather it evolved its particular structures as a consequence of our bodily engagement with the sensuous surroundings, and hence has a natural proclivity to help us orient and relate to those ambiguous and ever-shifting surroundings. Whenever we attempt to focus the brain back upon itself, or on any other dimensions—whether subatomic or galactic—it cannot help but bring those predispositions to bear, anticipating gravity, ground, and sky where they are not necessarily to be found, interpreting data according to the elemental constraints common to our two-legged species, yielding an image of things profoundly informed by our animal body and its accustomed habitat.

There is much to be gleaned from our investigations into other scales and dimensions, yet we consistently err by assuming our studies provide an objective assessment of the way these realms *really are* in themselves. In order to convince ourselves of the rigor and rightness of our investigations, we consistently ignore, or overlook, the embodied nature of all our thoughts and our theories; we negate or repress our carnal presence and proceed as though—in both our scientific and our spiritual endeavors— we were pure, disembodied minds, unconstrained by our animal form, or by our carnal and perceptual entwinement with the animate Earth.

Thus do our sciences, like our religions, perpetuate the age-old disparagement of sensorial reality. The experienced Earth lends something of its atmosphere to every world that we can conceive, and hence haunts these other worlds like a phantom. Each of the diverse and multiply divergent worlds that cacaphonously claim our attention in this era—whether scientific or sacred, virtual or psychodelic, submicroscopic or supercosmological—is haunted by the animate Earth. Each is haunted, in some fashion, by the distant draw of all our thoughts toward that vast and enigmatic horizon that first drew those thoughts forth. Of course many of our professors, priests, and scientists prefer not to confront such vague presences that threaten, out on the very edge of our awareness, to disrupt all our certainties. Still, even the most confident scientists must sometimes find themselves wondering, late at night, how we can have gleaned such marvelous insights into the hidden structure of the universe when the most evident and apparent world that materially surrounds us seems to be choking and retching, its equilibrium disrupted and its diverse plants and animals tumbling into oblivion as a result of our human obliviousness. Can we really trust our apparently brilliant discoveries regarding the unseen causes that move the cosmos when our own local cosmos seems to be falling apart all around us, apparently as a result of our collective inattention? Is it possible that we have forgotten something, that some crucial element of our intelligence has been overlooked or misplaced? Indeed, is it not likely that everything we think we know about other worlds (supersmall and supervast, technological and philosophical) has been distorted by our refusal to recognize our thorough embedment in *this* world—by our refusal to acknowledge and account for the utter entanglement not only of our bodies but of our *minds* (our rarefied intellects) within this mysterious lattice of intertwined lives and living elements that we call Earth?

ETHICS AND OTHERNESS

Of course, the fragmentation and loss of coherence experienced in our individual lives echoes a profound discombobulation within the larger community. In the absence of a common or broadly shared world, ethical instincts—including a basic respect for others, and the mutual restraint and conviviality that hold a community together—steadily lose their grip, and indeed morality gradually comes to seem a largely arbitrary matter. When each of us expends so much energy and time engaged in worlds not shared by our neighbors (or even by the other members of our family), when we continually direct our attentions to dimensions hidden above, behind, or beneath the shared world to which our senses give us access, it should come as little surprise that the *common* sense is impoverished, along with any clear instinct for the common good.

And yet an ethical compass—a feeling for what is right (or at least decent), and perhaps more important, for what is *not* right—is especially crucial in such an era as this, when our technological engagement in other dimensions gives individuals a far greater power to manipulate experience, to violate others' lives and privacy, to inflict large-scale terror, and even to eradicate whole aspects of the real. Yet how is a genuinely ethical sensibility instilled and encouraged? How is an ethical sense (or, more simply, a good heart) born? Real ethics is not primarily a set of abstract principles; it is not, first, a set of "rules" (or "commandments) that can be memorized and then applied in appropriate situations. Ethics, first and foremost, is a feeling in the bones, a sense that there's something amiss when one sees a neighbor kicking his dog, that there's something wrong about hastening to one's work past a stranger who has tripped and fallen, her grocery bags torn, with their pears, cabbage heads, and a busted bottle of olive oil strewn along the sidewalk. Yet from whence comes the impulse to stop and help? The impulse to intervene with the teenagers stomping on a line of ants, or simply to refrain from taking advantage of another's bad luck—where do these impulses come from?

It seems unlikely that the ethical impulse can be learned, simply, from the pages of a book (not even from a book as deeply instructive as the Torah or the Koran). Still less can it be learned from the screen of a computer. For while these media readily engage the cognizing mind in various of its aspects, they cannot engage the whole of the cognizing body (this animate, intelligent creature with its muscled limbs and organs and skin) in the way that any face-to-face encounter, in the flesh, engages the whole body. It is in the flesh and blood world of our bodily actions and engagements that ethics has its real bearing. It is here, in this irreducibly ambiguous and uncertain world in which we live with the *whole* of our beings— with our hands and our feet and our faces, with our bellies as well as our brains—that we are most vulnerable, most affected by the kindness of others, or by their neglect and disrespect. It is here, in this mortal world, that we are most susceptible to violence.

Of course we can strive to be basically responsible when engaged in those other, less palpable realms—for instance, when we are cruising the Internet, or responding to a mountain of e-mail, we can certainly try to respect electronic perspectives that are different from our own, or to refrain from violating the integrity and the privacy of other participants. Similarly, we can attempt to be ethical in our experimental researches with gene sequences, or in our laboratory experiments with nanotechnology, or in our electronic explorations of other planets. Yet unless we are already striving to act appropriately in our day-to-day, face-to-face interactions with the things and entities immediately around us, at the very scale at which we live—unless we are grappling with the difficult ambiguity of interacting with other persons and other beings without doing violence to those others—then we have no reason to trust that our more abstract, virtual engagements are genuinely ethical or good-hearted at all. For it is only in this corporeal, earthly world that we are fully vulnerable to the consequences of our decisions and acts.

In those less corporeal dimensions (whether religious, scientific, or technological) we may readily find ourselves interacting with certain ideal presences that have been richly envisioned by our religious traditions, or with various provisional entities hypothesized by our fellow scientists, or with virtual beings invented and programmed for our entertainment. In such abstract, transcendent, and virtual worlds, in other words, we commonly encounter phenomena that may or may not be our own creation—we find ourselves interacting, there, with the manifold artifacts and projections of our own, richly imaginative species. But in the more immediate, palpable world to which our bodily senses give us access, we encounter not only human creations but other *creative* entities—other persons as unfathomable as ourselves, and other earthborn entities whose sensations and experiences are even *more* unfathomable and mysterious. It is only here, in the earthly world of our bodily engagements, that we continually come into contact with beings (persons, deer, spiders, hawks) whom we can be sure are not primarily our own fabrications, but are really *other*—other selves, other centers of experience richly different from our own.

Even when we encounter another human person over the Internet (or via the telephone, or any other technological medium), it is but a filtered and flattened trace of that other person, mediated by electronic circuitry and satellite technology, a virtual presence with which we interact only by (unconsciously) filling out this phantom with our own inadvertent projections and assumptions regarding how our interlocutor really appears at this moment, what sort of things she is doing while tapping out these messages to us on her keyboard or while talking to us on the phone, what is or is not going on around her, what sort of mood she is in, and so on. Whenever we interact with other persons through electronic and digital media it is necessarily a somewhat abstract interaction, and it is difficult to discern whether we are not interacting more with our own projections than with the reality of this other being. However, when I encounter another person *in the flesh*—both of us immersed in the same context, or *place,* breathing the same air and enveloped by the same textures and colors and sounds— then I cannot so easily shield myself from the evident otherness of this other person. Assumptions and even projections still inevitably come into play, yet here our projections are far more constrained by the visible, audible, and tactile presence of this other breathing body (by a range of subtle facial expressions, gesticulations, and silent gestures that cannot readily be conveyed via any technological medium—indeed by the countless subtle cues by which breathing bodies in proximity communicate feelings and moods to one another beyond the horizon of our conscious awareness).

It is thus in the sensuous world that we most readily find ourselves confronted by what is genuinely, *and indubitably,* other than ourselves. It is only in this sensorial terrain that we continually find ourselves in relation to other active agencies that are clearly not of our own making, to a world whose elemental lineaments we can be sure we did not devise. It is only here that we know we are in contact with what really *exceeds* us. And hence it is here, in this earthly world, that ethical questions have their primary bearing. It is here, first and foremost, that ethical action *really matters.*

And thus it is here, in the sensorial world, that an ethical sensibility is first engendered in any person. The seeds of compassion are sown in the palpable field of our childhood encounters with other sensitive and sentient bodies, in that richly ambiguous land where we gradually learn—

through our pleasures and painful wounds, and through the rage and the tears of others—to give space to those other bodies, gradually coming to recognize in their sounds and gestures and expressions a range of sensations strangely akin to our own, and so slowly coming to feel a kind of spontaneous, somatic empathy with other beings and with our commonly inhabited world. It is this early, felt layer of solidarity with other bodies and with the bodily Earth that provides both the seeds and the soil necessary for any more mature sense of ethics; it is this nonverbal, corporeal ability *to feel something of what others feel* that, given the right circumstances, can later grow and blossom into a compassionate life.

The child's spontaneous somatic solidarity with others is inevitably a tentative and tenuous phenomenon, a layer of experience that emerges only when a child is free to engage, with the whole of her or his muscled and sensitive organism, in the animate world that immediately surrounds her. This quietly empathic layer of experience can arise, that is, only when the child is free to explore, at her own pace, this terrain of scents, shapes and textures inhabited by other sensuous and sentient forms (by trees and insects and rain and houses), and so to discover, gradually, how to resonate with the other palpable presences that surround. It can arise only when the child is not deflected from such spontaneous, sensory explorations by being forced to engage, all too quickly, in the far more abstract and disembodied dimensions that beckon through the screen of a television or a computer.

How much violence has been done, in the latter half of the twentieth century, by planting our children in front of the television! How many imaginations have been immobilized, how much sensorial curiosity and intercorporeal affinity has been stunted by our easy substitution of the television screen, with its eye-catching enticements, for the palpable presence of another person ready to accompany us on adventurous explorations of our mysterious locale? The screen of the computer, too, requires us to immobilize our gaze, and to place our other senses, along with our muscles, out of play. It isolates and engages only a narrow slice of a child's sensorium, inviting her to set aside the full-bodied world that she shares with the fiery sun and the swooping birds. We should be properly cautious, then, regarding all the new education initiatives aimed at "placing computers in every classroom." We should be profoundly skeptical about every exhortation by so-called experts to bring our children "on-line" as rapidly as possible in order to ensure their readiness and eventual competitiveness in the new "information economy." There is of course nothing wrong with the computer, nor with the astonishing realms now so rapidly being opened for us by the wondrous capability of our computers—*as long as we bring to these new realms both the curiosity and the restraint, the creativity and ethical savvy that grow out of our full-bodied encounters with others in the thick of the earthly sensuous.* But if we plug our kids into the computer as soon as they are able to walk, we short-circuit the very process by which they could acquire such creativity and such restraint.

BREAKING OUT OF MATERIALITY

The final years of the twentieth century bore witness to the spread of a new and heartbreaking form of violence among young people in the United States. In every part of the country, increasing numbers of teens were bringing firearms with them to school, and in the course of three years, from October 1997 to April 1999, seven different kids around the continent had opened fire on their schoolmates, killing twenty-nine people and wounding almost twice as many. Numerous other children, in other communities, were arrested or detained on the suspicion of intending to wreak similar havoc. The most collectively traumatic of these events—every one of which seemed to mirror, for the culture as a whole, a vast societal abyss previously unsuspected by most citizens—was the massacre at Littleton High School in Colorado on 20 April 1999, when two seniors, Eric Harris and Dylan Klebold, walked through the halls gunning down thirty-five students and a teacher apparently at random (thirteen of them fatally) before turning their guns on themselves. As the culture, along with the survivors, staggered through the cycle of shock, numbness, and outrage, the media straightaway began to focus the collective dismay on the two adolescent killers themselves: *Time* magazine placed the genial faces of Klebold and Harris on the cover of that week's issue, accompanied by the stark headline, in large block letters, "THE MONSTERS NEXT DOOR." Numerous other journals, as well, depicted the two as "monsters"; in later weeks *Time* went on to describe the boys as "bad seeds" and "Natural Born Killers." This easy demonization of Harris and Klebold gave many in the populace a precise target for their outrage; it also helped ensure that few of us would recognize and come to terms with our own complicity in such careless violence. For it is likely that Klebold and Harris were not at all deranged monsters, but rather impressionable kids who played out, and so made visible for all of us, a growing shadow that belongs to the culture a whole.

Predictably, many of those whose children were killed or wounded in the Littleton shooting have chosen to blame the parents of Harris and Klebold, and are pressing huge legal suits against these couples already struggling under a grief and shame unimaginable to most persons, having lost their own children in such an outrageous manner. (By all accounts of those who know them, including the repeated assertions of young Harris and Klebold on videotapes that they recorded just before their bloody rampage, their parents were good and caring folks—if a bit lax in monitoring their children's pastimes.) A few of the bereaved have channeled their anger in a more constructive manner, and are working hard to convince lawmakers to enact stronger and more comprehensive legal restrictions on the purchase of guns. Other persons have reacted to the spread of school killings by decrying the ubiquitous violence in the entertainment industry and, in particular, the vicarious mayhem and murderousness of several very popular video-games. Yet while such folks angrily critique the *content* of the interactive entertainments and diversions now so readily accessible over the Internet, few—if any—have noticed that the very *form* of the new digital universe, when continually engaged by children not yet fully awake to the wild complexity of the sensuous world, inevitably encourages a rather reckless disregard for this comparatively drab, difficult, and very mortal world in which they haplessly find themselves stuck whenever they're forced to go offline.

Young Klebold and Harris—like the other teenagers (ranging from eleven to seventeen years of age) who shot up their own schools in Mississippi, Kentucky, Oregon, and Arkansas—were members of the very first generation of youth that had been brought up online; the first generation that had essentially grown up in steady and prolonged involvement with the computer. Most had been eagerly encouraged, by both parents and teachers, to actively engage in the rapidly emerging technology—not merely to access information but to plunge in and participate in the ongoing evolution of electronic worlds. Interacting with other screen personas without having to endure the strangeness and vulnerability of a face-to-face encounter, activating their curiosities and exercising their instincts for exploration and adventure without risk of physical pain or suffering, many children enjoy a far more exciting and compelling life online than they do in the palpable, bodily world with its boring rules and its tiresome rule-keepers. All around them, these kids notice adults and elders visibly trashing the directly experienced world—fouling the air with the visible exhaust from their cars on the freeway, clear-cutting hillsides, and paving over wild lots and wetlands. They hear at school that growing numbers of species are tumbling over the brink of extinction due to the destruction of habitat by adult institutions and corporations supported by their country's government, and that still other species are being genetically "engineered" by highly respected scientists to better suit the needs of human beings. Kids and teenagers cannot help but notice, in other words, that the society of adults pays scant heed to the diverse otherness and integrity of earthly reality. Neither can they avoid noticing the innumerable gestures of obeisance made by those same adults toward a host of ostensibly more valuable realities clearly transcendent to the sensorial world—whether toward a religious heaven or afterlife hidden beyond the visible, or toward a subatomic reality hidden beneath the appearances, or toward that purely *numerical* heaven (composed of either abstract equations or huge sums of money) that seems to determine so much of what happens in the apparent world. American children, in other words, cannot help but imbibe the deep disdain of their parents' culture for the body's world—a disdain and a dismissal implicit in the collective assumptions, the discourse, and the actions of all who are "well adjusted" to the society.

Such a culture offers little, or nothing, to counterbalance the fascination that many children now have for the open-ended, interactive expanse of cyberspace. Is it any wonder that, having grown up spending far more time interacting with the digital screen than with palpable people, many teenagers begin to suspect that cyberspace is the truer and finer realm, and that fleshly, carnal reality is but a paltry substitute or delusion? Is not this suspicion a logical extension of their civilization's age-old disparagement of the earthly sensuous? (After all, Plato himself—launching the entire enterprise of Western philosophy—taught that the ambiguous, shifting world to which our senses give us access was at best a facsimile of that eternal, bodiless realm hidden beyond the stars, and that one's soul, or self, is trapped in this earthly body as in a prison). And if some kids conclude that their suspicion is correct, and that the bodily world of siblings and school is a bothersome illusion, are they not simply following the implicit lesson of a civilization that ceaselessly paves over the living land on behalf of technological progress and the technological dream of immortality?

It is possible, of course, that the two killers in Littleton were really "bad seeds"—two malignant and vicious "natural born killers" thirsty to inflict as much pain and death on as many of their cohorts as they could manage. Yet this seems unlikely, especially given the reports of those who knew them. What is far more likely is that these two boys lacked any clear sense of the real substantiality, the depth, the real weight and gravity and palpable *actuality* of this commonly shared material world, relative to the virtual universe of websites and videogames and richly designed virtual worlds in which they spent so much of their time. It is entirely possible that they were no more trying to really destroy people than they were trying to *liberate* people from the delusion that this rather painful material world—of schoolwork and taunts and family stresses and chores—has any meaningful reality or weight whatsoever.

The closest friend of Dylan Klebold and Eric Harris was Brooks Brown—a classmate who had been Klebold's best friend through much of their childhood, and had recently been hanging out with Harris as well. Brown acknowledges that Klebold and Harris had mischievous tendencies, that they were drawn—like many teens—toward darkly shadowed aspects of experience, and that they carried some real resentment toward the football jocks who often taunted them at school. Yet according to Brooks Brown, "What they did wasn't about anger or hate. It was about them living in the moment, like they were inside a video game." [1] A reporter interviewing Brooks Brown seems taken aback by Brown's honest inability to construe his friends as bloodthirsty murderers, and by his contrary sense that during their rampage "the flesh and blood of the maimed and dying was no more real to them than pixels on a video monitor," and hence that there was no great need to take their suffering seriously.[2] Yet Brooks Brown's perspective is an astute one, and it is probably far more insightful, and far more attuned to his friends' experience, than the myriad analyses of all the adult experts trying to parse the event and its causes.

Curiously, in the same month that the Littleton massacre unfolded, a remarkable new film, entitled *The Matrix,* began showing at the suburban cinemas across the United States. A richly conceived and audaciously filmed science-fiction thriller, *The Matrix* followed the story of its central character, the computer hacker Neo (played by Keanu Reeves) as he gradually awakens to the fact that the everyday world of sights and sounds and smells that he, and everyone else, inhabits is a complex fabrication, a carefully constructed illusion calculated to lull the minds of its human inhabitants and so to keep them from suspecting the horrific reality of their situation: that humankind has been overcome and enslaved by a vast machine that is steadily drawing their vital fluids to power its various schemes. The "matrix" is the name given to this fabricated reality that holds everyone—except for Neo and a motley crew of renegade comrades—in its thrall.

"Matrix," of course, is the Latin word for "womb"; it derives from the Latin word "mater" (meaning "mother"), and is cognate with the words "matter" and "material." The premise of the film is that the material world around us—the sensorial matrix in which we find ourselves immersed—is itself no more than a collective delusion, an entirely virtual reality that holds us enslaved, and from which we must liberate ourselves by arduous mental discipline—and by computer-hacking our way behind the visible world into the hidden machinery that holds that world in place. For all its contemporary technological trappings, *The Matrix,* in this sense, is a profoundly Platonic film, and its runaway success among youth suggests the remarkable extent to which the Platonic faith—the belief in a truer reality hidden behind the sensuous world—has persisted as a structuring leitmotif for Western civilization down to the present moment, and indeed has attained a kind of apotheosis in the age of cyberspace.

The action sequence at the film's climax takes place in a corporate building that houses the headquarters of the robot villains who are foisting the illusionary world on the oblivious human race. Neo and his partner, Trinity, walk into this institutional building dashingly dressed in black trench coats. The trench coats conceal a small arsenal of guns and explosives, which Neo and Trinity soon deploy in a artfully choreographed display of vengeful firepower, obliterating the various guards and demolishing the marble walls and pillars of the lobby. When watching the film it is difficult to avoid the resemblance between this pair of trench-coated heroes and young Harris and Klebold striding into their own institutional building, similarly bedecked with guns and explosives hidden under their own dark trench-coats, intent on their own Armageddon. Like the two figures in *The Matrix,* Harris and Klebold striding into their high school are ready and eager to loose their rage on an accepted everyday world that they find intensely oppressive and pathetically overrated, and as they launch their carnage they seem to feel justified in violently exposing this stultifying reality as a sham.

The convergence and similarity between these two events (one fictional, one actual) which became visible in the culture at precisely the same moment, each of them carefully planned and prepared long in advance, should make us all pause, and should stir second thoughts in those who would classify Harris and Klebold as aberrant monsters. Clearly these two were enacting impulses that were brewing more broadly under the surface of the collective culture. Similarly *The Matrix*—with its multiple guns concealed under gothic trench-coats, its fascination with computer-mediated virtual realities, its suspicion that the visible, tangible world is something of a hoax, and its righteous rage against the boring constraints of this all-too-complacently accepted world—crystallized the zeitgeist of the first generation of teenagers to have grown up online.

Klebold and Harris gave themselves to that zeitgeist with a vengeance. Did either of them ever doubt that they would have the guts to follow through with their scheme? Probably. Dylan Klebold had even made a date for the evening *after* the massacre at which he and Harris killed themselves.[3] On April 21st, he and two friends were going out to see a new film called *The Matrix*.

DRINKING THE RAIN

We can have little hope of rejuvenating a collective sense of the ethical without beginning to acknowledge and honor the forgotten primacy of the one world that we all have in common. Strangely, the only world we all have in common is the very world that we share with the other animals and the plants—this earthly dimension of wind and water and sky, shivering with seeds and warmed by the sun. Hence, it seems unlikely that we will locate a lasting ethic without rediscovering our solidarity with all those other shapes of sentience, without remembering ourselves to the swallows and the meandering rivers.

We are understandably fascinated by the rich promise of our technologies, and deliciously dazzled by the new experiential realms opened to us by the genius of the electronic and digital revolution. Yet our enthrallment with our own creations is steadily fragmenting our communities and our selves; our uncritical participation with technology risks eclipsing the one realm that *alone* can provide the guidance for all our technological engagements. Indeed, only one realm is sufficiently outrageous and inexhaustibly complex enough to teach us the use and misuse of our own creations.

Only by remembering ourselves to the sensuous Earth, only by recalling ourselves to this bodily land that we share with the other animals and the plants, and rediscovering this place afresh, do we have a chance of integrating the multiple and divergent worlds that currently vie for our attentions. Only by rooting ourselves here, recovering our ageless solidarity with this breathing world—feeling the fur on our flesh, drinking the rain, and listening close to the wind as it whirls through the city streets—only thus do we have chance of learning to balance and to nav-

igate among the multiple worlds that now claim our attention at the outset of a new millennium.

To paraphrase the words of Paul Eluard at the start of this essay: there
are many, many other worlds, yes, but they are all hidden within this one.
And so to neglect this humble, imperfect, and infinitely mysterious world
is to recklessly endanger all the others.

NOTES

1. Quoted in "Portrait of a Deadly Bond," in the May 10, 1999 issue of *Time* magazine,
p. 32.

2. Ibid. These are not Brown's words, but those of a reporter describing Brown's viewpoint.

3. Pam Belluck and Jodi Wilgoren, "Shattered Lives: Columbine Killers' Pasts Hid Few
Predictors of Tragedy," the *New York Times,* 6 July 1999.

9

Lived Body and Ecological Value Cognition

John R. White

INTRODUCTION

Constructing an environmental ethic assumes that there is some medium by which we cognize ecological values. But in spite of the importance of this assumption for environmental ethics, investigating the nature of ecological value cognition is something rarely undertaken. Nor is this surprising. Analyzing the nature of value cognition in general poses difficulties enough; but understanding what could characterize the cognition of ecological values, especially given the fact that many persons apparently sensitive to other morally relevant values can seem quite insensitive to the moral significance of the environment, creates what might appear an insurmountable task.

Nonetheless, in this essay, I would like to begin to tackle just this set of issues. It is my conviction that ecological values are not cognized first and foremost in "object" cognition but are given originally in terms of lived body experience. Human beings are "rational animals" and it is precisely *in* the experience of our animality, that is, of our vital and bodily being, that we attain our first access to understanding ecological values. In accord with this assumption, I aim in this paper to clarify how ecological values are given through lived body experience and to draw some significant consequences of this fact for understanding the nature of our value knowledge.

I proceed in the following manner. First I discuss a proposed link between lived body consciousness and the experience of vital values, taking as my cue certain hints from Merleau-Ponty's *Phenomenology of Perception*. I then turn to several ideas of Max Scheler on lived body and vital value, ideas which I believe round out the suggestions I take from Merleau-Ponty. I infer from these discussions that socially conditioned variations in lived body consciousness can affect the manner in which we perceive vital values, including ecological values. Finally, to illustrate this general proposition, I look to an example of contemporary capitalism's effects on lived body experiencing. I conclude that a comprehensive environmental ethics requires a body-ethic, one which accounts for the sociological conditioning of lived body experiencing.

LIVED BODY CONSCIOUSNESS

Merleau-Ponty's influential investigations in *Phenomenology of Perception* suggest that all our experiencing of the world is in some measure a function of lived body consciousness. But though there has been a good deal of research on many portions of Merleau-Ponty's analysis, one element not broadly developed is the link between lived body consciousness and *value*. Though he admittedly does not develop this point beyond a few suggestions, it is clear that Merleau-Ponty thinks there are value experiences associated with the lived body. For example, in chapter 4 of *Phenomenology of Perception,* while reiterating his critique of empiricism, Merleau-Ponty says:

> The pure *quale* would be given to us only if the world were a spectacle and one's own body a mechanism with which some impartial mind made itself acquainted. Sense experience, [in contrast,] invests the quality with vital values, grasping it first in its meaning for us, for that heavy mass which is our body, whence it comes about that it always involves a reference to the body. (52)

Lived body consciousness, therefore, includes "vital values," a notion which, I take it, refers to those values associated with us as living bodies, as animals, and to objects in the world insofar as they are advantageous or disadvantageous to our animal life.[1]

One might infer from this passage and others surrounding it that, for Merleau-Ponty, vital value is inherent to lived body consciousness and the perceptual field in general. Thus *all* our lived body experience is invested with vital values. Nor is this investing merely a product of the cognitive relation to an object. For value is not given either as a thinglike entity or objectually but as a characteristic of a *situation*: the value and meaning of a situation is not straightforwardly in an object or in the " body-subject,"[2] but exists somehow in the conscious, meaning-filled nexus of the two, coloring all our lived experience.

Indeed, in this same chapter, Merleau-Ponty tells us that sensuous experiences are associated with various kinds of (bodily) emotions and vital reactions.[3] Sensing is a vital process, "no less than procreation, breathing or growth" (PhP 10). Thus vital values permeate the whole of our sensuous life—and therefore the whole of our cognitive life—since emotions and reactions of this kind naturally relate to what is advantageous or disadvantageous to life, that is, to vital values. In contrast, therefore, to empiricist or intellectualist theories of perception, which tie all sensing only to object-qualities and mental or spiritual acts, Merleau-Ponty insists that vitality and vital values, are at the heart of all our experiencing.

Merleau-Ponty gives us an important key for understanding how our bodily experience can impact our experience of the environment. Lived body consciousness, on Merleau-Ponty's account, is not an *object* consciousness, but, as the term suggests, a *lived* consciousness. Based on the analysis above, this implies that we not only "experience" vital values—objectually—but "live" them, and in an immediate and bodily way. But this further suggests that *how* we live such values can affect our experience of vital values in general, for the manner in which we live vital values will tend to be the basic source of our interpretation and understanding of objectually given vital values. Thus, how we live our bodiliness, how we experience, for example, sex, vitality, health, bodily pleasures, and so on will tend to condition the extent and the depth of our cognition of vital values generally.

This point is important not only for the issue of vital value cognition in general but also for the cognition of ecological values in particular. Whatever else ecological values are—and that can be debated—they are presumably vital values, values that pertain to the existence and flourishing of the ecosystem and its subsystems and to all animate and inanimate beings, insofar as they are associated with that existing and flourishing. Thus it may well be that how it is we experience our own bodiliness, that is, our animality and its values, affects the clarity, depth, and even the extent of our understanding of ecological values.

If this point is basically on target, it suggests an important principle of the sociology of knowledge. For it would follow that, if one lives in a civilization where body experiences and body practices are not conducive to the experience of one's own vital values, one will quite likely fail to recognize and appreciate the values of the environment. And if, to take the matter one step further, the civilization in question is antagonistic to vital values, we might expect to discover kinds of value blindness or even transvaluations of vital values to be widespread in those living within and according to the social norms of that civilization. In fact, to return to the problem I began with, we would expect in such circumstances that even persons highly sensitive to other morally relevant values might fail to grasp the significance of ecological values, precisely because their body-praxis would act as a hindrance to such insight.

A Concept of Value

In order to give some justification to these speculations based on the hints from Merleau-Ponty, I turn to some ideas from Max Scheler. Scheler's thought was a significant source for Merleau-Ponty's early phenomenological work, though not one to which scholars typically turn for an understanding of his philosophy.[4] Whether or not Merleau-Ponty had the following points from Scheler in mind with his comments in *Phenomenology of Perception*, I of course do not know. But I think some of Scheler's ideas round out Merleau-Ponty's thought in a way helpful for constructing an epistemology of ecological value, one at least consistent with the points developed above. I turn first to a concept of value.

Value

As is well known, many early phenomenologists, among them Husserl, Scheler, Ingarden, and Hildebrand, developed philosophies of value. After the advent of Heidegger's *Being and Time* with its powerful critique of the philosophical study of value—at least as an ontological study— value philosophy became in some measure outmoded among phenomenological thinkers. While I cannot develop the point here, it appears to me that the acceptance of Heidegger's critique came a bit too easily to phenomenologists. In contrast to the bulk of post–*Being and Time* phenomenology, it seems to me that a concept of value along the lines of Scheler's developments is both useful and necessary for constructing an ethics. For my current purposes, I shall introduce Scheler's concept of value without argument, though I acknowledge from outset that the assumption of an ethics which includes intrinsic values à la Scheler is by no means uncontroversial in our time.

Though in our concrete moral experience objects are given as *goods,* Scheler thinks that we can distinguish intellectually between the good taken as a whole and the aspect or quality of the good that he terms its *value(s).* The term "value" refers then to a quality of a being, in virtue of which a being is "good" (in some respect) (Scheler 1973, 12-23).

Terming value a *quality* is meant to indicate at least two things. First, it refers to the fact that the existence of a value occurs only in a being which bears it: I do not perceive "justice," "genius" or "beauty," but a just act, the genius of Socrates or the beautiful sunset. These values are "qualities," therefore, at least in the sense that they exist *in* things, persons, communities, institutions, systems, and so forth and do not exist independently of some relation to a bearer.[5] Second, values are "qualities," for Scheler, in the sense that they are given with a full-bodiedness: that is, they are given *perceptually* (in value feeling) not merely intellectually or still less as something posited or inferred to (1973, 16, 18, 63–71, 253–64). This differentiation between goods and the values that render them good is significant for Scheler's philosophy because the difference in the notions of "good" and "value" suggest differing sets of essential laws referring to each.

Now focusing just on value (and not necessarily on the goods that posses them), we can differentiate a few more features. First, value is characteristically given not as a discrete entity but in terms of other values. This attribute of value experience Scheler refers to as their being given according to a "rank order" (ibid., 86–110). That is to say, we typically experience values not simply on their own terms, but in terms of other values, values which are understood as being higher or lower in axiological dignity than others. By way of example, Scheler thinks one not only experiences, say, a cultural value, but may experience it as "higher" than vital values and "lower" than religious values.[6] And for Scheler there is no question that perhaps the primary way of experiencing values is in an act of *preferring,* an act which does not give singular values, but gives multiple values in a rank order (ibid., 86–110). Scheler differentiates five such value ranks (given here in descending order): religious, cultural/spiritual, vital, pleasure, and utility values.

Scheler further spells out this notion of rank order by distinguishing values according to their *kind*: each of these value ranks suggests specific value kinds, such as religious, moral, or vital values. The differentiation into kind is important in that it suggests, to Scheler, that broad issues of ethics are not reducible to the realization of one kind of value, but comprise a complex picture of the good life, that is, a life in which all the various value kinds are represented in one's moral consciousness, according to some definite and presumably hierarchical order. If ethics is meant to express the aim of flourishing as a person, then it is not reducible to the set of values known as moral values.[7] Rather, moral values are realized only in the realization of the various value kinds and in accord with their right order.

Vital values

Like Merleau-Ponty, Scheler speaks of vital values. By "vital values" Scheler refers to those associated with organic life and its experience, with the flourishing and the declining of life. It must be confessed that, more often than not, Scheler's concern for these values (like Merleau-Ponty's) is anthropocentric: he concerns himself less with vital values as such than with their importance for human life.[8] Nonetheless, Scheler's insights will help us both to understand human vital experience and also the cognition of life values more broadly.

Scheler develops vital values mostly in the context of feelings of our own life.[9] Though values are always given, on Scheler's account, in specific modes of value feelings, vital values are given in a particularly pronounced subjectual way, that is, they are lived rather than given objectually. Among these feelings, Scheler mentions "the feelings of 'quickening' and 'declining' life, the feelings of health and illness, the feeling of aging and oncoming death, the feelings of 'weakness' [and] 'strength'" (1973, 106–107; cf. 338–342). But each of these is experienced not only factually, but axiologically and each of these experiences is founded on the more primordial lived experience of the value of one's own life.

But though Scheler concerns himself generally with our experiencing of our own vitality, he extends his considerations also to other vital beings. Feelings are not restricted to one's own experience of oneself, but also found what Scheler calls vital sympathy, that is, our sympathetic entering into another's vital experience, whether the Other refers to human or to nonhuman beings (1973, 340). Vital feelings of oneself, therefore, ground vital sympathy with other living beings, making it possible to enter into another's vital world, even to the point of a sympathetic, "subject-subject" relation to other beings, insofar as they are animate.[10]

These points from Scheler spell out in greater detail what Merleau-Ponty often leaves implicit. First of all, Scheler develops vital values in the context of a general theory of value. Thus, vital values are a specific value modality, one that can be characterized according to its determinate features and which has a specific and analyzable mode of givenness. Furthermore, though Scheler is, like Merleau-Ponty, concerned with issues of value givenness, his concept of a rank order of value suggests not only where vital values stand in a hierarchy but also what might count as a *distortion* in value experience: namely, when one's value experiences contrast with the value hierarchy. Finally, Scheler adds to Merleau-Ponty a cognitive tool for understanding how we move from our lived body knowledge of vital values to the values of other vital beings, including, therefore, also ecological values, that is, by means of vital sympathy. These points are important for our current considerations, as can be seen in the following way:

Even though the elements of an ecosystem include more than life and its values, it is at least plausible to assume that forms of life and their concomitant values act as keys to the nature and knowledge of the environment and that, therefore, our feeling for and knowledge of vital values become a central cognitive access to valuing the environment. On Scheler's account, this knowledge we have of others (and, presumably, of systems of vital others) attained through vital value cognition is closely associated with vital sympathy. This implies that the awareness of the meaning of vital values in others hinges on the meaning and nature of our experience of our own vitality and its values. It follows from this that how we experience and interpret our own vitality and its values is likely to impact—and impact decisively—how we experience and interpret forms of vitality and vital values outside ourselves, precisely because understanding vital values outside ourselves is dependent on how we experience and understand vital values within ourselves.

Consequently, if we experience our bodiliness, our vitality, our bodily pleasures as genuinely valuable—that is to say, if we positively *live* our vital values, as I put it above—we will equally tend, through vital sympathy, to appreciate vital values outside of ourselves as genuine values, including ecological values. On the other hand, any devalorization of our own vital values will tend to lead to an at least equivalent devalorization of other vital values, including ecological values, because the distorted value experience of our own vital values will inhibit a positive experience of another's vital values through vital sympathy.

LIVED BODY AND THE CAPITALIST ETHOS

We can perhaps illustrate the significance of this general principle through a brief look at our contemporary social and political climate. Anecdotally at least, there is a declining appreciation for ecological values, a trend that has been going on for the last few decades. This is evidenced, for example, in the general reduction of state and federal funding for the enforcement of environmental regulations; in a widespread lack of public sympathy for ecological issues, as compared, say, to the 1970s; in the various contemptuous epithets widely used to speak of those interested in ecological issues (e.g., treehuggers)

Whatever power units we might think to be the main source of this cultural shift—industrial interests, Republican control of government, corporate media or what have you—it appears that there is something even more fundamental at work, something rooted, as I will suggest, in certain sociological characteristics of capitalism. For the shift away from support for environmental programs may well be a function of a shift in how ecological values are experienced. If ecological values are not experienced *as values,* one has little or no rational justification for defending the environment: why defend what is not experienced as important or valuable?[11] I believe that there are not only widespread cultural obstacles to experiencing ecological values as values, but also that our meditations on Merleau-Ponty and Scheler have given us some insight into why this is. Let's look at this more concretely.

If there is one thing which recent developments in economic sociology suggest, it is that we can no longer conceive of "capitalism" as a singular, universal phenomenon.[12] While I grant that point and while I grant that contemporary American capitalism is thus in certain respects a phenomenon unto itself, there are nonetheless certain general characteristics of industrial and postindustrial (if there is such a thing) capitalism that have been cogently analyzed for nearly a century and are, I believe, still useful for understanding contemporary American capitalism. I am thinking here, in particular, of the analysis offered by Max Weber in his popular essay *The Protestant Ethic and the Spirit of Capitalism* (1958). I will not try to summarize this work, but only explore a few relevant points that I believe illustrate the link between lived body value experience and the experience of ecological values.

Weber notes many characteristics of the Calvinist ethos which, on his account, form twentieth-century capitalism, especially the American and Anglo-Saxon varieties. Among these we can mention the Calvinist drive for order, derived from the religious imperative for the Saints to order the world for God. A further associated characteristic is the aim of *rationalization,* that is, the aim of reducing the practical world to rational formulae, by means of which the world is dominated.[13] These two characteristics are essential to the Calvinist ethos, in that the present disorder "stinketh in the nostrils of God," as one Puritan sermon put it.[14] Thus these seemingly technical and deeply capitalist values at the same time arise from an energetic religious and cultural motive.

But more important for our purposes is a specifically *bodily* characteristic associated with the Calvinist ethos. This Weber terms its "worldly asceticism." Weber noted that the advent of Calvinism was associated both with resistance to a perceived moral corruption in the Roman Church, expressed in particular by what Calvinists saw as an excessive sensuality, and with the rise of a technical, bourgeois civilization (1958, 36–38). These two characteristics of the Calvinist ethos, combined with the will to order and rationalization mentioned above, tend to produce a particular picture of the body and its values. The body, from the standpoint of this ethos, is seen as something which tends one toward laziness, which tempts one to slack off. Examples of this attitude toward the body abound. If we compare the quality of our food to other industrialized countries, the amount of time spent eating or sleeping or caring for our bodies, the lack of sense for physical beauty associated with our productive life, we can see indications of the negative attitude toward the body associated with our capitalism: as if pleasure, beauty and care for the body are temptations against higher values. Furthermore, bodily pleasures, on this account, come to be associated with obstacles to the intellectual clarity of mind necessary for living life in a rational and orderly way, that is, for a life fitting the Saints (Weber 1958, 119–122). There are, therefore, both religious and cultural valuations which motivate this interpretation of the body and simultaneously a new set of value *criteria* for how to live bodiliness, criteria determined by the needs of industrial production, that is, by values of utility.

What I wish to draw from these points is that, if Weber is essentially correct, there is a constitutive body experience bound up with American capitalist praxis, in large measure due to its powerfully Calvinist coloration.

Lived body experience and the experience of vital values are profoundly conditioned in and through this ethos: it is a body experience that tends to devalorize our vital and animal experience since these latter—to revert to Schelerian language—appear to be hindrances to what are perceived as *higher* values, such as living out the religious and cultural values which we affirm. Simultaneously, it falsely reduces vital values to those of utility. So rather than living vital values in their proper rank order, as Scheler would describe the correct moral situation, the capitalist ethos demands we repress and reduce experienced vital values to values of utility.

There are many "societal symptoms" that might indicate just these points. Consider, for example, the widespread acceptance of the jargon of "natural resources" for the environment. Independently of the ethical and linguistic questions concerning the appropriateness of this jargon, it is safe to say that the widespread acceptance of this jargon suggests a basic *experience* of the environment in terms of resources. Now whatever else the jargon of resources implies, it fundamentally expresses the experience of utility: characteristically, we term x a resource when x is experienced as useful for the goals of some system y. Hence the language suggests an experienced reduction of vital values to utility values. Simultaneously, we find many religious neoconservatives—think, for example, of James Watt's famous statements against preserving "resources"[15]—who not only experience this reduction but treat the domination of the environment as a kind of religious imperative along with a capitalist necessity. It appears that religious and cultural practices lead to experiencing vital values as mere utility values—to the devastation of the environment.

Or again, consider genetically modified organisms. Living organisms that function as food for human beings are genetically manipulated, not because of the benefit or flourishing of life values, but primarily for gains in market share for food conglomerates. Food is therefore treated purely as a commodity—that is, according to utility values—in the name of economic advantage, in other words, cultural values. Once again, a culturally conditioned value experience reduces a distinctive vital value, the value of food, to a utility value—and brings with it the well-documented damage to the environment, the food chain, and human health.

I suggest that these symptoms arise from an experienced reduction of vital values to utility values, an experience which is a function of capitalist praxis with its denigration of body experience. Capitalist praxis tends to lead one not only to the well-documented devastation of the environment, but first to an inner devastation by which one distances oneself from one's own animality and bodiliness, a distancing that cannot but severely inhibit and/or distort the basic source of our vital value experience—our bodies—and, with it, the perception of ecological values. Indeed, it could be that the "outer" devastation of the environment is in the end a projection of the "inner" alienation we experience from our own animality. How could we come to appreciate the vital values of the environment if, in our innermost experience of vital values as such, we take them to be disvalues? And if vital sympathy requires that we become aware of our own vital values in order to appreciate others, how can the devalorization of our own vital values fail to produce a blindness and even a transvaluation of ecological values?

One of the consequences we will need to draw from this is that developing a sound environmental ethic is not simply a question of dealing with the values and norms which apply to "the environment," as if the latter is something extrinsic to ourselves; rather, it is also a question of coming to terms with our own animality and vitality, of facing the fact that our vitality is as much a part of us as our rationality and that therefore we are not "above" the ecosystem but are living members of it.

A further consequence is that, as we attempt to construct a sound environmental ethic, we should not rest satisfied with trying to understand the environment and its values. Rather, we need to understand the way in which our own cognition of ecological values becomes sociologically formed, according to the valuations embedded in the social life we live. Among other things, this means that an environmental ethics needs to concern itself not only with the environment but with constructing an ethics of the lived body: an ethics whereby we can understand the moral significance of the ways social life forms our body experience (and vice versa), so that we can learn to live and love our own bodiliness as one condition of our living and loving the environment.

NOTES

1. On this definition, of course, all living things, life systems, and also inanimate things insofar as they are relevant to organic life also imply vital values.

2. I will use this term since it is a common articulation of Merleau-Ponty's thought in secondary literature, though I do not think that it exactly expresses the concept of lived body Merleau-Ponty had in mind.

3. See especially PhP 55 ff.

4. For example, Langer's 1989 makes no reference to Scheler, though there are nearly as many notes referring to Scheler as to Sartre in the *Phenomenology of Perception.*

5. Frings refers to this as the "functional existence of value," in 1997, 22.

6. While analyzing these sets of relations in terms of hierarchical language may not be the best to way for Scheler to develop this thought, there is an important point here, namely, that some values seem to stand out as less expendable than others for persons, in part because of their axiological dignity. A person, for example, who acts as a martyr may very well think that the cause for which she fights possesses a higher value than the relevant vital value, namely, the value of her own life.

7. Scheler has several surprisingly Aristotelian-sounding passages in his ethics is meant to achieve. At the end of the preface to the second edition, we find Scheler describing the full flourishing of persons in language which resembles Aristotle on *eudaemonia.* Furthermore, Scheler understands his ethics as a virtue ethics, comprising virtues with reference to this complex picture of the good life.

8. For example, he considered much of modern culture to be expressive not only the loss of the sense of what he considered higher values, such as the religious or moral values, but in particular as expressive of *declining life,* that is, the lack of flourishing organic life, and the decline of those values and value experiences associated with our animality. See especially Scheler's 1998, 121–143.

9. In fact, Scheler thinks that all values, not only vital values, are given through various kinds of feelings. See his 1973, 239–353.

10. On Scheler's account, one would presumably have a more robust sympathy with animals than with plants and with higher animals as opposed to lower animals.

11. Strikingly enough, many in public office who oppose special protections for the environment often consider themselves quite morally superior to those who want such protection. This may suggest not simply value blindness but a transvaluation of ecological values.

12. Several of the contributions in Granovetter and Swedberg eds. 2001, justify this claim exceptionally well. See especially the introduction and the articles by Polanyi, Granovetter, and Portes and Sensenbrenner.

13. In practice, Weber treats of the desire for order and rationalization as the same, stressing rationalization over the lust for order, Weber 1958, 47-78. A different treatment of Calvinism with a stress on order rather than rationalization, see Taylor 1989, especially c. 13.

14. Quoted in Taylor 1989, 228.

15. James Watt was Reagan's Interior secretary and was famous for thinking that using environmental resources was a good thing since it hastened Christ's Second Coming.

REFERENCES

Frings, Manfred. 1997. *The Mind of Max Scheler.* Milwaukee: Marquette University Press.

Granovetter and Swedberg, eds. 2001. *The Sociology of Economic Life.* Cambridge MA: Westview Press/Perseus Book Group.

Langer, Monika. 1989. *Merleau-Ponty's Phenomenology of Perception. A Guide and Commentary.* Tallahassee FL: Florida State University Press.

Scheler, Max. 1973. *Formalism in Ethics and Non-formal Ethics of Values.* Translated by Manfred Frings and Roger Funk. Evanston: Northwestern University Press. Originally published as *Der Formalismus in der Ethik und die materiale Wertethik. Max Scheler, Gesammelte Werke, Bd. 2.* 1954/1966. Bern: Francke Verlag.

————. 1998. *Ressentiment.* Translated by Lewis Coser and William Holdheim, with an introduction by Manfred Frings. Milwaukee: Marquette University Press. Originally published as *Das Ressentiment im Aufbau der Moralen.* 1915. Leipzig: Verlag der Weissen Buecher.

Taylor, Charles. 1989. *Sources of the Self,* Cambridge MA: Harvard University Press.

Weber, Max. 1958. *The Protestant Ethic and the Spirit of Capitalism.* Translated by Talcott Parsons, with an introduction by R. H. Tawney. New York: Scribner's & Sons. Originally published as *Die protestantische Ethik und der Geist des Kapitalismus.* 1904–1995. *Archiv fuer Sozialwissenschaft und Sozialpolitik,* vols. XX and XXI.

10

"Fleshing" Out an Ethic of Diversity

Molly Hadley Jensen

The current ecological crisis can be framed as a crisis of diversity. This crisis involves both dwindling biodiversity and increasing homogeneity in agricultural production and knowledge systems. Sociobiologist E. O. Wilson in *The Diversity of Life* details the dramatic plunge in the number of species worldwide. He explains that the extinction of species is much worse than even field biologists, like himself, had previously understood. In his words, rare species are disappearing just beyond the edge of our attention, entering oblivion: "leaving at most a name, a fading echo in a far corner of the world" (1992, 244). The fading echo reverberates in a host of figures: approximately 20 percent of the world's freshwater fish species are either extinct or in a state of dangerous decline; population densities of migratory songbirds in the mid-Atlantic United States have plummeted by more than 50 percent and many species have become locally extinct; tropical rain forests containing more than half the species of plants and animals on earth are disappearing at a rate of one area the size of a football field per second (256, 275). Wilson attributes the alarming decline of diversity to human beings and their consumption patterns. He traces the connection between human settlement and consumption with the mass extinction and argues that the increasingly intrusive and destructive modes of harvesting have produced unparalleled rates of extinction.

Some environmental justice advocates blame the dwindling diversity in human knowledge systems and food production practices for disrupting non-Western and marginalized cultures and for exacerbating the loss of nonhuman species. Vandana Shiva, an Indian physicist and leading environmental justice researcher and activist, chronicles the effects of global, corporate industrialized agriculture. She explains that just as converting natural forests into monocultures of pine and eucalyptus robs the forest of biodiversity and its capacity to conserve soil and water, so too industrial agriculture creates homogeneity and scarcity. Shiva refers to a "phenomenon of stolen harvest" that is being experienced in every society, "as small farms and small farmers are pushed to extinction, as monocultures replace biodiverse crops, as farming is transformed from the production of nourishing and diverse foods into the creation of markets for genetically engineered seeds, herbicides, and pesticides" (2000, 7). As agricultural patterns are supplanted with corporate monocultures, indigenous farming practices and local medicinal knowledge are threatened. A counter movement among Indian environmentalists and farmers launched to protect the local agricultural practices and food supply—and to preserve indigenous knowledge that rely on biodiversity— is called Navdanya, "Save the Seed." By selecting, saving, and replanting the best seeds from year to year, these Indian activists hope to stem the encroaching tide of corporate monocultures and perpetuate their own unique local cultures.

While movements like "Save the Seed" offer a glimmer of hope amidst a sea of sameness, the global crisis of diversity beckons persons, particularly those in the western world, to strongly consider the value of diversity. A first step in this process is to identify some of the philosophical and ethical systems that have denied the significance of difference. Immanuel Kant, for instance, developed a moral philosophy predicated on the universal structures of human reason. Morality, in this system, depends on those structures that are supposedly shared by all rational beings. Those beings who fall outside of this scope of sameness, including all other species in the more-than-human world, are denied inherent moral worth. Another step toward the recovery of diversity is to highlight those philosophies that do embrace the value of diversity. One such philosophy is Maurice Merleau-Ponty's philosophy or ontology of the "flesh."

The significance of diversity is evident in Merleau-Ponty's other work prior to his elaboration of the flesh in *The Visible and the Invisible*. In his essay "The Child's Relations with Others," Merleau-Ponty describes the diverse world of others as the origin of conscious life (PRI, 96–155). He argues that conscious life begins not as a sphere of sameness or self-centeredness, but as coexistence with others. Recognition of oneself as a distinct being develops from and through bodily relations with *multiple* others.

According to Merleau-Ponty's analysis of infant development studies, diverse others are necessary to the perception of oneself as an "I." The child gains, through others, an awareness that different perspectives can be taken on her. The child's awareness that she can be an "other" for others initiates her own self-cognition. A child must first learn to see herself as a body for different others before she knows herself as a body for self (Dillon 1988, 123). Merleau-Ponty explains that the "I arises when the child understands that every you that is addressed to him is for him an I" (PRI, 150). This level of self-recognition is a product of a reciprocity of points of view and entails the recognition of the other's body as a distinct self. The bodies of others are therefore integral to the process of self-consciousness. I perceive my body as *my* body only by perceiving it in relation to other bodies and other things that are not me (Dillon, 123).

For Merleau-Ponty, the presence and awareness of diverse bodies is a building block for the awareness of self. Not only do we come to recognize ourselves as a distinct being by others' recognition of us, but we transfer our recognition of other bodies onto our own. He observes that a baby can discern between a parent's image in the mirror and the parent's body before he can discern between his own image and his body (PRI, 128-129). The ability to consider an external perspective or view of oneself, to trace an image of oneself back to a self, then relies on and develops out of the ability to trace the image of another back to his or her body. Merleau-Ponty finds that one challenge for the child is to identify parts of her body as her own and to integrate the parts of her body that she sees into a recognition of one unified body seen by others. The bodies of others facilitate this recognition. He notes that after six months of age, the child is seen scrutinizing the parts of the other's body and "systematically relating" to himself "the different things he has learned about the other's body from looking" (PRI, 125). Like the process of identifying parts of her body, the process of integrating these bodily parts depends on the bodies of others. When a child observes that the body of an other forms a distinct whole, she is able to understand how the parts of her body do the same.

Merleau-Ponty's posthumously published chapters and working notes on the "flesh" elaborate on this theme of difference and diversity. He surmounts the philosophical split between the mind and body by detailing the intermingling of the body sensed and the body sensing and of diverse bodies of the world. The one element of "flesh" encompasses both the sensed and sensing (of the self and of the world) but this flesh is characterized by difference. There is, most generally, the difference of the sensing and sensed. Merleau-Ponty insists that we must admit that (from one side) our body is a thing among things and also (from another side) that which

sees and touches things (VI, 137). The body therefore unites two proper-
ties within itself and has a "double-belongingness." Each side of being
"calls for the other" (VI, 137). David Abram reinforces the difference
inherent to Merleau-Ponty's account of sense perception by commenting
that we "implicate our own sense, and indeed our own sentience in every
perception" (Abram 1997, 66). Though these sides of being are bound
together, intermingling and flowing back and forth, their difference is
never collapsed. It is the differentiation and distance that enables sense
perception. Merleau-Ponty describes perception as the fission of flesh:
"[T]he fundamental fission or segregation of the sentient and the sensible
. . . makes the organs of my body communicate" (VI, 143). Through the
self-distancing, my flesh hollows out a clearing or field through which
the sentient and sensible sides of my self can exchange. This exchange of
the two sides, the side that senses and the side which is sensed, is perception. According to Merleau-Ponty, both the sensing and the sensed are
involved in perception. Sue Cataldi explains that, in Merleau-Ponty's
"flesh," "no sense can be made of disembodied percipience" (Cataldi
1993, 61). Percipience is animated by the transitivity of the sensed and
sensing flesh.

A fullness or distance preserves the difference of the flesh. Engaged in
a mutual exchange between the two sides of flesh, each self has an openness. Merleau-Ponty admits that the language of sides is inadequate for
capturing the fullness through which the two sides interweave. He says
that "to speak of leaves or layers is still to flatten and juxtapose" the sides
of being. A more adequate metaphor for the two-sided flesh, he suggests,
might be two segments of a sole circular course. Merleau-Ponty explains
that within this one sole movement in its two phases "there is a reciprocal
insertion and intertwining of the one in the other" (VI, 137–138). The
two segments of being can encounter and enfold one another. Important
in this metaphor, says Cataldi, is that the two sides of being are not flattened into a back and front like "a buttered [and unbuttered] side of
bread" (1993, 61). She mentions the metaphor of two caves which connect at their entrances. Perhaps, two windows provide an even more
evocative metaphor for the intermingling within fleshly being. A fresh
breeze flows in through a west window dances around the house enliven-
ing the calm air within it, and is taken through an east window. As the
breeze which invigorates the air within my home depends on the distance
between the two windows, the animation of a fleshly being relies on the
self-distancing of the two sides of the one flesh. The self-distancing of the

two sides of my flesh facilitates my self-consciousness as one who senses and is sensed. In the openness between the two sides of being, a reversibility between the sensed and sensing takes place: the two sides continually encounter and interact with one another in their difference.

The differentiation extends beyond the distinction of sensing and sensed. With the continual exchange of the sensed and sensing, a being of the flesh is a complex array of sense relations. Merleau-Ponty explains that sense experience reveals that we are constituted not only by the relation of sensed and sensing sides, but also by the synergy among diverse senses. In the splitting open or bursting forth of the sensing and sensed body, that Cataldi likens to the opening of a seed capsule, the general element of the flesh "begins to touch, see, hear, smell and taste itself and eventually begins to understand itself or become aware of itself" as a particular self (1993, 61). The occurrence of a particular expression of selfhood is actually a synergy of various senses collected across the contours of a sensing body. Merleau-Ponty contends that sense experience refutes the understanding of self-unity as a sole consciousness. If we have two hands that open on one sole world, he claims, we cannot argue that these two are given to one sole consciousness. He suggests that we must not only renounce the bifurcation of 'consciousness of' and the object to embrace an understanding of two-sided being; but, we must also acknowledge the multiple and synergic quality of the body's consciousness to explain how two hands are unified.

Sense perception demonstrates the "fundamental polymorphism" of the sensing body. Merleau-Ponty expressed an early recognition of the synergy of the senses in *Phenomenology of Perception*. He observes that "any object presented to one sense calls upon itself the concordant operation of all the others" (PhP, 318). And unlike "flowers in a bouquet," senses intermingle with one another. The cooperation and interweaving of the various senses is evident in the extension of sense experience: each contact with a part of our body-self is "a contact with the whole of the present or possible" being (PhP, 317). The synergy of multiple senses that we experience in sense perception influences Merleau-Ponty's view of consciousness. He states that the "unity and identity of tactile phenomenon do not come through any synthesis of recognition in the concept, they are founded upon the unity and identity of the body as a synergic totality" (PhP, 317). This interpretation of consciousness is further explicated in *The Visible and the Invisible*. Merleau-Ponty explains that the "synergic body . . . assembles into a cluster the 'consciousnesses' adherent to its hands, to its eyes" so that "each touching is bound to every other sense—bound up in such a way as to make up with them the experience of one sole world and one sole body" (VI, 141–2). The diversity, multiplicity, and complexity of senses do not *compromise* the unity of the consciousness; rather the transitivity and cooperation of the various senses *comprise* a unity of consciousness.

Though Merleau-Ponty began to articulate the diversity of the sensing body early in his career, he extends this synergy of the senses to include other beings in his flesh ontology.[1] The separation of and openness between the two sides of a being admit the exchange of the sensing and the sensed and the cooperation of diverse senses; but this openness also admits the exchange with the myriad of beings in the world. Merleau-Ponty explains the "fundamental fission" that makes the organs of my body communicate also "founds transitivity from one body to another" (VI, 143). The bond that unites the diversely constituted self also unites one flesh with diverse other beings. If, Merleau-Ponty reasons, a synergy is possible within each of us, then why would it not be possible among different organisms? These other bodies share the world with me and have bodies which can be sensed like mine. If I can perceive myself as sensed flesh, then these other bodies must also be accessible to my perception.

The exchange or reciprocity with other fleshly beings is not incidental in Merleau-Ponty's account of sense perception. The relations with diverse others, which is possible through our own sensual diversification, is an entangling of our senses with others. Merleau-Ponty lyrically expresses encounters between fleshly beings as sensual involvement or intimacy: "[t]heir landscapes interweave, their actions and passions fit together exactly" (VI, 141–142). This intimate interweaving with others that occurs in perceptual experiences constitutes who we are. For Merleau-Ponty, intercorporeality is fundamental to our selfhood. We, as sensing/sensed beings, are relational beings—beings *with* others.

In his examination of sense experience, Merleau-Ponty finds that diverse others are integral to perception and to self-coherence. David Abram refers to sense encounters with others as an "interpenetration" and a "magical participation that permits me, at times, to feel what others feel" (1997, 125). But he also indicates that, for Merleau-Ponty, encounters with others are fundamental to experience. He notes that in Merleau-Ponty's sense phenomenology, the experiencing self is "not a self-enclosed object, but an open, incomplete entity . . . an open circuit" (Abram 1997, 125). Cataldi agrees with this assessment. She explains that "Merleau-Ponty does not regard perceptual experiences as interior, worldless activity" (Cataldi 1993,

71). Instead, the sensing self "completes itself only in things, and in the world" (Abram 1997, 125). Only through relations with the sensible world and its diverse beings, is my sensing self realized.

Each sensible being is fundamentally relational and bound to others. Abram maintains that, in Merleau-Ponty's account of the flesh, we "are destined for relationship" and that "[i]t is primarily though my engagement with what is not me that I effect the integration of my senses, and thereby experience my own coherence" (1997, 125). Bodied beings in a shared sensible world, we cohere in and through connection with others.

Merleau-Ponty's exploration of sense experience reveals that "self-hood" is not a demarcation of a simple and autonomous entity. Instead, the self is a site of relation between dual aspects or sides and this self flourishes through intercorporeal encounters. This view of the self as elementally open and reciprocally involved with others is an ethically potent interpretation. The rigid separation of the human being from different others, the natural world and other nonhuman species is impossible to maintain if the self is no longer singular and closed.[2]

That the self is a continual and complex exchange between one body and the bodies of others implies that we not only can, but *must* encounter different others. The self, an intertwining of modalities ignited by contact with other bodies, is diminished when the senses are dulled by isolation and seclusion. Mutuality exists between me and other. If I dismiss or disregard encounters by erecting barricades along lines of difference, I effectively damage myself for I am constituted by differentiation and exchange. The interdependence and mutuality of Merleau-Ponty's flesh dispel the philosophical bifurcation of the world and thrusts humans into encounters with a world of diversity. His flesh is a vision across the boundaries of human-nonhuman separation. Such a vision parallels the arguments and pleas of concerned ecologists and biologists.

Wilson, the preeminent sociobiologist, characterizes the human pretension of independence from the more-than-human world as "an amnesiac reverie" (1993, 347). He remarks that humans must begin to identify themselves more closely with the rest of life and that the more quickly we do so, the more quickly we will become aware of the sources of human sensibility (1993, 348). That which he intimates as the source of sensibility is the life-sustaining matrix of biodiversity. Wilson warns that "[t]o disregard the diversity of life is to risk catapulting ourselves into an alien environment . . . like the pilot whales that inextricably beach themselves on New England shores" (1993, 347). He advises that humans must "judge every scrap of biodiversity as priceless" and work toward a deep understanding of our connection with the diversity of life (1993, 351).

Wilson's emphasis on diversity as the seedbed of consciousness is remarkably consistent with Merleau-Ponty's discussion of the flesh. Wilson finds that the "undeniable trend of progressive evolution has been the growth of biodiversity" (1993, 187). Human life is one fruit of expanding diversity. Five hundred and fifty million years into the Phanerozoic era, adaptive radiations (the spread of species of common ancestry into different biological niches) brought biodiversity to an all-time high (Wilson 1993, 211). The human species is a "late product" of these radiations, of this zenith of biodiversity.

Human dependence on ecological diversity has not waned, despite our amnesiac affliction. Wilson describes the human race as a "newcomer," less than two million years old, holding but a "tenuous grip on the planet" (1993, 211). The human grasp on its existence depends on the unfathomable diversity that preceded it. This dependence is not merely a relation of linear causality, something of the past. Biodiversity is no mere prelude to the main event of human existence. Wilson uses the example of insects, the most diverse animals on the planet. Insects exist in an astounding variety of millions. Due in large part to their diversity, insects have lived for more than 400 million years. The image of invincibility in our modern "pest-control" paranoia, insects enable larger and less diverse animal species to exist. Wilson states his case in unequivocal terms, "Insects can thrive without us, but we and most other land organisms would perish without them" (1993, 211). Heeding Merleau-Ponty's philosophy of the flesh and warnings such as Wilson's, the human community may yet acknowledge the value of a diversity of beings.

The acknowledgment and embrace of a fundamental "fleshly" and ecological diversity can promote a revision of Kantian morality of the autonomous rational ego. First of all, difference need not imply separation or opposition. Merleau-Ponty's work indicates that difference or diversity can be a basis for coherence and connection. Each being of his "flesh" is comprised of difference. The different sides of these selves are reciprocally engaged with one another. The multiple senses also cooperate and collaborate to form a unified percipience. Merleau-Ponty's work goes beyond merely describing a self as diversely constituted; he describes a harmony and symmetry of the multiple senses. With this account of sensing beings, Merleau-Ponty undermines the assumption that difference poses a threat to self or community. Different others need not be shunned, resisted, or dominated in order to protect the one's own. In fact, he implies that difference and diversity must be welcomed, that it is within difference that identity is forged.[3] Martin C. Dillon argues that the only way to resist the polarizations of dualism is to embrace the "fundamentally ambiguous identity-encompassing difference" adopted by Merleau-Ponty (1988, 159).

Merleau-Ponty's "evasion" of the "trap of polarizations" has powerful ethical ramifications. One who is separate, isolated, and removed from others lacks the capacity for sharing with, feeling for and responding to others. With his diversely constituted, reciprocally involved fleshly being, Merleau-Ponty conceives of the possibility that human and more-than-human can cohere for the flourishing of life.

The diversity of the flesh presents ever emergent and unimagined possibilities for the human self, other beings and the shared sensible world. Merleau-Ponty depicts a dynamic depth of the flesh that unfolds in and through encounters with difference. The flesh, he explains is "a new type of being," pregnant with potential sense expressions, with an ever-expanding horizon of possibility (VI, 149). These possibilities rest in the depth of the flesh that maintains difference. Difference and diversity are then fundamental to one's body and selfhood *and* to the emergent expression of the world's body. Merleau-Ponty dramatically details the value, indeed necessity, of difference and diversity for the flourishing of the world. His ontology of the flesh can serve as a counter to a prevailing logic of sameness, a logic that legitimates dominance of one species to the detriment of diverse others. With the fecundity of the flesh, Merleau-Ponty also undermines the correlation between progress and homogeneity. His work poses a direct challenge to the models of "development" which suppress diversity. The ethic of diversity that can be "fleshed" out from his ontology can promote efforts to nurture and expand ecological diversity.

Human development patterns that threaten biodiversity and promote monocultures can be seen as a denial of the basic ontological significance of diversity. Merleau-Ponty's ontology can help to recover the value and potential of ecological diversity. His work indicates that the singular and solipsistic self rests on a flawed ontology that breeds a dualistic and self-referential morality. Merleau-Ponty's relational ontology provides the basis for a relational ethics in which reciprocity and diversity are primary values. His work offers concrete guidance for ecological ethics. In ethical evaluations of various courses of action, Merleau-Ponty's ontology would place the burden of proof on the exclusive concern for one species and on any course that would substantially diminish diversity. Domination by one species impoverishes and starves the world's being by limiting possibilities of diverse encounters among beings.

Merleau-Ponty's philosophy implies a different theory of value. Value in this theory is not concentrated in or confined to certain supreme beings or species. Rather, value is an expression of relations and interactions among species. Merleau-Ponty does not establish absolutes of truth or value; instead, his resistance of absolutes undermines the supreme value of a particular being or species. In this theory of value, human consumption patterns and agricultural practices would be evaluated within a larger ethical framework. Ethical evaluation would include consideration of the network of diverse fleshly relations—present and potential—in which humans share. Ethical considerations would include such questions as: How will corporate monocultures disrupt the ecological balance of a bioregion? How do consumption patterns in one part of the world impact those in other parts of the globe? According to this relational ethics, that which is a good or right course is one which is good or right for relations of diverse beings of the one flesh. An ethics informed by Merleau-Ponty's flesh summons us to seek a course of action that promotes exchanges and relations among a diversity of beings within the ecological community and preserves rich possibilities of ecological relations in the future. Such an ethics can never be reduced or abstracted from the world of experience and relations. Merleau-Ponty's work introduces a new ethics altogether—one that is more adequate for addressing the current crisis of diversity and for the task of moral discernment and analysis in an ecological age.

Notes

1. His consideration of child development expressed in "The Child's Relations with Others" certainly helped to effect this "extension" of a previous insight into the formulation of the "flesh."

2. The theme of the intertwining of human with the rest of nature is one that Merleau-Ponty was developing in *The Visible and the Invisible,* as evident from his notes and outlines. See VI 267/274 where Merleau-Ponty outlines ideas of Nature and of "man-animality" intertwining.

3. Douglas Low argues that Merleau-Ponty asserts what has to be one of the earliest expressions of multiculturalism. Low refers to Merleau-Ponty's call to attend to the diversity of language in *Signs,* but the same claims can be made of his other works. See Low 2000, 92–93.

REFERENCES

Abram, David. 1997. *The Spell of the Sensuous: Perception and Language in a More-than-Human World*. New York and London: Routledge.

Cataldi, Suzanne L. 1993. *Emotion, Depth and Flesh: A Study of Sensitive Space—Reflections on Merleau-Ponty's Philosophy of Embodiment*. Albany, New York: State University of New York.

Dillon, Martin C. 1988. *Merleau-Ponty's* Ontology. Evanston, ILL: Northwestern.

Low, Douglas. 2000. *Merleau-Ponty's Last Vision: A Proposal for the Completion of The Visible and the Invisible*. Evanston, ILL: Northwestern.

Shiva, Vandana. 2000. *Stolen Harvest: The Hijacking of the Global Food Supply*. Cambridge, MA: South End Press.

Wilson, Edward O. 1992. *The Diversity of Life*. New York: W. W. Norton.

11

Social Ecology and the Flesh

Merleau-Ponty, Irigaray, and Ecocommunitarian Politics

Sally Fischer

Merleau-Ponty never shied away from radical philosophical reexamination. In the chapter of *Signs*, titled "Everywhere and Nowhere," Merleau-Ponty criticizes Hegel's prejudice of Western philosophy over the philosophies of the Orient, which Hegel calls a distant approximation of conceptual understanding. Merleau-Ponty says: "Our idea of knowledge is so demanding that it forces every other type of thought to the alternative of resigning itself to being a first sketch of the concept or disqualifying itself as irrational. Now the question is whether we can claim as Hegel did to have this absolute knowledge . . . If we do not in fact have it, our entire evaluation of other cultures must be re-examined" (S 137). From this fine example I think that we can glean the possibility that we need to reexamine and reevaluate our *own* culture, perhaps even its foundations in very strong versions of anthropocentrism, its historical concept of nature as not only mechanistic but also atomistic, its egoistic and individualistic notions of the self, and so forth. In light of the environmental crisis, it seems to me quite clear that the need to question our fundamental ideologies and institutions has never been more urgent. Because of his emphasis on our embodied existence *in* the world, and on our dialogical relation *with* the world and others, it is not difficult to see the possibilities of Merleau-Ponty's philosophy toward such a reexamination. In his early work, Merleau-Ponty presents a phenomenological description of behavior as embodied intentionality, which does not bifurcate mind from body, nor body-subject from the world. His critique of the Cartesian tradition, of scientific objectivism, and of transcendental idealism deepens in his later work, and culminates in a wholly new ontology by which he describes the very soil that makes possible the intentional relation. Indeed, by *The Visible and the Invisible,* Merleau-Ponty claims that we must "recommence everything," and in doing so he creates an ontological concept, "flesh," which he says is neither thought nor thing, but rather an epistemological and ontological *relation,* that includes the sentient-sensible and the sensed-sensible (i.e., perceiving being and perceived being) as its two lips or leaves. Flesh, then, is neither subject nor object, but the "formative medium" of the two—a "general manner of being" (VI 147). By means of this new ontology Merleau-Ponty attempts a radical reevaluation of our most basic conceptual presuppositions of the tradition of Western metaphysics: our ontological categories of thought, thing, selfhood, and alterity.

Despite her critique of Merleau-Ponty's indifference to gender-biases sedimented in his understanding of embodiment, Luce Irigaray shares remarkably similar views with Merleau-Ponty regarding the present task of philosophy. She, too, says we must "recommence everything," go back to experience and rearticulate "all the categories by which we understand things, the world, subject-object divisions, and so forth" (Irigaray 1993, 151). In the later thought of both Irigaray and Merleau-Ponty we find a call for a discursive and ontological shift, for a new horizon of understanding that, taken together, has fecund possibilities for a social ecology and for ecocommunitarian politics. Social ecology in very general terms asks us to re-create socially and ecologically sound ideologies and institutions; that is, it, too, calls on us to recommence everything. The social ecology of John Clark, for example, argues for the need to replace the egoistic, individualistic notion of selfhood with a social-ecological self; asks that we rethink the dualism of mind and body; and proposes a new ecological imaginary to replace our current economistic imaginary. But a social ecology must not, as Clark correctly asserts, give causal priority to either ideologies or to institutions; it must avoid one-sided idealism and one-sided materialism (Clark 1998, 431). Merleau-Ponty's concept of flesh, particularly in regard to alterity, offers a more ecologically beneficial alternative to Cartesian dualism and to the sovereign, individualistic subject of Modernity. Moreover, with the aid of Irigaray's demand for a recognition of differenced embodiment, Merleau-Ponty's philosophy suggests fruitful possibilities for the understanding and practice of responsible social and ecological relations. In the final section of this paper, I make a case for a Merleau-Pontyan social ecology that begins with a general *shift* in the way we understand ourselves and live our lives with others, rather than for a set of ahistorical maxims. I interpret this shift politically as a kind of ecocommunitarian politics, which, in Merleau-Pontyan terms, must be realized through the dialectic of concrete intersubjectivity.

ONTOLOGY OF THE FLESH: FROM EGOLOGY TO ECOLOGY

Merleau-Ponty's concept of "flesh" is an attempt to *root* his previous phenomenology in its fleshy (ontological) soil and to radicalize his critique of dualism by thinking anew the space between the subjectivist and objectivist alternatives. It is a term meant to maintain the blurring of subject and object not only in the body, which he argues in his earlier phenomenology, but in all of the Sensible. He says, "If the distinction between subject and object is blurred in my body…it is also blurred in the thing, which is the pole of my body's operation…and which is thus woven into the same intentional fabric as my body" (S 167). Yet he is not espousing an eradication of all duality. Rather, it is through a kind of deflection or "divergence" in Being, an *écart*, that the two lips of the flesh open up in an intertwining of noncoincidence. Maintaining a "reversibility" of the two lips, *without* coincidence, Merleau-Ponty is able to alter the notion of subjectivity that he offered earlier in *Phenomenology of Perception,* without abandoning it altogether. He speaks about an anonymous visibility, a pre-reflective intercorporeality out of which reflective life and ideality arise—a generality that constitutes the unity of my body and opens it to other bodies (VI 142). It is perhaps a part of our own sedimentation in the Western tradition, particularly Cartesian thought, which emphasizes the *individualism* of subjectivity along with its technological control and power over/against objectivity that may lead us to conclude that this new way of understanding the relation of self/other in such nonhierarchical terms, in terms of an intertwining which arises out of an anonymous flesh, would have to mean an abandonment of subjectivity altogether. But if we live as these two dimensions of a single flesh, we need not abandon, but only to rethink the "I" in terms of a blurring (but not fusion) of ego-boundaries between self and world. In *Signs,* for example, he claims that we are woven into the same intentional fabric as things and as other *animalia*. There is a reversibility in terms of a chiasm or crossing between the sensing-sensible (*animalia*) and the sensed-sensible. Perception is possible because there is a preestablished harmony with things: he says, "Between the exploration and what it will teach me, between my movements and what I touch, there must exist some relationship by principle, some kinship . . ." (VI 133).

Social ecologists often describe our relation with nature as a dialectic that refuses to either conflate or to bifurcate mind and body, and individuals from society and nature. John Clark says, for example, that "a social ecology applies its holistic and dialectic approach to the nature of the self" and that "Part of the social ecological project of comprehending 'unity-in diversity' is to theorize adequately this duality [of mind and body, self and nature] and the necessary experiential and ontological moments of alienation, separation and distance within a general nondualistic, holistic framework" (Clark 1998, 425). Social ecologist, Joel Kovel describes our connectedness, but not fusion, with nature in ontological terms: "In the universe as a whole, there is no real separation between things; there are only, so far as the most advanced science can tell us, plasmatic quantum fields; one single, endlessly perturbed, endlessly becoming body" (Clark 1998, 423). Both Clark and Kovel reveal the way we are *ecological* beings, not simply *egological* beings—and we find the seeds of this already in Merleau-Ponty's thought with his description of the ontological roots of our perceptual "communication" (VI 135) or dialogue with the world—a dialogue that becomes too easily lost or forgotten when we think of the human-other relation solely in terms of instrumental reason and of the environment as a giant supermarket, a manageable storehouse of (potential) commodities.

The notion of "dialogue" is central to his understanding of subjectivity as an opening in the flesh. Our very existence is founded on a kind of corporeal dialogue with the world and others. In fact, even in his earlier phenomenology, Merleau-Ponty calls perception itself "a sort of dialogue" (PhP 320).[1] He describes dialogical interpersonal relations in terms of an "intercorporeality" (S 168), where the body, in its power of lived expression, is the "medium of communication" (PhP 181). The lived body, as the site of the relation of reversibility, as the movement of touching-touched, as a perceiving-thing is the *opening* to alterity. Merleau-Ponty thinks that the notion of reversibility (really only a *partial* reversibility) does not only apply to my body, but also "overturns our idea of the thing and the world" (S 166). The transition or movement of partial reversibility can also take place between my body and another, because "he and I are like organs of one single intercorporeality" (S 168). Bodies dialogue in a kind of "compresence" where I perceive (prethetically) a different "sensibility" before I perceive a different person's thoughts.

He writes:

> Other persons are there too (they were already there along with
> the simultaneity of things). To begin with they are not there as
> minds, or even as "psychisms," but such for example as we face
> them in anger or love—faces, gestures, spoken words to which
> our own respond without thoughts intervening. (S 181)

The flesh is the field for an intercorporeality that "I do not form, which
forms me, this coiling over of the visible upon the visible, can traverse,
animate other bodies as well as my own" (VI 140). One could even say
here that Merleau-Ponty is writing a holism, something like a "systems
theory," where landscapes interweave, where my singular existence is
bound to every other, and where a synergy exists among different organisms (VI 142).

EMBODIMENT AND SOCIAL RELATIONS

To be sure, Merleau-Ponty's philosophy of embodied existence can be useful toward the kind of ontology for which many ecologists seem to be
searching. But regarding alterity in terms of social relations, just how radical is his attempt to recommence everything? On the one hand, the perceiving body as an inherently communicative intentionality provides the
condition of possibility for dialogical life with others. Yet on the other
hand, even in his explicit attempt to reconceive our categories of experience, for the most part Merleau-Ponty himself has a blind spot regarding
sex, race, and gender.[2] My goal here is not to blame him for this oversight,
but rather to claim that recognition of real differences is an essential element for a *social* ecology, since social ecology links domination of nature
with social domination, and the lack of ethical recognition of difference
can be a factor in social domination. This missing element must be considered if we are to find Merleau-Ponty's thought beneficial for a social
ecology.

In her work, *The Ethics of Sexual Difference,* Luce Irigaray criticizes
his ontology for this very problem, namely his indifference to sexual difference. While her critique is beautifully insightful, it is questionable,
since, although it is not his explicit concern, his philosophy of embodied relations *can* incorporate difference, or, "real others." Nevertheless,

my purpose in this paper does not center around a defense of his thought regarding her critique, but rather my interest lies in the way that Irigaray's thought can provide a fecund reopening of Merleau-Ponty's texts and can aid in the development of a Merleau-Pontyan social ecology.

Irigaray has argued that subjectivity has not been represented in terms of real, sexed speaking subjects, but instead, historically has been predicated on male morphology and on a masculine style of embodied experience. There has been no place for the subject *as* woman, since this so-called neutral subjectivity is already represented and structured as that which is not female/feminine. Most liberal feminists, she thinks for example, "describe what a woman is within the horizon of a male subject's culture" (Irigaray 1996, 61). The creative aspect of Irigaray's task thus centers around envisioning the beginnings of a new ontology of embodiment and a new symbolic order. *Asserting* sexual difference, she thinks, is a necessary strategy if we are going to suppose that we can have an intersubjectivity that arises out of two sexed subjects, in other words, that asserts a place for the woman-subject to speak as a woman, and not as that falsely neutral subject. Irigaray uses the notion of the "two lips" as a metonymic device that links a new discursive and ontological order to the female body. The "two lips" serves as a concept meant to disrupt the traditional categories of Western thought by blurring the dichotomies of subject/object, inside/outside, active/passive, unity/plurality, and so on, and by offering a new notion of alterity.

While Irigaray is concerned with creating an ontology of *sexed* embodiment, tied to female morphology and to traditionally feminine experience, the ontological relation she imagines is remarkably close to Merleau-Ponty's own notion of the flesh, which also disrupts these same categories. First, Irigaray speaks of an ontology of female embodiment that is neither one, nor a two—not "one" in the sense of an essential identity, yet not two in the sense that the relation of the two lips is a kind of double self-reflection, not of two separate "parts," but rather as a contiguity between two sensing-sensibles. Merleau-Ponty describes an ontology of a world "that is neither one nor two," and of a flesh that is neither identitiy nor nonidentity. Second, her concept of "mucosity" (another metonymic devise) resembles the chiasmus of the flesh, that contiguous and fluid relation between the two lips (reinterpreted now), in its *re*doubling as two sensing-sensibles. The central dynamic inherent in both the concept of flesh and of mucosity is the mechanics of fluidity, which serves to deconstruct traditional categories in a dynamic movement. While Irigaray seems to think that her concept of mucous differs significantly from Merleau-Ponty's concept of flesh, I do not think that it does, particularly if we understand flesh as a fluid, diachronic movement.

Despite the similarities of their *ontologies* of embodiment, Irigaray thinks that in order to obtain a genuine intersubjectivity in practice, there must be a relation between persons "as real others" and not simply swept up in a falsely neutral conception of subjectivity. But since there is no One proper universal body-subject, the achievement of a genuinely intersubjective, nonimperialistic relation may not be so facile as Merleau-Ponty sometimes seems to describe, for example, when he talks about intersubjectivity as a "consummate reciprocity." In her book, *I Love to You,* Irigaray argues that in order to have genuinely intersubjective relations, two things must obtain: First, we must create and represent new symbolic orders of sexed identity. She claims: "[I[f the other is not defined in his or her actual reality, there is only an other me, not real others" (Irigaray 1996, 61). And second, in terms of lived experience, we must also approach the other with the acknowledgment that "I am not everything." This is an important facet of Irigaray's ethics—what she calls the role of the "negative"—that interval between myself and other that is protective of the reduction of myself to the other, and of the other to me. The negative in sexual difference means an acceptance of the limits of my gender and recognition of the irreducibility of the other.

Yet both of these same conditions for ethical intersubjectivity are at least consonant with Merleau-Ponty's thought; namely, that others are recognized as real others, rather than as universal subjects, and that the kind of consummate reciprocity he describes requires a reciprocal recognition that "I am not everything." Because he rejects the individualist and solipsistic subject in favor of a decentered and dialogical subject, already we have a subject "poised" for the possibility of a genuine intersubjectivity. Bodies for Merleau-Ponty are always communicative and expressively open and accessible, which necessarily presupposes an *other,* a possible *interlocutor* in the dialogue. In other words, despite his blind spot I think that his account of intersubjective relations can account for real, and not simply ideally or falsely universal others.

Now, it is certainly possible that we habituate ourselves and others to ignore the call of the other and simply impose our own desires onto a situation. But to do this is to lose the very "symbiotic" sense that Merleau-Ponty describes as part of our dialogical nature. To maintain our dialogical nature demands that we recognize that call, and while our interpretation may shift, both in our individual experience and culturally or historically, if the relation really is a kind of symbiotic communication, then the other's being places limits or constraints on our interpretation of that experience.[3] Nevertheless, when we consider many current social and environmental practices (e.g., sweat shops and factory farming), we might ask what understanding of our selves we are living where the other being's communicative intentionality is ignored. Perhaps it is a view, returning to Irigaray's point, simply where I *am* everything. To alter our pathologically detached and imperialistic mode of experience that has been incorporated into our lived experience with human and nonhuman beings requires a new conception of ourselves, and of our relations to others and to the natural world. It furthermore requires that this in turn become incorporated into our everyday experience. This demands a commitment on our part to restore and maintain dialogical relations—not only ecologically, but socially.

MERLEAU-PONTYAN SOCIAL ECOLOGY IN PRACTICE: CONSTRUCTING A COMMON GROUND

I think that from Merleau-Ponty's philosophy one can elicit a kind of social ecological ethics that includes a call for a *general shift* in the way we understand ourselves and live our lives with others, rather than a call for an ahistorical set of maxims. It is not just a matter of simply recognizing *that* there is another, with a view different from my own. Rather, ethical recognition is a *mode* of being with another; it *demands* that the other be listened to as *another* possible perspective while still attempting to maintain the goal of a genuine reciprocity. Merleau-Ponty writes: "In the same way, the perception of a veritable alter ego presupposes that his talk be capable of remaking us in his image and to open us to another meaning...He is able to get across to me inasmuch as I am also speech, that is capable of allowing myself to be led by the flow of talk toward a new state of knowledge" (PM 143). Respect demands not that I agree with the other's perspective (this is not sheer ethical relativism), but that there is an obligation, a pact to keep the communicative process *alive*. This kind of ethical demand is consonant with an ecocommunitarianism that does not presuppose some kind of facile fusion of perspectives or horizons, but only that, as Clark suggests, we develop and promote institutions which foster direct democracy. One of the goals of ecocommunitarian direct democratic assemblies is to "attempt to balance adversary politics by nourishing the mutualistic art of listening," and to "seek common rhetoric evocative of a common democratic discourse" (Clark 1998, 433). The communicative process that Merleau-Ponty describes is our capacity of reflection, expression, and gathering together (the dia-*logos*) the separate elements into a whole that does not subsume all the "parts" (since Merleau-Ponty's idea of the movement of the *dia*-logos is not Hegelian). Ethical relations hinge on a communicative rationality, not of the Habermasian sort, but rather what Merleau-Ponty calls a "presumptive" universality, grounded in the communicative body, and ultimately in the reversibility of the flesh. This is a *historical, lateral,* and *presumptive* universality, not an a priori given or one that can be known through disembodied reason, but one realized through dialogue and concretized in interpersonal relations and social institutions. Merleau-Ponty distinguishes his own understanding of "universality" from that of Kantian liberal thought: "With the assumption of impersonal Reason and rational Man, and by regarding itself as a natural rather than an historical fact, liberalism assumes universality as a datum, whereas the problem is its realization through the dialectic of *concrete* intersubjectivity" (HT 35).

We must be careful not to "smooth over" the difficulties that particularity or difference brings to the dialectical process of this new kind of presumptive universality. In spite of his otherwise excellent reading of Merleau-Ponty's philosophy, Gary Madison, for example, seems to assume what I would call a too facile or optimistic belief in the inevitable progress of communicative rationality. For example, he claims that "we have come to realize thanks to the phenomenon of globalization, the freedom of each is inseparable from the freedom of all. Postmodernity and Postmodern globalism have given us a new beginning and have freed us from many of the avatars of our past. Let us hope, as Merleau-Ponty would surely have, that there is some unshakable truth to Hegel's belief that human history is, in the last resort, the history of the progress of the consciousness of freedom" (Madison 2001, 179–180). It seems to me, rather, that many aspects of current globalization do not take place in the kind of dialogical community that Merleau-Ponty seems to have in mind, but rather as monological (i.e., with one view dominating the relation) and sometimes oppressive and imperialistic practices of current consumer capitalism. These practices, such as the use of Third World labor in the form of sweatshops, certainly seem to leave the particularities of those "others" behind in that global "dialogue." Thomas Busch explicitly recognizes this important aspect of the ethical dimension in Merleau-Ponty's works that Madison sometimes seems to smooth over. Busch writes: "Invoking abstract principles implies, for Merleau-Ponty, a process of depersonalization, distancing us from 'the social totality we live in.' A universality based on abstraction, which would be achieved by a transcendence of particularity in the sense of leaving it behind, is a false universality" (Busch 1999, 81). Madison's understanding of globalization seems to embody this sense of "transcendence of particularity." The new kind of universalism or common ground set forth as a goal in the dialogical process of a Merleau-Pontyan communicative rationality must be recognized as a difficult, open-ended, and continuous process. Part of its difficulty lies in the fact that the oppression of others' perspectives, and therefore suppression of genuine dialogue, is often deeply sedimented in our social institutions, including and especially in our discourses, as Irigaray would argue. In turn, this becomes part of the complex web from which social relations arise. In the Introduction to *Signs,* Merleau-Ponty writes: "There is equal weakness in blaming ourselves alone and in believing only in external causes . . . Evil is not *created* by us or by others; it is born in this web that we have spun about us—and that is suffocating us. What sufficiently tough new men will be patient enough to really reweave it?" (S 35). It is clear that, for Merleau-Ponty, the process of communicative rationality through which we try to forge a common ground involves both the clear recognition of the other, and at the same time takes place within a shared intentional fabric and a shared social and historical field.

In his essay, "A Note On Machiavelli," Merleau-Ponty writes: "The suffering that I cause rends me along with my victim . . the evil that I do I do to myself, and in struggling against others I struggle equally against myself" (S 212). What we commonly call "self-interest" perhaps ought to be rethought as something like Aristotle's notion of "self-love" (albeit grounded in the affective embodied subject) since our own self-respect and our respect for the other are inherently tied together. Although one cannot escape from the shared soil of the interworld, self-interest would tend to close off the dialogue, while self-love requires dialogue. Rather than viewing self-love and altruism as dichotomous, a Merleau-Pontyan social ecology can show us that the move from monocularity (my particular view) to binocularity, which the others' perspective can give me, is what allows for depth. Those other eyes, ears, and voices give depth to my own.[4]

I have argued that the seeds of ethical behavior toward others are already present in the very structure of communicative intentionality arising out of that common fabric of the flesh, but these must be *realized* in our habitual actions, and become incorporated into the very (dia)logic of the self. Like all social ecologists, Merleau-Ponty clearly recognizes that values are not simply ideals, but must become embodied in interpersonal relations and in social institutions:

> . . . a society is not the temple of value-idols that figure on the fronts of its monuments or in its constitutional scrolls; the value of a society is the value it places upon man's relation to man. It is not just a question of knowing what the liberals have in mind but what in reality is done . . . To understand and judge a society, one has to penetrate its basic structure to the human bond upon which it is built; this undoubtedly depends upon legal relations, but also upon forms of labor, ways of loving, living, and dying. (HT xiv)

As selves already woven into the same tissue as others, norms apply to the interwoven community, and they shift as our human history is a movement through time. As reflective, embodied persons, we are both the subject and object of history. Values, then, have a historical character, but, as I would argue, if they are based in Merleau-Ponty's understanding of human reality and of the flesh, then they are not completely relativistic. Of course there is a slowly evolving dialectical movement between our lived behavior and cultural discursive representations, so that we cannot ignore either when considering an ethics. Recognizing the historical dialectic of perception and values, Merleau-Ponty says, "The way we perceive depends upon our wishes and our values, but the reverse is also true" (HT 96). In redefining our understanding of the self as ecological, we must create and *represent* not only in discourse but also in our *institutions,* relations with others and the natural world based on the goal of genuinely dialogical relations. To do this, surely would be to recommence everything.

NOTES

1. Perception is described as dialogical throughout the *Phenomenology of Perception*. One's body provides a "certain way of linking up with the phenomenon and communicating

with it" (PhP 317). Furthermore, this is grounded in the fact that the lived body, according to Merleau-Ponty, is "connatural with the world" and through prereflective behavior, is able to "discover a sense in certain aspects of being without having myself endowed them with it through any constituting operation" (PhP 217).

2. In "The Child's Relations with Others," however, Merleau-Ponty does address racism and gender roles in a secondary, but nevertheless interesting way. He uses Else Frenkel-Brunswik's analysis of the personality trait, "psychological rigidity," and its connection to racism and rigid gender roles to argue that "it is impossible to establish a cleavage between what will be 'natural' in the individual and that will be acquired from his social upbring-ing" (CRO 108). In other words, the subject's psychological disposition, family and social structures are taken-up in a "global project," at the heart of which is an ambiguity where neither can be given causal priority. Merleau-Ponty addresses racism and gender roles in this context, namely as phenomena that appear in this "global project," that is, as phenom-ena that show up in that ambiguous dialectic of individual traits and social context operat-ing in our individual perceptions and projects. While he addresses racism and gender here ultimately in order to highlight the "profound relation of the two phenomenal orders [the functions of the intellect and the subject's relation to society] that are part of a single global project of the individual" (CRO 108), nevertheless, the general way in which racism is described—as a psychologically rigid subject's attempt (given the right social conditions) to project onto the "other" those characteristics that the subject himself does not want to have, is ashamed of, or has deemed not proper—may be useful to bear in mind as I attempt to open up a more direct and deeper Merleau-Pontyan understanding of gender and race (in terms of the possible ethical recognition of difference in general) than is addressed here in "The Child's Relations with Others."

3. Indeed, I would argue that the fact that owners and managers of sweat shops and factory farms go through so much trouble to conceal their practices from the public suggests that they already recognize that there is something wrong with these practices. If the owners of factory farms, for example, really believed that the animal's call of psychological and phys-ical pain is acceptable, then I would think that they would try to, and would eventually be able to convince the public. Mill and Taylor made a somewhat similar argument in *The Subjection of Women.* He (or they) asked if men really did believe that women were *natu-rally* incapable of intellectual endeavors, then why did the men go through so much trou-ble to *prevent* the women from *attempting* these endeavors? In both cases, the subjugating persons already perceive something about the being at the other pole of the relation, and have reasons to prevent its being acknowledged. John Stuart Mill and Harriet Taylor, *The Subjection of Women,* in *Modern Political Thought,* edited by David Wooten. (Hackett Pub-lishing Company, 1996), p. 688.

4. For example, in his essay, "From Mauss to Claude Lévi-Strauss," Merleau-Ponty writes: "At the point where two cultures cross, truth and error dwell together . . ." Our own view and approach of what is other can either "hide what there is to know of us" (i.e., if we are stuck in a kind of monocular view); or it can become "a means of incorporating other peo-ple's differences." But to be open to these differences requires that the inquirer "let himself be taught by another culture. For from then on he has a new organ of understanding at his disposal . . ." (S 120).

References

Busch, Thomas. 1999. *Circulating Being*. New York: Fordham University Press.

Clark, John. 1998. "A Social Ecology," in Michael Zimmerman, ed. *Environmental Philosophy*. New Jersey: Prentice Hall.

Irigaray, Luce. 1993. *An Ethics of Sexual Difference*. Translated by Carolyn Burke and Gillian C. Gill. Ithaca: Cornell University Press. Originally Published as *Ethique de la différence Sexuelle*. 1984. Paris. Les Editions de Minuit.

———. 1996. *I Love to You*. Translated by Alison Martin. New York: Routledge. Originally published as *J'aime a toi*. 1995.

Madison, Gary Brent. 2001. "The Ethics and Politics of the Flesh." In Duane H. Davis, ed. *Merleau-Ponty's Later Works and Their Practical Implications*. New York: Humanities Books.

12

Harmony in a Dislocated World

Jocelyn Dunphy-Blomfield

Merleau-Ponty's philosophy is . . . a philosophy of relation.

—Enzo Paci

It does not show much love for reason to define it in such a way that it is the privilege of a Western elite released of all responsibility toward the rest of the world. To seek harmony with ourselves and others, not only in . . . solitary thought but through the experience of concrete situations and in a living dialogue with others . . . is the exact contrary of irrationalism, since it accepts our incoherence and conflict with others as constants but assumes we are able to minimise them . . . Existentialist philosophy, they say, is the expression of a dislocated world. Indeed, and that is what constitutes its truth.

— Merleau-Ponty: *Humanism and Terror*

The topic "Merleau-Ponty and Ecology" starts with a problem. Ecology, the science of relations, has come to mean by extension our natural and human environment and—extended again—this environment's destabilizsation by industry and economic development. Widening further, the semantic field takes in notions of care, social movements and policy-formation. This is an extension of an abstract term that looks like a case of Whitehead's (1933) "misplaced concreteness," except that an increasing human population and the thrust of technology make ecology in its current sense an urgent challenge for thought.

Merleau-Ponty did not use the word *ecology*, but both its core concept *relation* and the associated term *environment* are central in his writing. But we do not find environment used in its biological sense as in Uexküll (1926; cf Agamben, 2004), or in the systemic sense of human ecology or Bateson's (1973) "ecology of mind." For Merleau-Ponty the term *environment* translates Husserl's *Umwelt*—our being-in-the world as

Heidegger recast it. In this sense it functions within a phenomenology of human existence that uses its own impetus to go beyond Husserl and Heidegger so as to express a new ontology. So in what way can we approach Merleau-Ponty now so as to include conceptual shifts in thinking, and respond to the cultural distress contained in current use of the word *ecology*?

Enzo Paci points out that Merleau-Ponty is preeminently a philosopher of relations (Paci 1958/2000, 21). David Abram establishes that his philosophy of Nature offers research a "clarified epistemology, and the language of perceptual experience" that makes it possible to "speak of ecological systems without positing our immediate selves outside of those systems" (Abram 1988, 87).

My aim is to bring these themes together in Merleau-Ponty's philosophy of nature, then to relate this to the perspective opened by his philosophy of action. Since his work in dynamic psychology parallels the development of both, his study of love as both union and oppression at the end of the unfinished essay "The Child's Relations with Others" (PRI, 154–155) will form a bridge between these two aspects of his philosophy, opening a way to ecology.

MERLEAU-PONTY AND NATURE

We can take up three aspects of Merleau-Ponty's thought on nature: nature as the interrelation of subject and object; nature and twentieth-century physics; and finally the correlation of the physical and psychological worlds.

Merleau-Ponty's interrelation of subject and object

Merleau-Ponty's philosophy of nature is encapsulated in his 1946 summary of *Phenomenology of Perception* in the address he gave to the French Society of Philosophy, published as "The Primacy of Perception":

> . . . the perceived world is not a sum of objects (in the sense in which the sciences use this word), . . . our relation to the world is not that of a thinker to an object of thought . . . The perceived world is the always presupposed foundation of all rationality, all value and all existence. (PRI, 12–13).

He presents his method as radical. *Phenomenology of Perception* had begun: "Probably the chief gain from phenomenology is to have united extreme subjectivism and extreme objectivism in its notion of the world or of rationality." For phenomenology the world is

> . . . the sense which is revealed where the paths of my various experiences intersect, and also where my own and other people's intersect and engage each other like gears. (PhP xx)

Merleau-Ponty does not aim to split off "objective" nature from "subjective" feelings or meaning. That would be proposing a familiar two-sided world, a duality debated in arguments about the natural versus the social sciences.[1]

I shall follow his "extreme" path towards the formulations of *The Visible and the Invisible* without giving special emphasis to that unrevised work. Ricoeur's "Hommage à Merleau-Ponty" (1961/1992, 162–163) and James Morley's discussion of Merleau-Ponty's "circularity" (1999, 243–245) emphasise across forty years that the aim to integrate dualist approaches and go beyond them characterises his thought from the beginning.

From *Phenomenology of Perception* things hold together as a world through our embodiment: "The relations between things or aspects of things having always our body as their vehicle, the whole of nature is the setting of our own life . . . in the last analysis we cannot conceive anything which is not perceived or perceptible" (PhP 320).

The world is the correlate of our action: "Perceiving is pinning one's faith, at a stroke, in a whole future of experiences, and doing so in a present which never strictly guarantees the future; it is placing one's belief in a world" (PhP 297). Merleau-Ponty's "world," like Kant's (1933, A418, B446), is a conceptual unity, both "thing" and value. It is what we relate our selves and our actions to. The freshness of Merleau-Ponty's metaphysics of nature is its presentation through the body, and its identification with perception as creating and guaranteeing it by ongoing "belief."

Nature and the new physics

Students' notes of Merleau-Ponty's "Cours de Sorbonne" lectures from 1949-1952 on psychology and child psychology (Prunair 2001) show him developing the themes of the perceiving self, the other and the world, bringing out that problems in psychology overlie conceptual issues. These are the problems of oneself and the other for "pure empiricism"; problems of the body and the other for "pure reflection" inherited from Descartes; problems of conceiving self and experience from Kant through to Husserl and to the question of Being. Their best hope of being resolved is to be brought together by "examining how we need to conceive the world," for "these three problems are internally linked" (Prunair 2001, 539–540, my translation). So how are we to conceive the world, practically speaking?

There is a theoretical leap between the earlier writings on nature of the 1940s and the early 1950s and the plans that Merleau-Ponty drew up from 1956–1959 for his lectures at the Collège de France, *The Concept of Nature* (1968). These lectures are marked by the integration of the advances of twentieth-century physics. The integration is paired with a renewed focus on ontology that holds to a "double conviction": if the philosophy of nature "cannot by itself solve the ontological problem . . . neither is it a subaltern or secondary element in any such solution" (RC 62–98).

In these later lectures, through Newton and Kant, Schelling and Hegel, to Bergson, and arriving at Husserl, Merleau-Ponty seeks a containing ontology to reposition his initial conviction that nature is the interrelation of world and perceiver as embodied mind, and that perception is a nascent *logos*. This more developed ontology has to avoid anthropomorphic accounts of nature and offer, without idealism or mysticism, "the idea of an exchange between Nature and consciousness within man, an internal relation between man and Nature" (RC 76).

Husserl belongs in this enterprise because of the ontological force of his pursuit of the "things themselves," the "blosse Sachen." Starting from a first position where nature appears as "the correlative of the sciences of nature—as a sphere of 'pure things'"—and avoiding "extreme idealism," Husserl integrates "objective and scientific thought" by revealing "the intentional life that sustains, grounds and constitutes it," and is "the measure of its truth" (RC 79). In the Collège de France lectures of 1956–1957 Merleau-Ponty sees the body as pivot of this intentional unity of nature and consciousness. Quoting Husserl as he had in *Phenomenology of Perception* (137), he emphasises that it is "my body" as the "organ of a motor power, of an 'I can,'" and as a "field of localisation" of sensations, that makes possible this ontology, the Being of a world through the mutual involvement of human consciousness and objective beings (RC 80).

Introducing the academic year 1957–1958 he at first reviews the problem in the impasse of the idea of nature, of man and of God in the moderns—as he writes, the equivocations in naturalism, humanism, and theism, which he sees as currently sliding into each other. The impasse derives from two senses of the word *nature* in Descartes - "natural light" and "natural inclination" (RC 88–89). They mark two ontologies—of the object and of the existent—and as he says, Leibniz had in fact pointed to a "labyrinth of first philosophy" (ibid., 90) needing elaboration to give its various contradictions their place. Merleau-Ponty's aim is to go beyond the "predialectical ontology" (ibid. 91) that has cluttered modern dialectical thinking and to seek a renewal by following recent development in the notion of nature. He presents the transformation of this notion by scientific practice as full of philosophical significance:

> Physical action is no longer conceived as a trace in absolute space and time, passed on from one absolute individual to other equally absolute individuals. Physical entities, like mathematical entities, are no longer seen as "natures," but as structures in an ensemble of operations. (ibid.)

He sums up: "As Niels Bohr has remarked, it is no accident that there is a harmony between the descriptions of psychology (we would say, of phenomenology) and the conceptions of contemporary physics" (RC 93). He notes that psychological concepts too are having their principles over-turned, and finds changes in the life sciences as well, though not on the same scale as in physics and not as achieving theoretical unification.

At this point nature is for Merleau-Ponty first and foremost an onto-logical concept, one that modern scientific practice has opened to new for-mulation. As he puts it:

> What is called nature is certainly not a spirit at work in things whose aim is to resolve problems by "the most simple means"—but neither is it simply the projection of a power of thought or determination present in us. It is that which makes there be, simply, and at a single stroke such a coherent structure of a being, which we then labori-ously express in speaking of a "space-time continuum," or "curved space," or simply of "the most determinate path" of the anaclastic line. Nature . . . stands at the horizon of our thought as a fact which there can be no question of deducing. (RC 93)

The plans for 1959–60 on *Nature and Logos: The Human Body* touch on embryology and phylogenesis, stating that the goal of the course has been "to come to the appearing of man and the human body in nature" (RC 128). At the center of both man and nature the human body is the connecting concept that has taken the place of consciousness:

> We are not dealing here with two natures, one subordinate to the other, but with a double nature. The themes of the *Umwelt,* of the body schema, of perception . . . popularised in psychology and nerve physiology, all express the idea of corporeality as an entity with two faces or two "sides." (RC 129)

His conclusion rephrases a core theme of *Phenomenology of Perception,* this double aspect of the body as more than subjective:

> . . . the body proper is a sensible, and it is the "sensing"; it can be seen and it can see itself; it can be touched and it can touch itself, and, in this latter respect, it comprises an aspect . . . open in principle only to itself. (ibid.)

The language of these last lectures is that of *The Visible and the Invisible:* the "body proper embraces a philosophy of the flesh as the visibility of the invisible" (RC 129).

Just as the focus on physics came from Husserl's approach in the *Krisis,* the central place given to the body was due to Gabriel Marcel, as noted by Paul Ricoeur in his Obituary (1961/1992, 159). Merleau-Ponty recapitulates the role of the human body in constituting nature when he turns to psychoanalysis: "The body which possesses senses is also a body which has desires, and thus esthesiology expands into a theory of the libidinal body" (RC 129). In Melanie Klein's development of Freud he notes "corporeality taken as . . . the search of the external in the internal and of the internal in the external, that is as a global and universal power of incorporation" (ibid., 130). Through the libidinal body, not only perception but desire operate to constitute nature.

How can one sum up the harmony of his philosophy of nature as developed in *Phenomenology of Perception,* then related to the sciences and social sciences in the *Lectures,* to be taken up again in his later critique and reformulation of ontology? Martin Dillon (1989, 77) orients this development towards *The Visible and the Invisible,* pointing out that Merleau-Ponty's key notions of subject, object and meaning are the categories of traditional ontology and that his later terminology indicates the replacement of unworkable concepts. The overhaul of ontology makes sense of this change of terminology, Merleau-Ponty's philosophy remaining consistent despite it. What is evident if one measures the outline of his philosophy against Dillon's conclusion is that a major element in Merleau-Ponty's shift in language is his openness to the scientific advances of his time.

Throughout the changes his theme of interrelatedness remains central. Reviewers of his reading of the late Husserl in the 1950s show him at work on the foundations on his new ontology. Among these, Claude Lefort (Merleau-Ponty, 2003) presents the Collège de France lecture notes of 1954–1955 on Husserl's concept of *Stiftung* (beginning or "institution," as distinct from Kantian constitution) and on passivity (sleep, the unconscious, memory, dream), to show a re-working of Husserl's idea of sense as "sedimentation" or deposition. These notes show understanding emerging over time through multiple, aleatory, converging selections that make up reception with its unpredictable switches and conflicts.

Leonard Lawlor (Merleau-Ponty, 2002) analyses the later 1959–1960 lecture notes on Husserl's *The Origin of Geometry* in terms of their comparative study of Husserl and Heidegger regarding the nature of coming-to-be. For Husserl this is genesis of sense: for Heidegger, advent of being; for Merleau-Ponty, Husserl's idea of *Verflechtung* (interrelation, entwinement) is "inaugural," originary. Over the decade his rethinking of the philosophy of nature is seeking the fine point of coming-to-be.

Through his term *intertwinement* the concepts of flexibility, change and conflict in time, as well as the genesis of being and meaning, unite science and philosophy in an ontology that connects emergence with uncertainty. Perceiver and perceived are interrelated in a dynamic process.

The correlation of the physical and psychic worlds

Two psychological monographs connect Merleau-Ponty's interest in human development to the "I can" of *Phenomenology of Perception*. *Consciousness and the Acquisition of Language* from the Sorbonne lectures on child psychology reviews studies of language and concludes that the child's imitation of others' speech is not the result of copying or identifying with others. On the contrary, it *produces* identification. Like nature, speech "must be considered as a total structure, a system by which one can attain communication with others . . . I exist through language in a relationship with others" (CAL 68).

"The Child's Relation with Others" (PRI 96–155), reworked from lectures of the early 1950s, covers affective development and sense of one's body up to the age of three: learning one's name and using it, and perceiving oneself in a mirror in relation to the family group. The essay takes up a major observational and theoretical synthesis by Henri Wallon (1931) that brought together a half century's clinical research. For Merleau-Ponty saying one's name and learning one's identity spring, like the acquiring of speech, not from simple copying, but from action, desire, intersubjectivity, and reciprocity. From the experience of one's body to relating with others via the "I can" in speech, the child builds his world, a world that is the basis of the adult one.

The essay is contemporary with the late Collège de France lectures on Freud. Tracing its implications as psychology's contribution to the ontology of nature we can first note the child's building the world from the place of his own body, then Merleau-Ponty's establishing that this identity springs from action. Underscoring this view in the psychoanalytic theme itself, he writes in his Preface to Hesnard's *L'Oeuvre de Freud* (1960/1993, 67): "Freudian thought confirms phenomenology in its description of a consciousness that is not so much knowledge or representation as investment." Investment involves purpose, wish, self-interest. In the context of a philosophy of nature that is centred on the reciprocity of perceiver and perceived, of perceiver and sayer, speaker and agent, it is this reciprocity as *action* that gives shape to the world. In 1960, Merleau-Ponty also made a noted intervention on theoretical formulation at the conference on the Unconscious organized at Bonneval by the dynamic psychiatrist Henri Ey, leading Ey to comment in the *Proceedings* (Ey 1966, 143) on the energy of this intervention that gave no hint of approaching death. According to the reporter, J-B. Pontalis, Merleau-Ponty replaced a dualist notion—conscious/unconscious—with a continuous one based on Kant's concept of "negative magnitudes." If we pair this note with the Collège de France study of Husserl's *Stiftung* or "institution" outlined above we again see his psychodynamic research working in harmony with his philosophy of nature.

Following this philosophy across its development through observational and dynamic psychology, it is evident that for Merleau-Ponty nature is not a given. Our relating what we experience to our sense of our identity originates in childhood with acts that express our power to be. This interrelation is what his late work expresses by terms such as *intertwining, chiasm,* and *Flesh.*

Marcel Gauchet (1997, 202) glosses "flesh" as "the continuous living tissue of the world." It is remarkable that the discoveries in Merleau-Ponty's lifetime—of relativity and quantum mechanics; new thinking in psychology, the social sciences, and linguistics; the explosion of psychoanalytic thinking in France; and the flowering of post-Impressionist art where he was inspired by the work of Cézanne—all exemplify the ontology that he works to articulate. The coincidence of exceptional developments in the sciences and arts with the penetration of his mind forms a particular historical moment, a high point of modernity. This period also saw the creation of postwar organizations aiming at a restabilised world: at peace, disarmament, and international justice; health, and education; the elimination of poverty, financial stability, and development.

MERLEAU-PONTY AND ACTION

Merleau-Ponty's philosophy rearticulates "Nature" as the converse of human perception, reconstituting it as interconnection and coming-to-be. His first published book, *The Structure of Behaviour*, combines a study of empirical psychology with underlying reflection on Husserl's idea of "passivity" as inaugural beginning of thought. This allows him to identify action as a "progressive and discontinuous structuration" (SC 177), and to end by pointing to his work to come: ". . . all the problems . . . touched on are reducible to the problem of perception."

Two postwar works of political philosophy, *Humanism and Terror* (1947) and *Adventures of the Dialectic* (1955), deal like Husserl's *Krisis* (1936), with rupture in the human-natural bond. *Humanism and Terror* analyses the collapse of Resistance hopes and solidarity in France. Its center is "the relations between men" and the power of thinking to go beyond a society's "basic structure to the human bond upon which it is built." This bond "depends upon legal relations, but also upon forms of labor, ways of loving, living, and dying" (HT xiv). Perception as action, and action as interconnectedness, are the conceptual hinge that allows for a redescription of the world.

Merleau-Ponty's problematic of action

In extending his thinking to political philosophy, Merleau-Ponty joins the influence of Husserl and the sciences to that of Hegel and Marx which he also comes to question. *Humanism and Terror* formulates the postwar crisis as "an inextricable situation . . . The Marxist critique of capitalism is defined as still valid, and it is clear that anti-Sovietism today resembles the brutality, *hybris,* vertigo and anguish that already found expression in fascism. On the other side, the Revolution has come to a halt . . ." (HT xv). A conceptual shock, this recognition of the end of the revolution (for French thinkers the French Revolution—their own historic triumph over oppression—as well as the Russian Revolution with its early promise) gives rise to the term "a dislocated world" (ibid., 187). This dislocation is the "truth"—the philosophical justification—of his reply to Koestler's (1942) Cold War dualism.

Adventures of the Dialectic, more developed conceptually, groups articles published in *Les Temps modernes* on the crisis of Marxism in the postwar years. If "the Marxist critique of capitalism is still valid" (AD 3) a philosophy of both history and spirit is needed to deal with the problems touched upon. The book's middle section shows communism's progressive self-distancing from the historical dialectic it started with, while the last chapter condemns Sartre's support for Soviet Stalinism, marking the historic break between the two friends. Its polemic relies on the argument that, as both theory and action of liberation, Marxism has misunderstood and abandoned its own history, and even its very *understanding* of history derived from Hegel. Merleau-Ponty concludes "What remains of the dialectic if one must give up reading history and deciphering in it the becoming-true of society?" (AD 204).

Merleau-Ponty's insistence on "understanding" rather than "dogmatism" is crucial here. Husserl's *Krisis* had shown the European crisis as that of the "sciences." Accordingly, Merleau-Ponty portrays understanding as the basic concept of social science. Rephrasing Husserl, he opens with "The Crisis of Understanding" on the work of Max Weber, "a liberal" who "admits that truth always leaves a margin of doubt" (AD 9). Weber goes beyond Marxist theory and "demonstrates under what conditions a historical dialectic is serious" (ibid., 29).

For Merleau-Ponty, Weber's demonstration has a threefold strength. First, his critique of capitalism provides a deeper source for Marxist principles than the worn-out dialectic. It penetrates to the social meaning of an apparently objective economic system so as to show capitalism in its *origin.* This origin is more than a simple developmental chronology via the evolution of medieval "nonventure capitalism": it is the historical moment when "the maturity of Puritanism" encountered that of preexisting economic structure, allowing "transition from one to the other" and revealing to later observers "a certain logical structure which is the key to a whole series of other facts." Capitalism's origin is thus not just an aspect of a determinist historical structure but a unique coming-to-be: "(N)o other civilization has a theology which sanctifies daily labor, organizes a worldly asceticism, and joins the glory of God to the transformation of nature . . . (O)nce crystallized in the world by the Protestant ethic, capitalism will develop according to its own logic . . ." (AD 15).

Second, Weber allows Merleau-Ponty's central operative concepts of "truth and freedom" (AD 9) to relate thought to action. Not only capitalism, but other Marxist principles as well are rooted in unique experience. The emancipation of oppressed workers is inspired by an underlying reality, "our irreplaceable life, our fierce freedom" (ibid., 11). Since freedom is paired with truth from the start of the essay (ibid., 3), the great principle of the Revolution is potentially a doubtful one. "(Weber) is against the revolution because he does not consider it to be revolution—that is to say, the creation of a historical whole. He describes it as essentially a military dictatorship" (ibid., 25)—the contradiction of the freedom it proclaims. For Weber a leader who aims at a historical whole "makes truth work together with decision, knowledge with struggle . . . he makes sure that repression is never justified in the name of freedom" (ibid., 26–27). Political truth is not assured by doctrine or possessed by those at the top. It is unique to each situation, and a key phrase states that it is only known by perception after the event: "In politics truth is this art of understanding what will appear to have been required by the time" (ibid., 29).

Third and last, Weber transmits to the Cold War world Husserl's theme of the "institution," or primary conceiving, of human experience as a coming-to-be:

> (History's) meaning arises in contact with contingency, at the moment when human initiative founds a system of life by taking up anew scattered givens. And the historical understanding which reveals an interior to history still leaves us in the present of empirical history, with its density and its haphazardness, and does not subordinate it to any hidden reason. Such is the philosophy without dogmatism which one discerns all through Weber's studies. (AD 16)

Where Merleau-Ponty's philosophy of nature describes the coherence he finds in interrelation, his philosophy of action addresses his perception of disruption. On this point I would disagree with Castoriadis (1997, 310) who, though he too recognizes a dislocated or "fragmented" world, claims that Merleau-Ponty lacks "an ontology of genesis." On the contrary, Merleau-Ponty's extension of Husserl through Weber's operative use of "understanding" hinges on just such an ontology of genesis that includes action in the world. His philosophy of action develops from Husserl's idea of possibility and origin and is completely consistent with his philosophy of nature. His exposure of dislocation transmits Husserl's critique to the postwar age.

However this ontology of genesis requires him to confront a further problem. How can a philosophy with neither dogmatism nor dualism account for negativity inherent in nature through human action such as destruction and oppression?

Nature and action

Here we return to "The Child's Relations with Others." Providing a third conceptual crisis—the "three-year-old crisis" when children move into reciprocity with adult life—it links Henri Wallon's study to the work of Piaget and Freud, to end with the passage on love noted above (1960/1984, 154–155). Wallon had discussed the three-year-old's struggles with adults with regard to gifts, lying, and shame. These struggles raised the issue of separateness and "indistinction between me and the other."

In "The Child's Relations with Others," Merleau-Ponty asks about love and freedom:

> Could one conceive of a love that would not be an encroachment of the freedom of the other? If a person wanted in no way to exert an influence on the person he loved and consequently refrained from choosing on her behalf or advising her or influencing her in any way, he would act on her precisely by that abstention… There is a paradox in accepting love from a person without wanting to have any influence on her freedom. If one loves, one finds one's freedom precisely in the act of loving, and not in a vain autonomy. (PRI 154)

This leads him to reflect on questions of sharing and identity, and of sureness about others' feelings toward me, with a consequent risk of pathological demand: "The ensnaring love of the child is the love that never has enough proofs, and ends by imprisoning and trapping the other in its immediacy" (PRI 155).

Merleau-Ponty extends love's uncertainty beyond the question of a child's maturation to adults:

> . . . all relations with others, if deep enough, bring about a state of insecurity, since the doubt we mentioned always remains possible and since love itself creates its own proper truth and reality. The state of union with another, the dispossession of me by the other, are thus not suppressed by the child's arrival at the age of three years. They remain in other zones of adult life. (PRI 155)

In this way the "three-year-old crisis" reveals the logic of interrelatedness throughout life, showing the principles of truth and freedom as fragile.

This brief study is clearly relevant to adult sexual love.[2] However its gender-specific translation into English here reduces its significance for the ontology of emergence and interaction brought out in the previous section. The literally translated pronouns *elle* and *la* of the French text refer to the neutral word *la personne*—a person who may be male or female. An alternative translation might read:

"Someone who would never want to influence a person he loved, and so tried never to make a decision for that person, never give advice or exert influence, would still be doing so through the act of refraining . . ." In this way Merleau-Ponty's study of love extends to all struggles of reciprocity. Human interaction involves unavoidable conflicts and oppression.

Here his philosophy of action expresses the notion of a world dislocated not only by the failure of the Revolution, but by the ambiguity that action must take into account: the "paradox" of interrelation as both empowering and destabilising. Like freedom and truth, love is fragile.

In a far-reaching implication for ecology, this casts doubt on any one-sided solutions to problems of interrelation. Such solutions may include relying on benevolence, cooperation or good will to resolve conflicts, or even on principles such as deep ecology when what is at stake is pragmatic degradation of the environment by human interests. How can such complexity be conceptualized?

William Hamrick (Hoeller 1998, 181) notes that Merleau-Ponty's phenomenological tools enable his work on psychology to describe behavior that is called abnormal or pathological. This is a step forward. Taking this into account, can we bring together the ambiguous aspects of good-will, and the pathological ones that have to be included in thinking about action and public policy?

Charting a philosophy of action

Two articles published between *Humanism and Terror* and *Adventures of the Dialectic* chart Merleau-Ponty's steps towards formulating an answer to this problem. "A Note on Machiavelli" of 1949 (S 211–223) wrestled with the issue of nonsimplistic solutions to power. Those in power "seek to seduce consciousness" so as to practice tyranny, while the people "ask nothing except not to be oppressed." Recognizing Machiavelli's interest as the shift in his time from power as fact, to power as public discourse based on the requirement that those governed accept the power that is over them, he analyses this shift in terms of practical reason or prudence (cf . Garver 1987) that acknowledges the role of force: "What he [Machiavelli] is reproached for is the idea that history is a struggle and politics a rela-tionship to men rather than principles" (S 219).

Myriam Revault d'Allonnes in her study of his political thought (2001, 28) gives particular emphasis to Merleau-Ponty's approval of Machiavelli's image of multiple mirrors illustrating transformations—"of softness into cruelty and harshness into value." As Merleau-Ponty sum-marises:

> As mirrors set around in a circle transform a slender flame into a fairyland, acts of authority reflected in the constellation of con-sciousnesses are transfigured, and the reflections of these reflec-tions create an appearance which is the proper place—the truth, in short—of historical action. (S 216)

Mutual perceptions of the multiple images generated by a circle of mir-rors illustrate the interactive nature of public action, even in harsh regimes. Contemporary with his work on the mirror-experience of the three-year-old, Merleau-Ponty's choice of this example situates the emer-gence of political action in our developing self-awareness through mutual, often conflicting, activity. The political world with its obligations and violence is continuous with the vulnerability and potential "I can" of childhood.[3]

Two years later, the 1951 lecture-discussion "Man and Adversity" (S 224–243) extends the problem of conflict to the "origin" of creative thought itself in describing adversity as the "dead weight" of the "already-thought" that we confront in thinking (Prunair, 2000, 334). In the discussion following this lecture the conservative audience was nonreceptive. The dialogue recalls both Merleau-Ponty's use of Machiavelli's multiple perceptions, and the understanding gained from Weber that in dealing with public issues, truth is what will later "appear to have been required by the time."

Conclusion

The idea of ecology, not explicit in Merleau-Ponty's generation, belongs centrally within his philosophy of the complexity of perception, and interperception, of the world. I have presented this under two aspects: his philosophy of nature, well explicated in works on his ontology, and his philosophy of action on which studies are now appearing.

From theory, to issues of public process, understanding, and the handling of conflict, this philosophy develops consistently from his earliest work to his late essays, where a firm reply of 1958 to a question on French Algeria speaks to us now:

It is said, and it is true, that torture is *the* answer to terrorism. This does not justify torture. We ought to have acted in such a way that terrorism would not have arisen. (S 328)

Though within the logic of pragmatism torture is, as it always has been, the answer-riposte to terrorism, Merleau-Ponty shows in *Adventures of the Dialectic* that the criterion for social action is "the becoming-true of society." Thus pragmatism as stimulus-response is not self-justifying.

At stake in his philosophy of action, as in his ontology of nature, is the view of an interrelated world that includes diversity we do not yet understand, and consequent need for a matching politicocultural discourse. Machiavelli's example of an interrelating circle of mirrors shows such discourse arising from mutual reflections of multiplicity. Merleau-Ponty's audience's reaction to his lecture "Man and Adversity" showed that bringing about such new understanding is a precarious task. Like the aleatory, intertwined processes of nature described in the Merleau-Ponty and

Nature section above, and the ambiguity inherent in human reciprocity, our intervening in the processes of a "dislocated" ecology will be uncertain. Ecological dynamics is not a matter of simple cause and effect, violence and counterviolence. Assessable only in the future within "the becoming-true of society," it is a reflective and active process resulting in "what will appear to have been required by the time."

NOTES

1. A sophisticated discussion of the objectivism-subjectivism issue in the debate between the natural and human sciences is the article by Clifford Geertz "The Strange Estrangement: Taylor and the Natural Sciences," in the Festschrift volume edited by James Tully : *Philosophy in an Age of Pluralism: The Philosophy of Charles Taylor in Question*. Cambridge: Cambridge University Press, 1994.

2. The work of Simone de Beauvoir, and Bair's (1990, 147, 468) biography of her, show that over the years Merleau-Ponty discussed sexual love with her and Sartre in terms of its potential for oppression. His essay takes the discussion to its wider implications, though without completing the argument as affecting his philosophy overall. That is a loss to us, since Sartre remained unable to go beyond dualism. His reply to Merleau-Ponty's critique, in the Obituary that he wrote for him (1965), ends with the words: "this is how men love—badly," a phrase limited neither to men nor to a "romantic" reading, but trapped by pessimism.

3. It can be noted in passing how different such robust recognition of conflict and interaction is from later interpretations of the mirror-image by Baudrillard (1983) and others as endless and futile iteration.

REFERENCES

Abram, David. 1988/1996. "Merleau-Ponty and the Voice of the Earth." In David Macauley, ed. 1996. *Minding Nature: The Philosophers of Ecology*. New York, London: The Guilford Press.

Agamben, Giogio. 2002/2004. "Umwelt." In *Open*. Stanford: Stanford University Press.

Bair, Deirdre. 1991. *Simone de Beauvoir: a Biography*. New York: Simon and Schuster.

Bateson, Gregory. 1973. *Steps to an Ecology of Mind*. St. Albans: Granada Publishing Limited, Paladin Books.

Baudrillard, J. 1983. *Simulations*. New York: Semiotext(s).

Castoriadis, Cornelius. 1997. *World in Fragments: Writings on Politics, Society, Psychoanalysis, and the Imagination*. Edited and translated by David Ames Curtis. Stanford, California: Stanford University Press.

Dillon, Martin C. 1989. "Merleau-Ponty and the Reversibility Thesis." In Henry Pietersma, *Merleau-Ponty, Critical Essays*. Washington, DC: The Center for Advanced Research in Phenomenology and University Press of America.

Edie, James M. 1964. Introduction to Maurice Merleau-Ponty. *The Primacy of Perception And Other Essays*.

Ey, Henri. 1966. *L'Inconscient* (VIe Colloque de Bonneval) sous la direction de Henri Ey. Paris: Bibliothèque Neuro-Psychiatrique de Langue Française. Desclée de Brouwer.

Garver, Eugene. 1987. *Machiavelli and the History of Prudence*. Wisconsin: The University of Wisconsin Press.

Gauchet, Marcel. 1997. *The Disenchantment of the World: A Political History of Religion*. Translated by Oscar Burge; with a foreword by Charles Taylor. Princeton, NJ: Princeton University Press.

Geertz, Clifford. 1994. "The Strange Estrangement: Taylor and the Natural Sciences," in James Tully. *Philosophy in an Age of Pluralism. The Philosophy of Charles Taylor in Question*. Cambridge: Cambridge University Press.

Hamrick, William. S. 1994. "Language and Abnormal Behaviour: Merleau-Ponty, Hart and Laing," in Keith Hoeller, ed. *Merleau Ponty and Psychology*. Atlantic Highlands, NJ: Humanities Press International.

Kant, Immanuel. 1787/1978. *Immanuel Kant's Critique of Pure Reason,* Translated by Norman Kemp Smith. London: The Macmillan Press.

Koestler, Arthur. 1940/1964. *Darkness at Noon*. Translated by Daphne Hardy. Harmondsworth: Penguin.

Lawlor, Leonard. 2002. *Husserl at the Limits of Phenomenology: Including Texts by Edmund Husserl, Maurice Merleau-Ponty*. Edited by Leonard Lawlor with Bettina Bergo. Evanston, ILL: Northwestern University Press.

Merleau-Ponty, Maurice. 1960/1993. "Phenomenology and Psychology," in Hoeller, Keith (ed.). 1994. *Merleau Ponty and Psychology*. Atlantic Highlands, NJ: Humanities Press International.

———. 2001 *Psychologie et pédagogie de l'enfant, Cours de Sorbonne 1949–1952*. Edition établi par Jacques Prunair. Paris: Editions Verdier.

———. 2003 *L'Institution dans l'histoire personnelle et publique: le problème de la passivité, le sommeil, l'inconscient, la mémoire: notes de cours au Collège de France, 1954–55;* textes établis par Dominique Darmaillacq, Claude Lefort et Stéphanie Melnasel; preface de Claude Lefort. Paris: Belin.

Morley, James. 1999. "Afterword," in Dorothera Olkowski and James Morley (eds.) *Merleau-Ponty: Interiority and Exteriority, Psychic Life and the World*. Albany: State University of New York Press.

Paci, Enzo. 1958/2000. "Introduzione a *Elogio della filosofia*," *Chiasmi 2*, Milano: Vrin, Mimesis, University of Memphis.

Prunair, Jacques. 2000. Maurice Merleau-Ponty *Parcours deux*. 1951–1961. Paris: Editions Verdier.

———. 2001. Maurice Merleau-Ponty. *Psychologie et pédagogie de l'enfant, Cours de Sorbonne 1949–1952*. Edition établi par Jacques Prunair. Paris: Editions Verdier.

Revault d'Allonnes, Myriam. 2001. *Merleau-Ponty. La Chair du politique*. Paris: Editions Michalon.

Ricoeur, Paul. 1961/1992. "Hommage à Merleau-Ponty" in *Lectures II*. Paris: Editions du Seuil.

Sartre, Jean-Paul. 1965. "Merleau-Ponty" in *Situations*. Translated from the French by Benita Eisler. London: Hamish Hamilton.

Uexküll, J. von. 1926. *Theoretical Biology*. Translated by D. L. MacKinnon. International Library of Psychology, Philosophy and Scientific Method. London: Kegan Paul, Trench, Trubner & Co.

Wallon, Henri. 1931. "Comment se développe chez l'enfant la notion du corps proper," in *Journal de Psychologie*. Republished in Wallon, Henri. 1949/1987. *Les Origines du caractère chez l'enfant*. Paris: Presses Universitaires de France.

Whitehead, A. N. 1933. *Science and the Modern World*. Cambridge: Cambridge University Press.

13

Merleau-Ponty's Transversal Geophilosophy and Sinic Aesthetics of Nature

Hwa Yol Jung

In memory of Petee
Only connect!

—E. M. Forster

PRELUDE

At stake is the Earth in its totality, and humanity, collectively. Global
history enters nature, global nature enters history: this is something
utterly new in philosophy.

—Michel Serres

Ecology has rightly become our ultimate concern. It has a religious
magnitude. It has turned into the question of *"to be* or *not to be."* The
ecological crisis persists: there is no waning sign to it. It is a permanent
fixture of the human condition everywhere. Alarmingly this earth, our
dwelling place, has progressively become an inhospitable, precarious,
ruinous, and even deadly place for all earthlings both large and small,
human and nonhuman. The ancient Hindu scriptural saying of *Bha-
gavad Gita* captures the dire predicament of the earthly condition
today: "I am become death." Indeed, we stand at the edge of history
since the end of the earth or nature *is* also the end of history. Is there
then a saving measure on earth to overcome our human-induced ecological crisis?

The ecological crisis signals human disembodiment from the earth as a "household" (*oikos*) whose "deed" is being taken away by nature's mutiny or silent revolt. In sinography, *crisis* is spelled with two ideograms: *danger* and *opportunity*. It means to seize an "opportunity" to save a situation from "danger." To overcome the ecological crisis, we are in need of inaugurating a geophilosophy grounded in fundamentals which, according to Deleuze and Guattari, "brings together all the elements within a single embrace" (1994, 85)—only in fundamentals since, in following the advice of Einstein, not everything that counts can be counted. Merleau-Ponty's ontology or "there-being" ("*il y a*") of intercorporeality establishes and secures the firm foothold in such fundamentals for erecting the edifice of geophilosophy *as if the earth really matters*.[1] Only by way of his intercorporeal ontology, are humanity and the earth said to be bonded or intertwined. Without doubt the intercorporeal "generosity" (see Diprose 2002, 190) of the whole earth will be a promising and defining moment of humanity in the new millennium.

THE WAY OF TRANSVERSALITY

[T]hinking about One is not thinking about All.

—Edouard Glissant

Transversality is meant to be a term of connectivity, of lateral connectivity. It makes "connections in the face of difference" in the environment in which everything is connected to everything—the principle of which is called by the biologist Barry Commoner "the first law of ecology" (1971, 33).[2] Difference marks the *conditio sine qua non* of connectivity. Difference and connectivity are correlative: but for difference, there would be no need for connectivity. Akira Kurozawa's famed film *Rashomon* portrays the reality that truth or truth-telling is diverse and thus search for it, too, is truly "an adventure of difference" (Gianni Vattimo's phrase).

Transversality is the term used in geometry (as well as in physics) that refers to the two diagonally connecting lines of any parallelogram. Félix Guattari, who was drawn to what he calls "ecosophy" in resonance with the Norwegian "ecosopher" Arne Naess, proposed transversality as a new way of thinking about the "politics" of psychiatric institutions (see 1972, 72–85 and 1984, 11–23, and see also Genosko 2000). Transversality, for Guattari, *interrupts* the idea of "the institutional transference" and allows "undisciplined creativity" (*chaosmosis* in Joyce's term), which means to prevent us from falling into *seriality* (Sartrean term) and "bureaucratic sclerosis." It is a genre of "social creationism" in a multidimensional environment in which the individual subject, too, is conceived of "polyphonically."

For Calvin Schrag (1997), transversality is the new way of overcoming the impasses of modernity and postmodernity. In other words, it is the way of defining or redefining the task of philosophy *after* postmodernity. His transversal shifter is meant to scale the continental divide between modernity and postmodernity and intends to dissolve, as it were, their differences. By way of transversality, Schrag means to subvert and transgress the dichotomy between "the Scylla of a hegemonic unification"/"a vacuous universalism" on the one hand and "the Charybdis of a chaotic pluralism"/"an anarchic historicism" on the other (cf. Jung 1995).

The relevance of Merleau-Ponty's "lateral universal" (S 120) to cross-cultural geophilosophy cannot be underestimated. He uses "lateral" and "transversal" interchangeably. In opposition to the Eurocentrism of Hegel for whom universal knowledge is certified by the Occidental seal of approval alone, Merleau-Ponty insists that the Oriental past also has an honored place in the famed hall of philosophies to celebrate its hitherto "secret, muted contribution to philosophy" (S 140).[3] He contends that Western philosophy can learn from Indian and Chinese philosophies to rediscover our relationships to Being. He challenges: "If Western thought is what it claims to be [universal], it must prove it by understanding all 'life-worlds'" (S 138). It would indeed be presumptuous to claim that what is particular in the West is universalizable, whereas what is particular in the non-West remains particular or ethnophilosophical. For Merleau-Ponty, the "lateral universal" is acquired through ethnological experience by testing transversally one culture by way of the other and vice versa. It is a passport, as it were, that allows us to cross borders between diverse cultures, enter the zone of intersections, and discover cross-cultural connections in pursuit of truth. It, in short, promotes the cross-fertilization of ideas and deeds by negotiating differences and facilitates the confluence of differences. While Eurocentrism claims its validity as universal truth, Merleau-Ponty's "lateral universal" takes into account "local knowledge" before global or planetary knowledge by espousing the Gadamerian "hermeneutical autonomy" of the other who may very well be right. Thus, it demands an open and unending dialogue as an end in itself. It opens up the uninterrupted flow of cultural dialogue based on difference or, in the terminology of Heidegger, *Differenz* as

Unterschied, which may be neither reified nor erased, neither assimilated nor annihilated, but negotiated and compromised (com/promised) (Chakrabarty 2002, 140). As "an adventure of difference," the transversal dialogue, like a Zen garden, which allows no dialectical closure, is never finished or—as Mikhail Bakhtin's dialogism has it—is "unfinalizable."

Transversality is, in a manner of speaking, a phoenix rising from the ashes of universality wedded to Eurocentrism. By decentering or deprovincializing Eurocentrism, it may be spelled "trans(uni)versality"; it intends to go beyond and transfigure the Eurocentric metanarratives of universality. As a paradigm shift in our thinking, it may be likened to a *lateral* movement of digging a new hole instead of digging the same hole deeper and deeper with no exit in sight. Michel Foucault's lateral projection may have been right when he remarked in his dialogue with a Japanese priest in 1978: "The crisis of Western thought is identical to the end of imperialism . . . [I]t is the end of the era of Western philosophy. Thus, if philosophy of the future exists, it must be born outside of Europe or equally born in consequence of meetings and impacts between Europe and non-Europe" (1999, 110–114).

As a paradigm shifter in our thinking and doing, transversal geophilosophy, no less than transversality itself, is analogous to the famous wooden statue of Buddha at a Zen temple in Kyoto whose face marks the dawn of "enlightenment" (*satori*) or signals the beginning of a new regime of knowing and morals. From the crack in the *middle* of the old face in the Buddha's statue, there emerges an interstitial, liminal face that signifies a new transformation. Since the new face emerges from the middle, it also symbolizes the arrival of Maitreya (i.e., the future "enlightened" One) or Maitreyan *Middle Way.*[4] Thus the "new face" of transversal geophilosophy points to the emergence of the "middle" or "third" term, which mediates and facilitates (1) cultural, (2) disciplinary, (3) speciesistic, and (4) sensorial border-crossings. In other words, it is concerned with those matters that are intercultural, interdisciplinary, interspeciesistic, and intersensorial border-crossings.

Intercorporeality and Geophilosophy

Body am I entirely, and nothing else; and soul is only a word of something about the body.

—Friedrich Nietzsche

For twenty-five centuries, Western knowledge has tried to look upon
the world. It has failed to understand that the world is not for the
beholding. It is for hearing. It is not legible, but audible.

—Jacques Attali

The Enlightenment contains the principal ethos of Western modernity. Its
unbridled optimism, which awakened (Western) humanity from the
slumber, as Kant put it with clarity, of self-incurred tutelage or immatu-
rity, has promoted the idea of infinite progress based on the cultivation of
pure (Cartesian) and instrumental (Baconian) Reason which spells out the
lingua franca of Western modernity. While privileging and valorizing Reason above all the other human faculties for allegedly human, material
progress, and emancipation, European modernity marginalizes and disem-
powers the (Reason's) other whether it be (1) nature, (2) body, (3) woman,
or (4) non-West (see Jung, 2002), all of whose categories are genderized
interestingly as feminine.

Descartes erected the canonical institution of the *cogito,* which is by
necessity disembodied, monological/narcissistic, and ocularcentric. He
built an epistemological Panopticon[5] whose influence at least in France
has been so extensive that Deleuze and Guattari declare: "The French are
like landowners whose source of income is the cogito" (1994, 104). As it is
the act of the mind as "thinking substance" (*res cogitans*), the *cogito* (the "I
think") is the epitome of an incorporeal man in splendid isolation from
others, both other minds and other bodies. As a thinking substance, the
mind claims to be independent of the body (*res extensa*); it needs nothing
other than itself to exist. Once the self and the other are viewed as disembodied substances, two self-contained substances, monologism—or even
solipsism in extremis—is inevitable. Merleau-Ponty puts it succinctly:
"Sociality . . . is a scandal for the 'I think'" (1973, 155). In geophilosophy,
sociality refers to both interhuman and interspeciesistic relationships.

Francis Bacon (see 1955) is unquestionably the most eloquent and
"Enlightened" voice of Western modernity as the age of science, technology,
and quantitative economy. He advocated the convergence of theory and
practice, of knowledge and utility, and of knowing and making. Experimentalism, the utility of knowledge, power over nature, and philanthropia,
when combined together, become a paradigmatic attempt to replace the old
"cult of books" by the new (experimental) "cult of nature" or the "inquisi-
tion of nature," which promotes the "direct commerce of the mind with
things" themselves. He formulated the principles of *Herrschaftswissen* in

which knowledge and power converge for the sake of utility. The framework of modern technology was laid down by Bacon when he insisted on the meeting of human knowledge and power in one (i.e., *scientia et potentia in idem coincidunt*) and discovered "in the womb of nature many secrets of excellent use." Speaking against the "degenerate learning" of Scholastics, Bacon felt that they had "sharp and strong wits" and "abundance of leisure" in "the cells of monasteries and colleges" but they knew little history of nature or "no great quantity of matter," that is, their "cobwebs of learning" produced "no substance or profit."

Enough has so far been said about the grand narratives of European modernity in the language of the Cartesian bifurcation of mind and body and the Baconian domination and exploitation by humanity of nature. Merleau-Ponty, however, offers a radically different scenario in terms of the lived body or embodiment, which is not only the "umbilical cord" to the world both social and natural but also the "stage director," as it were, of the body. He speaks of the lived body as "the zero point of orientation" that serves as the "canon" or "norm" of perception (1965, 262). The body founds and funds perception as a web of the human sensorium. There is indeed the "primacy of perception" in everything we do and think. To cite the often-quoted passage of Merleau-Ponty in defense of his main philosophical thesis of *Phenomenology of Perception*: "The perceived world is the always presupposed foundation of all rationality, all value and all existence. This thesis does not destroy either rationality or the absolute. It only tries to bring them down to earth" (PRI, 13).[6] Not only are all forms of consciousness perceptual or earthly perception, but also "the perceived world promises [transversal] *relations*" (1973, 13, italics added). Insofar as perception is a "nascent logos," there can be neither "disembodied reason" nor alienation of humanity from nature.

For Merleau-Ponty, to perceive natural things in the world is to sense them as they are through embodied consciousness, to sense the (*sauvage*, "wild") nakedness of nature. The act of perception as embodied consciousness is then neither representation nor idea. Rather, perception participates in or inhabits each reality it senses. It intertwines or interlaces the flesh of the body and the flesh of the world: the body and the world form one inseparable flesh-fold. Marjorie Grene is perceptive when she writes: "it is always as lived bodies that we sing the world, maybe out of key, maybe forgetfully, maybe with ingenious novelty, but really, in the flesh" (1980, 378).

Only in terms of the body as the participatory locus of perception do we come to grips with Merleau-Ponty's deep notion that the world is made of the same stuff as the body or "my body is made of the same flesh as the world (it is a perceived)" (VI, 248). In each act of perception, the body participates in the world. Each perception is an instance or moment of the sensuous unity, and it is enclosed in the synergic work of the body, that is, intersensorial. The body is the carnal field in which perception becomes localized as seeing, hearing, smelling, touching, and tasting this or that particular. Merleau-Ponty, therefore, contends: "la conscience perceptive n'est pas une alchimie mentale, elle est globale, totale" ("perceptive consciousness is not a mental alchemy; it is global, total"), that is, synergic (1965, 260). The synergic organization of perceptual acts is unimaginable without one of the most important discovery of phenomenology: the lived body or the body as subject. The body as subject is never an inert matter or mass but rather a sentient subject. As such the body as flesh is capable of "authoring" the world first before "answering" it. Thus, Merleau-Ponty writes with a touch of eloquence: "Mon corps n'est pas un objet, mais un moyen, une organisation. J'organise dans la perception avec mon corps une fréquentation avec le monde. Avec mon corps et par mon corps, j'habite le monde. Le corps est le *champ* dans lequel se localisent les perceptions" ("My body is not an object, but a means, an organization. In perception I organize with my body an association with the world. With my body and through my body, I inhabit the world. The body is the *field* in which perceptions localize themselves.") (1965, 261; italics added).

The body is an "earthword" as much as the earth is a "bodyword." The body and the earth inscribe each other in/as one flesh-fold. As such the body is quintessentially a place name, a name of location. The feminist Rosi Braidotti describes it concisely: "the primary site of location is the body" (1994, 238). One does not have to be a woman or feminist to be vindicated by Braidotti. The Anglo-Saxons knew the body as dwelling place and they named it *banhus* (bonehouse) and *lichama* (bodyhome) (Mairs 1989, 7). In locating the identity and humanity of African Americans, Ralph Ellison begins his narratives in purely carnal terms in his classic work *The Invisible Man:* "I am a man of substance, of flesh and bone, fiber and liquids—and I might even be said to possess a mind. I am invisible . . . simply because they refuse to see me" (1982, 3).

Merleau-Ponty's conception of the body as flesh is radically and preeminently geophilosophical across the measured template of time and space: to cite his celebrated passage: "(the body as) flesh is not matter, is not mind, is not substance. To designate it, we should need the old term 'element,' in the sense it was used to speak of water, air, earth, and fire, that is, in the sense of a *general thing* [*chose*], midway between the spatio-temporal individual and the idea, a sort of incarnate principle that brings a style of being wherever there is a fragment of being. The flesh is in this sense an element of Being. Not a fact or a sum of facts, and yet adherent to *location* and to the *now*" (VI 139–140). Inasmuch as an "element" is matter (*chose*), the body is said to be the *material condition* of our being-in-the-world or *l'intermonde*. There is no "thing" which does not occupy space. Only by way of the body are we said to be connected to the world which is both interhuman and interspeciesistic: as we are *social* through and through, intercorporeality is nothing other than that term which expresses our primordial and primary way of connecting or socializing ourselves to the world which is inhabited by other bodies, other minds, and other things. The body, in other words, is our *primum relationis* in which it and world are correlational: one cannot exist without the other. The mind itself becomes a term of relation only because the body is always already populated in the world with and among other bodies. Intercorporeality inscribes what Pierre Bourdieu calls "the performative magic of the social," which partakes of "*le sens pratique*" (1990, 57), not of "disembodied reason."

By the synergy of the body, Merleau-Ponty means to emphasize the transversal "circulation"[7] of the senses, that is, the intersensorium or intersensoriality. As the "sensible sentient" (*sentant sensible*), the "two dimensional" body is the chiasmic coupling of the sensible and the sentient. There is the synergic sociality of all the senses. As Merleau-Ponty describes it:

> We must habituate ourselves to think that every visible is cut out in the tangible, every tactile being in some manner promised to visibility, and that there is encroachment, infringement, not only between the touched and the touching, but also between the tangible and the visible, which is encrusted in it, as, conversely, the tangible itself is not a nothingness of visibility, is not without visual existence. *Since the same body sees and touches, visible and tangible belong to the same world.* (VI 134; italics added)

Therefore, the transversal movement or circulation of the sensorium cannot be painted with one particular sense along by disallowing the other senses to "inter-be" with each other and thus by ending in reductive abstraction against which Merleau-Ponty warns from *The Structure of Behavior* to *The Visible and the Invisible*. This reductive abstraction is a

Cartesian trap in which everything is streamlined to edify the epistemo-logical Panopticon of the *cogito* which, by being mesmerized by the eye, is turned into a scopic regime and ocularcentric machine. Here we should take heed of Johann Gottfried Herder who, as a cultural pluralist, questions the presentation of reason as "the single summit" of all human cultures in a single sentence: "Is the whole body just one big eye?" (1969, 199). Although vision may be an "exemplar sensible," Merleau-Ponty warns that "there is a fundamental narcissism of all vision" (VI 139). He also cautions the philosopher not to become a "spectator" or, better yet, *"kosmostheoros"* at whose sovereign gaze the world turns into "a panorama." Merleau-Ponty concludes that "a philosophy of reflection which identifies my being with what I think of it" (VI 48) scandalizes "sociality" (1973, 155). He claims that philosophy is in need of direct and immediate contact with the world prior to reflection. To be sure, the world is not something at which we merely gaze, but it is also something we can touch, taste, smell, and hear.

In philosophy, sight is thought of as a "rational" and masculine sense, whereas touch is denigrated to a pariah status as an "irrational" and feminine sense (see Gilman 1991, 29–49). José Ortega y Gasset argues against visual primacy: it would be "a grave mistake" to think that sight is the most important sense of all and that "touch was the original sense from which the others were gradually differentiated" and that "the decisive form of our intercourse with things is in fact touch."[8] Therefore, Ortega claims that "touch and contact are necessarily the most conclusive factor in determining the structure of our world" (1957, 72). Not unlike Merleau-Ponty's interlacing of the sentient body and sensed body as in a hand-shake, Ortega argues for the inseparability and the reversibility of "the body that we touch, and our body with which we touch it" (1957, 72). The synesthesia of touch inseminates and disseminates the sociability of the senses and performs the "magic of the social."

The primary but not exclusive organ of touching is the hand. Rodin's sculptural masterpiece *Cathedral* in which the caressing of two right hands (the "rite" of sociality) incarnates, certifies, and celebrates the "sacrament of coexistence"—to use the elegant expression of Henry G. Bugbee, Jr. (1958, 159).[9] Here I wish to draw attention to the *jouissance* of tickling and being tickled which, again like the handshake, is a reversible phenomenon. It cannot transpire in the absence of the other for the reason that it is a con/tact (*tactus*) sport. This is the reason why one cannot tickle oneself.

In the footsteps of Irigaray and Levinas, Cynthia Willett speaks of "tactile sociality" (1995, 31–47) which begins and comes with the *caress* or *contact* between the mother and the infant. So she declares: "In the beginning is not the word; it is the touch" (1995, 47). Without doubt it is the "natal bond" (Merleau-Ponty's phrase) between the two sentient beings. It is a skin-to-skin or epidermic sociality that is never just "skin-deep." In *The Visible and the Invisible*, Merleau-Ponty has a cryptic instruction to himself: "Do a psychoanalysis of Nature: it is the flesh, the mother" (VI 267). When accent is put on "Nature," "flesh," and "mother," it turns into a "geo-psychoanalysis," that is, Mother Nature and Mother Earth (*Terra Mater, Gaia*), that personifies the caring and nurturing mother. The breast-feeding, which is the privileged rite of the mother, is the contact between the "skin-mouth" and "skin-breast," which is deeper than any other contact we can imagine. Breast-feeding as the biological act of caring instantiates the ethic of care.

We would be remiss if we forget to mention Irigaray's feminist philosophy, which bucks the mainstream or, better yet, "malestream" language of Western philosophy. She is determined to unpack or denigrate monistic "phallogocentrism," which, as vision has emasculated touch, is rooted in "scoptophilism" or the love of sight (see 1985 and Jay 1993, 493–542). By upholding the sense of touch or—to use Merleau-Ponty's expression—"tactile palpation," Irigaray embraces the caress of the two sexes—man and woman. For Irigaray, touch or caress enriches and cultivates the intercorporeal contact of proximity.

Following the thread of Irigaray's thought, it is worth lending our ears to the important and fascinating study of women in Tantric (*Vajrayana*) Buddhism in Nepal and Tibet, of *yogini-tantra* by Miranda Shaw in *Passionate Enlightenment* (1994, 140-178 in particular). Tantric Buddhism eulogizes the body or flesh as an "abode of bliss" or *jouissance*, as it were, by embracing the "jewel" of sexuality or sexual union in which asceticism and celibacy have no place.[10] It "enlightens" the body's passion. Shaw's work presents a gynecological view of Tantrism where *yoginis* or female Tantrics, who are female practitioners of yoga, engage in the teachings and practices of blissful intimacy as a path to enlightenment. However, Shaw contends that the body of *yoginis's* teachings and practices has been overlooked in the West because of the "androcentric bias" of Western (male) scholars and interpreters.

Yoginis revolutionized Buddhism, just as Irigaray's feminist philosophy overturned the "malestream" phallic-logocentric legacy of Western philosophy since Plato, in comprehending the nature of the three *S* words: sensuality, sexuality, and spirituality. No wonder, Irigaray has turned to the East for her philosophical illumination in *Between East and West (Entre Orient et Occident)*, in which she expands the horizon of her "logic" of "two" (or "betweenness") to the East/West connection. Whatever her critics say about the work (see Deutscher 2002, 164–184), it is the journey worth taking, which, I suspect, is far from being finished or completed. She might very well benefit from tossing a peek at Shaw's work as she expands her feminist horizon from corporeal "singularity" to intercorporeal "community" (ashram). The attainment of spiritual enlightenment, according to female Tantrics, is extremely difficult without a male partner. They seek their spiritual illumination in intimate partnership with men, which includes a mixing of sexual fluids. In a relationship with a man, touching and massaging a woman's feet and ingesting a woman's body are also allowed: a man sips, upon request, sexual fluid and menstrual blood from her vulva and licks any part of her body.

In the final analysis, there is a direct geophilosophical or ecological message or lesson to be had in Irigaray's feminist philosophy in conjunction with female Tantrics: The gyn/ecological self is the ecological self par excellence. It is an "earthlink" to the flesh of the world where everythng *touches* everythng else (cf. Sjöö and Mor 1987, 428). In rejecting the facile dichotomy between nature and culture, her "morphology" of *jouissance* and the sociability of the senses in touch connects what she calls "the calendar of the [feminine] flesh" (1991, 170) or "the cyclical character of feminine sexuality" (2002, 46) with the repeated cycle of seasonal changes in nature or the "myth of the eternal return."[11] There is indeed something "jouissanced," if you will, as well as deeply healing and comforting in the repeated refrains of nature in the serene expression of the incomparable American ecofeminist Rachel Carson who writes:

> Those who dwell, as scientists or laymen, among the beauties and mysteries of the earth are never alone or weary of life. Whatever the vexations or concerns of their personal lives, their thoughts can find reserves of strength that will endure as long as life lasts. There is symbolic as well as actual beauty in the migration of the birds, the ebb and flow of the tides, the folded bud ready for the spring. There is something infinitely healing in the repeated refrains of nature—the assurance that dawn comes after night, and spring after the winter. (1965, 88-89)

So does Merleau-Ponty with Paul Valéry listen to and rejoice in "the very voice of the things, the waves, and the forests" (VI 155).

The Eastern Body and Geophilosophy

> He who knows himself and other,
> Will also recognise that East and
> West cannot be separated.
>
> —Johann Wolfgang von Goethe

Silence is appreciated in the East as a priceless jewel. This may be the reason why Asians are called "inscrutable." Foucault was rightly curious about silence, which defines Japanese Zen culture. It may be said that the East is to silence, what the West is to talk. There is the "diacritical" or "hyperdialectical" connection between the East and the West as the inexorable pairing of *yin* and *yang* as complementary, not as a binary opposition.

Norman O. Brown's *Love's Body* has a mystical touch of Taoism and Zen. It is strikingly Eastern. It resonates with the Eastern conception of silence, which is quintessential to the magic of the body's performance(s). For Brown, "silence is the mother tongue" (1966, 264). It "speaks" eloquently. As it "speaks," its deed is performed in silence. As the (m)other tongue, silence has a double meaning: first, the genesis of language lies in silence and second, silence is the other of language or the other language. As a "virgin," silence invaginates language.[12] In the beginning was silence, not the word. Only when the word becomes flesh is there silence. "To recover the world of silence . . . ," Brown sums up with brevity, "is to recover the human body" (1966, 265).

In Sinism, which encompasses Confucianism, Taoism, and Ch'an (Sinicized) and Zen (first Sinicized and then Japanized) Buddhism and blankets the lands of China, Korea, and Japan, there are fortunately or unfortunately no hardheaded logocentrists—like Descartes and Bacon— who separate the mind (*res cogitans*) and the body (*res extensa*), on the one hand and humanity from nature, on the other. In Sinism it is said that there are four human "dignities," which are all bodily postures and movements: standing, walking, lying, and sitting (see Snyder 1990, 99). Among these "dignities," sitting as in *zazen* ("seated meditation") in Zen is best known to the Western audience. Without *zazen*, that is, without meditative "training" (*keiko*) or "cultivation" (*shugyo*) (see Yuasa 1987, 18), there would be no possibility of "enlightenment" (*satori*) which, as a thoroughly embodied phenomenon, may be juxtaposed to the logocentric and disembodied European "Enlightenment." In *zazen,* the body is the "heart" (*kokoro*) and vehicle of meditation and enlightenment. As *hara* (abdomen) is the "heart" of the body, there is the interesting Japanese expression *kufu* which is identified with "thinking with the abdomen" (Suzuki 1959, 104, n. 12). *Kufu*, not unlike Rodin's *The Thinker,* depicts thinking itself as an embodied activity. It comes as no surprise that Dogen Kigen (the founder of Soto Zen),[13] who is the most renowned Japanese carnal hermeneuticist, proclaims the primacy of the body, which is not far apart from Merleau-Ponty's primacy of perception whose locus is none other than the body itself.

The language of ideograms embodies the soul of Sinism. Therefore, it may be called sinography. Language and culture are inseparable twins. Language is a product of culture as much as culture expresses itself by the communicative medium of language: as Merleau-Ponty puts it, what the mind is to the body, thought is to language (1973, 102). They are all intertwined. The American philosopher Ernest Fenollosa (see 1936) is the inventor of "etymosinology" in which the study of things Sinic is correlated to the etymological anatomy of ideograms. Chinese ideography—calligraphy in particular—is a kinetic art: it is the human body in graceful motion. By the same token, calligraphy is kinaesthetic. The Chinese revere the art of calligraphy as much as, if not more than, painting: calligraphy is the ritualized painting of ideograms. In the genealogy of form, calligraphy precedes painting. In very significant measure, Chinese ideography is a choreography of human gestures (including *jen* or the human rendered in its upright posture) and, as a family of signifiers, "a conversation of gestures," which, because of the presence of meaning, is not to be reduced to human physiology. Picasso's *Swimmer* and *Acrobat* are two choreographs of the human body in fluent and rhythmic motion, which approach ideography or calligraphy.[14] They are, in essence, balletic and frolicking anthropograms. Marshall McLuhan, who had the romantic vision of writing his antitypographic treatise (1962) in the ideogrammic medium (with the sensorium of touch as its synesthetic epicenter), thought of—rightly, I think—the Chinese ideogram as "a vortex of corporate energy" (*ch'i*) (see McLuhan and Parker 1968, 183).

Merleau-Ponty would have been delighted to know that the term *lived experience* (*Erlebnis, expérience vécue*) in Japanese phenomenology is translated as *taiken* (*tai/ken*) in two sinograms (*kanji*), "bodily" or "embodied" (*tai*) "experience" (*ken*) (see Yuasa 1987, 48 n). Moreover, the contemporary Chinese philosopher Li Zehou coined the neologism "subjectality" (*zhu/ti/xing*) in distinction to "subjectivity," that is, the former is "embodied" while the latter is "idealized" (1999, 174). The Chinese *ti* and the Japanese *tai* are one and the same sinogram although they sound or are pronounced differently. To Sinicize "subjectivity" (or the body as subject) in Merleau-Ponty's phenomenology is to rename it as "subjectality" to follow the hermeneutical injunction of Confucius for whom the "rectification of names" belongs to the first order of performing moral acts, of speech acts and performing deeds. Third, for Watsuji Tetsuro who still lives, justifiably or not, under the shadow of Nishida Kitaro and wrote an important geophilosophical treatise on the impact of "climate" (*fudo*) (1961) on human civilization, the temporal and spatial difference marks the difference between the East and the West: the East is spatial, whereas the West is temporal. As he is critical of Heidegger's *Daseinsanalyse* in *Being and Time* that is alleged to focus on time rather than space, Watsuji propounds and defends the thesis that the spatiality of the body maps the social and environmental issues. In fact, the body is the connecting tissue of humanity to its environing world both interhuman and interspeciesistic. For Heidegger, the "ex-istential" condition of the human is temporally defined by the ecstatic "in" of *Dasein* as Being-in-the-world (*In-der-Welt-sein*). Watsuji, in contrast, defines the human in terms of the spatial "betweenness" (*aidagara*) as the human itself is spelled *ningen* (*nin/gen* in two sinograms), that is, (the upright pictogram of) "man" (*nin*) and "betweenness" (*gen*) (see 1996, 29–45). For Watsuji, accordingly, the true humanity of humans is located in "betweenness" as spatial relationality. The body is the specific location of human existence (*sonzai*). As the world is inhabited by other bodies or embodied beings, intercorporeality belongs to the frontier of Interbeing. Watsuji speaks of "a *carnal* interconnection" (Yuasa 1987, 47, and see further 37–48) that constitutes the first order of spatial "betweenness" (see Jung 2005).[15]

Sinism, which is expressed in the communicative medium of the corporeal language of ideography, also incorporates a rich corpus of geophilosophy (see Jung 1991). It is rich in the corporeal poetics of topophilia. The Sinic slogan "the body and the land are not two" (but one) is the celebration of the body in defense of the land.[16] The Sinic eco-art called *feng/shui* (geomancy or ideographically spelled "wind"/"water"), which is widely practiced as a conventional art of everyday living even in highly modernized, urbanized Asia, sanctifies and ritualizes the inseparability of humans from the land and the energy (*ch'i*) of the cosmic "elements." The eco-art of *feng shui,* whether it be used in building houses or in planning ancestral burials, means to harmonize human activities with the land, with the cosmic "elements." In the land of Zen where for some even Heidegger appears to be anthropocentric, the aesthetic principle that "small is beautiful" in advancing the conventional lifestyle of simplicity and frugality, the Cartesian and Baconian possession and mastery of nature is unthinkable. The Japanese have perfected the horticultural art of *bonsai,* which began in China. It is no accident that *haiku* poetry was invented in the land of Zen. By economizing words, *haiku,* which is meant to "enshrine words," expresses the feeling of reverence for small creatures and things in nature ("ten-thousand things") in accord with the circulation of the seasons.

The way of Taoism as a geophilosophy is synonymous with the way of *homo ecologicus.* It deflates rather than inflates or magnifies the importance of both the self and the human in conceptualizing the earth or cosmos. It is, in brief, neither egocentric nor anthropocentric. According to the *Tao Te Ching,* there is a "circulation" of "four greatnesses" in the universe: Man, Earth, Heaven, and Tao. Tao is the "mother" of Heaven and Earth or the world:

> In the universe we have four greatnesses, and man is but one.
> Man is in accordance with earth.
> Earth is in accordance with heaven.
> Heaven is in accordance with Tao.
> Tao is in accordance with that which is. (Chang 1975, 71–72)

At the heart of the circulating wheel of the four greatnesses lies "that which is" (*tzu-jan*), "being natural," or "thusness" in the sense of "thisness" or "thatness" in depicting the singularity of a particular thing. As it is spelled with two sinograms, it has a twofold meaning. One is physical in that it refers to myriads of beings and things in nature or "ten-thousand things"—mountains, rivers, animals, trees, plants, and so on. The other, more importantly, is ontological. As "thusness," it signifies the intrinsic and spontaneous (or uncontrolled) propensity of beings and things which may be called "*Natursein*" (see Cho 1987).

In Confucianism, too, there is no absence or lack of geophilosophical ideas. In it, filial piety (interhuman), for example, is connected to geopiety as reverence for "ten thousand things" in nature. The fifteenth-century neo-Confucian philosopher Wang Yang-ming, who yielded considerable influence inside and outside China (in Korea and Japan), declared that "The great man [or sage] regards Heaven, Earth, and the myriad things as one *body*" (1963, 272). The sage's feeling of commiseration for a child falling into a well, his inability to bear the suffering of birds and animals, his feeling of pity for broken and destroyed plants all show his "humanity" or humaneness (*jen*), which is regarded as the highest Confucian virtue, with all the sentients as they together form *one body* as the "sensible sentient"—to use Merleau-Ponty's expression. The feeling of humaneness (*jen*) embraces the sage's feeling of regret even to shattered tiles and stones (Wang 1963, 272). Wang extends the Confucian notion of humaneness to nonhuman things both animate and inanimate and incorporates the body into the mapping of his geophilosophical ideas. Seven centuries earlier, the Confucianist Chang Tsai envisioned in an encompassing way when he wrote the following reputed passage: "Heaven is my father, and earth is my mother, and even such a small creature as I finds an intimate place in their midst. Therefore that which fills the universe I regard as my body and that which directs the universe I consider as my nature. All people are my brothers and sisters, and all things are my companions" (Chan 1963, 497). Indeed, Wang and Chang celebrate the human as quintessentially an earthly being who is interconnected by way of the body with other beings and things on earth.

CODA

> We all stand only together, not only all men, but all things [in harmony].
>
> —Henry G. Bugbee, Jr.

We have for sometime been disenchanted with the ecological condition of the whole earth. We are out of touch with and displaced from our dwelling place called the earth as *oikos*. Reenchanting the earth may be as difficult as repairing a torn spider's web with our fingers—to use the evocative expression of Ludwig Wittgenstein. Nonetheless, disenchantment is a promising precondition for transcendence toward the reenchantment of all earthlings, that is, humans and "ten thousand things" alike.

To sum up: the aim of this essay is to explore Merleau-Ponty's geophilosophy as if the whole earth really matters with an accent on intercorporeality by means of which we humans, as the first principle of ecology dictates, are said to be interconnected to all other earthlings. The heart of Merleau-Ponty's contribution to geophilosophy, I submit, is his carnal ontology that provides us with the earthly comprehension that all relationships necessarily begin with the intercorporeality or interweaving of lived bodies both human and nonhuman. Indeed, intercorporeality is truly an "earthword" which means to "inter-be" with all earthly bodies or "earthbodies"—to borrow Glen Mazis's befitting term (see 2002). The body as flesh, according to Merleau-Ponty, is our *social placement* in the world with other species as well as other humans. As such it is, in essence, the *primum relationis*. Intercorporeality belongs to the first order of Interbeing: but for intercorporeality, there would be no Interbeing. The former is a species of the latter. If the human body is "a boundary symbol" (see Olson 1986), intercorporeality or intercorporeal "betweenness" marks boundary-crossings for the self to "inter-be" with other bodies on earth. All relationships begin first with intercorporeal symbiosis. The body is the primordial "earthlink" of the self to the flesh of the world which humans and "ten thousand things" inhabit together.

Moreover, transversality is to be taken as the radically new way of facilitating *lateral* border-crossings by decentering all the centers from one culture to another (intercultural), from one species to another (interspeciesistic), from one discipline to another (interdisciplinary), and from one sense to another (intersensorial). First, transversality as a lateral movement deconstructs and replaces universality as a Eurocentric idea. Second, it unpacks anthropocentrism (as well as egocentrism), which regards humanity as the apex of all creation and the measure of all things and as such is the cause of wanton ecological destruction and the accelerated disappearance of biodiversity. The arrogance of humans as allegedly rational beings breaks off the ecological continuum of Being or ecological Interbeing and results inevitably in an incurable nihilism. In anthropocentrism all beings and things exist only for the sole benefit of humans as rational beings. By inflating the human self, anthropocentrism destroys the transversal "circulation" of all beings and things and is oblivious to the aesthetic principle that "small is beautiful." Anthropocentrism queries: Why do animals cross the road we build? rather than Why do we build the roads where animals cross? Third, as the body is the locus of perception or the human sensorium and the *fundamentum* of everything we do and think, the inflation or domination of one sense deflates the other senses and violates what Merleau-Ponty calls the body's "synergy" or synesthesia as the chiasmic intertwining of all the senses. Vision or sight has been the "brahmmic sense" in Western philosophy and the others, particularly the sense of touch, have been reduced to "untouchable" senses. However, vision anaesthetizes the other senses and objectifies things, whereas touch synesthetizes them. The feminist Irigaray downplays ocularcentrism or "scoptophilism," which is also identified with the "malestream" grid of Western philosophy. By replacing the masculine sense of sight with the feminine sense of touch, she also means to recover not only the place of femininity in philosophy but also the (feminine) earth (*Terra Mater, Gaia*). As Irigaray puts it elegantly, the calendar of the feminine flesh is consonant with nature's rhythmic circulation of the seasons.

In the final analysis, the synesthesia of the human sensorium is synchronized with the harmony of music. The end of transversality is to measure and take into account the harmony of sentient beings and insentient things in the world. "All music is harmonious," Mikel Dufrenne proclaims, "because harmony is the primary condition of musical being" (1973, 255). Inasmuch as the sound of music surrounds the environing world and thus promotes the (round) circulation of beings and things, harmony maintains and preserves the wholesomeness of the whole earth which requires, according to Merleau-Ponty, "no *hierarchy* of orders or layers or planes" (VI 270).[17] John Dewey evokes the Greek conception of harmony (*kalon-agathon*) and extends it to human moral conduct (1934, 39). By so doing, he is not far removed from Confucius, who, as an *appassionata* of music, champions the kinship between music and the Sinic cardinal virtue of *jen* (humaneness) which attends to all living creatures. Thus, the "earthword" *harmony* becomes most *promising* for the future cause of geophilosophy in advancing the lateral relationships of all beings—human and nonhuman—primarily as *sentient beings* who are in need of the ethics of compassion, civility, hospitality, care, responsibility, kindness, and generosity (see Jonas 1984, Hamrick 2002, and Diprose 2002). In this respect, Erazim Kohák is forthright and unimpeachable when he declares that "To recover the moral sense of our humanity, we would need to recover first the moral sense of nature" (1984, 13). For the Amerindians, the first inhabitants of America, the entire embodied "Turtle Island" is the (sacred) *kiva* where all living creatures are called "peoples." The Japanese, too, enshrine not only *Fujiyama* but also the island of their inhabitation as *jinja* (sacred temple, the dwelling place of gods). Merleau-Ponty's transversality as lateral movement opens up a floodgate for gathering and fashioning the cross-cultural corpus and library of earthwords or geophilosophical ideas that give credence to the ecological motto of "thinking globally."

NOTES

1. Abram's work (1996) is thus far the unsurpassed and most creative interpretation of Merleau-Ponty's philosophy in applying and communicating it to the language and world of nonhuman beings and things.

2. The term *Interbeing* is borrowed from Nhat Hanh (1993) who is a Vietnamese Zen Buddhist and founded the Buddhist order of *Interbeing* (in two sinograms pronounced *Tiep Hien*). The idea of Interbeing characterizes Sinism and the all-encompassing ethos of Asian thinking. By virtue of it we can say without reservation that "Asians, indeed, can think"!

3. Glissant, who is a Caribbean francophone, uses such terms as *transversality* and *diversality* to criticize in part Hegel and Eurocentrism in praise of "*créolité*" (see 1989 and 1997).

4. When transversality is said to be complicit with the Buddhist's "Middle Way," we should keep in mind what Abe says: "This Middle Way, however, should not be taken as a middle point between two poles. On the contrary, the Middle Way breaks through dipolarity; it is the overcoming of dipolarity itself" (1985, 157).

5. The Panopticon is Jeremy Bentham's masterly architectural blueprint for an ideal prison system. For Foucault, it is "a figure of political technology" which has multiple applications. It is also "a type of location of bodies in space" (1977, 205).

6. "Perception," Levinas also writes, "is a proximity with being which intentional analysis does not account for" (1987, 118).

7. For a superb essay on Merleau-Ponty's notion of "circularity" or "Being circular," see Busch (1999, 80–106). Concerning the "circularity" of philosophy, Merleau-Ponty notes that "the end of a philosophy is the account of its beginning" (VI 177). Cf. Bachelard who writes that "being is round" (*das Dasein ist rund*) and that "everything round invites a caress" (1964, 234 and 236).

8. Cf. Levinas who says that "sensibility must be interpreted as touch *first of all*" and "contact is tenderness and responsibility" (1987, 116–118, italics added).

9. Bigwood (1993) is ambidextrous in synchronizing Merleau-Ponty's philosophy of embodiment and the aesthetics of Constantine Brancusi's sculpture in praise of "Earth Muse," that is, in developing a feminist ecosophy.

10. There is indeed a stark contrast between female Tantrics and the early Christian Fathers such as Origen who believed that "Human life, lived in a body endowed with sexual characteristics, was but the last dark hour of a long night that would vanish with the dawn. The body was poised on the edge of a transformation so enormous as to make all present notions of identity tied to sexual differences, and all social roles based upon marriage, procreation, and childbirth, seem as fragile as dust dancing in a sunbeam" (Peter Brown 1988, 168).

11. The "myth of the eternal return" is the primordial way of correlating historical time with the cyclical rhythm of nature. For a critique of "historicism" including the modernist view of progress against this primordial legacy, see Eliade (1954, 139-62).

12. According to Barthes (2005, 23), *silere* (to be silent) denotes "a sort of timeless virginity of things."

13. For a comparison between Dogen and Merleau-Ponty, see Olson (1986).

14. What Foucault says about the calligram would apply to the ideogram: "the calligram aspires playfully to efface the oldest oppositions of our alphabetical civilization: to show and to name; to shape and to say; to reproduce and to articulate; to imitate and to signify; to look and to read" (1983, 21).

15. The author's contention that what Being is to the West, Interbeing is to the East is supported by Robert E. Nisbett's recent empirical findings (2003).

16. Cf. Dee Brown (1970) who describes the attachment of the native Americans to nature and the earth: for them, "the earth is part of our body"; and "the measure of the land and the measure of our bodies are the same."

17. For my two experimental essays on environmental ethics based on music and its metaphors, see Jung (1981 and 1989).

REFERENCES

Abe, Masao. 1985. *Zen and Western Thought.* Edited by William R. LaFleur. Honolulu: University of Hawaii Press.

Abram, David. 1996. *The Spell of the Sensuous: Perception and Language in a More-Than-Human World.* New York: Pantheon Books.

Bachelard, Gaston. 1964. *The Poetics of Space.* Translated by Maria Jolas. Boston: Beacon Press.

Bacon, Francis. 1955. *Selected Writings of Francis Bacon.* Edited by Hugh G. Dick. New York: Modern Library.

Barthes, Roland. 2005. *The Neutral.* Translated by Rosalind E. Krauss and Denis Hollier. New York: Columbia University Press.

Bigwood, Carol. 1993. *Earth Muse.* Philadelphia: Temple University Press.

Bourdieu, Pierre. 1990. *The Logic of Practice.* Translated by Richard Nice. Stanford, CA: Stanford University Press.

Braidott, Rosi. 1994. *Nomadic Subjects: Embodiment and Sexual Difference in Contemporary Feminist Theory.* New York: Columbia University Press.

Brown, Dee 1970. *Bury My Heart at Wounded Knee.* New York: Holt, Rinehart and Winston

Brown, Norman O. 1966. *Love's Body.* New York: Alfred A. Knopf.

Brown, Peter. 1988. *The Body and Society: Men, Women, and Sexual Renunciation in Early Christianity.* New York: Columbia University Press.

Bugbee, Jr., Henry G. 1958. *The Inward Morning: A Philosophical Exploration in Journal Form.* State College, PA.: Bald Eagle Press.

Busch, Thomas W. 1999. *Circulating Being from Embodiment to Incorporation: Essays on Late Existentialism.* New York: Fordham University Press.

Carson, Rachel. 1965. *The Sense of Wonder.* New York: Harper and Row.

Chakrabarty, Dipesh. 2002. *Habitations of Modernity: Essays in the Wake of Subaltern Studies*. Chicago: University of Chicago Press.

Chan, Wing-tsit. 1963. *A Source Book in Chinese Philosophy*. Translated by Wing-tsit Chan. Princeton, NJ: Princeton University Press.

Chang, Chung-yuan. 1975. *Tao: A New Way of Thinking*. New York: Harper and Row.

Cho, Kah Kyung. 1987. *Bewusstsein und Natursein*. Freiburg: Karl Alber.

Commoner, Barry. 1971. *The Closing Circle: Nature, Man, and Technology*. New York: Alfred A. Knopf.

Deleuze, Gilles and Félix Guattari. 1994. *What Is Philosophy?* Translated by Hugh Tomlinson and Graham Burchell. New York: Columbia University Press.

Deutscher, Penelope. 2002. *A Politics of Impossible Difference: The Later Work of Luce Irigaray*. Ithaca, New York: Cornell University Press.

Dewey, John. 1934. *Art as Experience*. New York: G. P. Putnam.

Diprose, Rosalyn. 2002. *Corporeal Generosity*. Albany: State University of New York Press.

Dufrenne, Mikel. 1973. *The Phenomenology of Aesthetic Experience*. Translated by Edward S. Casey. Evanston, IL: Northwestern University Press.

Eliade, Mircea. 1954. *The Myth of the Eternal Return*. Translated by Willard R. Trask. New York: Pantheon Books.

Ellison, Ralph. 1982. *Invisible Man*. 30th Anniversary Ed. New York: Random House.

Fenollosa, Ernest. 1936. *The Chinese Written Character as a Medium for Poetry*. Edited by Ezra Pound. San Francisco: City Lights Books.

Foucault, Michel. 1977. *Discipline and Punish*. Translated by Alan Sheridan. New York: Pantheon Books.

———. 1983. *This Is Not a Pipe*. Translated and edited by James Harkness. Berkeley: University of California Press.

———. 1999. *Religion and Culture*. Translated by Richard Townsend. New York: Routledge.

Genesko, Gary. 2000. "The Life and Work of Félix Guattari: From Transversality to Ecosophy." In Félix Guattari, *The Three Ecologies*. Translated by Ian Pindar and Paul Sutton. London: Athlone Press, pp. 106–159.

Gilman, Sander L. 1991. *Inscribing the Other*. Lincoln: University of Nebraska Press.

Glissant, Edouard. 1989. *Caribbean Discourse: Selected Essays*. Translated by J. Michael Dash. Charlottesville: University Press of Virginia.

———. 1997. *Poetics of Relation*. Translated by Betsy Wing. Ann Arbor: University of Michigan Press.

Grene, Marjorie. 1980. "The Sense of Things." *Journal of Aesthetics and Art Criticism* 38: 377–389.

Guattari, Félix. 1972. *Psychanalyse et Transversalite: Essais d'Analyse Institutionnelle*. Paris: François Maspero.

_____. 1984. *Molecular Revolution: Psychiatry and Politics*. Translated by Rosemary Sheed. New York: Penguin Books.

Hamrick, William S. 2002. *Kindness and the Good Society*. Albany: State University of New York Press.

Herder, Johann G. 1969. *J. G. Herder on Social and Political Culture*. Translated and edited by F. M. Barnard. London: Cambridge University Press.

Irigaray, Luce. 1985. *This Sex Which Is Not One*. Translated by Catherine Porter with Carolyn Burke. Ithaca, New York: Cornell University Press.

_____. 1991. "Love Between Us." In Eduoardo Cadava, Peter Connor, and Jean-Luc Nancy, eds. *Who Comes After the Subject?* New York: Routledge, pp. 167–177.

_____. 2002. *Between East and West: From Singularity to Community*. Translated by Stephen Pluhácek. New York: Columbia University Press.

Jay, Martin. 1993. *Downcast Eyes: The Denigration of Vision in Twentieth-Century French Thought*. Berkeley: University of California Press.

Jonas, Hans. 1984. *The Imperative of Responsibility*. Chicago: University of Chicago Press.

Jung, Hwa Yol. 1981. "The Orphic Voice and Ecology." *Environmental Ethics* 3: 329–340.

_____. 1991. "The Way of Ecopiety: An Essay in Deep Ecology from a Sinitic Perspective." *Asian Philosophy* 1: 127–140.

_____. 1995. "The *Tao* of Transversality as a Global Approach to Truth: A Metacommentary on Calvin O. Schrag." *Man and World* 28: 11–31.

_____. 2002. "Enlightenment and the Question of the Other: A Postmodern Audition." *Human Studies* 25: 297–306.

_____. 2005. "Interbeing and Geophilosophy in the Cultural Topography of Watsuji Tetsuro's Thought," in Joseph F. Kess and Helen Lansdowne, eds. *Why Japan Matters!*, vol. 2. Victoria, BC, Canada: Centre for Asia-Pacific Initiatives, University of Victoria, pp. 691–702.

_____ and Petee Jung. 1989. "The Way of Ecopiety: A Philosophic Minuet for Ecological Ethics," in David W. Black, Donald Kunze, and John Pickles, eds. *Commonplaces: Essays on the Nature of Place*. Lanham, Maryland: University Press of America, pp. 81–99.

Kohák, Erazim. 1984. *The Embers and the Stars: A Philosophical Inquiry into the Moral Sense of Nature*. Chicago: University of Chicago Press.

Levinas, Emmanuel. 1987. *Collected Philosophical Papers*. Translated by Alphonso Lingis. Dordrecht, The Netherlands: Martinus Nijhoff.

Li, Zehou. 1999. "Subjectivity and 'Subjectality': A Response." *Philosophy East and West* 49: 174–183.

Mairs, Nancy. 1989. *Remembering the Bone House: An Erotics of Place and Space*. New York: Harper and Row.

Mazis, Glen A. 2002. *Earthbodies: Discovering Our Planetary Senses*. Albany: State University of New York Press

McLuhan, Marshall and Harley Parker. 1968. *Through the Vanishing Point: Space in Poetry and Painting*. New York: Harper and Row.

Merleau-Ponty, Maurice. 1965. "Husserl et la Notion de Nature (Notes Prises au Cours de Maurice Merleau-Ponty)." *Revue de Metaphysique et de Morale* 70: 257–269

Nhat Hahn, Thich. 1993. *Interbeing*, rev. ed. Edited by Fred Eppsteiner. Berkeley, CA: Parallax Press.

Nisbett, Richard E. 2003. *The Geography of Thought*. New York: Free Press.

Olson, Carl. 1986. "The Human Body as a Boundary Symbol: A Comparison of Merleau-Ponty and Dogen." *Philosophy East and West* 36: 107–120.

Ortega y Gasset, José. 1957. *Man and People*. Translated by Willard R. Trask. New York: W. W. Norton.

Phillips, Adam. 1993. *On Kissing, Tickling, and Being Bored: Psychoanalytic Essays on the Unexamined Life*. Cambridge, MA: Harvard University Press.

Schrag, Calvin O. 1997. *The Self After Postmodernity*. New Haven, CT: Yale University Press.

Shaw, Miranda. 1994. *Passionate Enlightenment*. Princeton, NJ: Princeton University Press.

Sjöö, Monica and Barbara Mor. 1987. *The Great Cosmic Mother: Rediscovering the Religion of the Earth*. New York: Harper and Row.

Snyder, Gary. 1990. *The Practice of the Wild*. San Francisco: North Point Press.

Suzuki, Daisetz Teitaro. 1959. *Zen and Japanese Culture*. New York: Pantheon Books.

Wang, Yang-ming. 1963. *Instructions for Practical Living and Other Neo-Confucian Writings*. Translated by Wing-tsit Chan. New York: Columbia University Press.

Watsuji, Tetsuro. 1961. *A Climate: A Philosophical Study*. Translated by Geoffrey Bowas. Tokyo: Ministry of Education.

———. 1996. *Rinrigaku*. Translated by Seisaku Yamamoto and Robert E. Carter. Albany: State University of New York Press.

Willett, Cynthia. 1995. *Maternal Ethics and Other Slave Moralities*. New York: Routledge.

Yuasa, Yasuo. 1987. *The Body*. Edited by Thomas P. Kasulis and translated by Shigenori Nagatomo and Thomas P. Kasulis. Albany: State University of New York Press.

14

Merleau-Ponty and the Ontology
of Ecology or Apocalypse Later

Martin C. Dillon

What can a philosopher contribute to the contemporary debate about ecology? As philosophers, we have no claim to technical knowledge about how to stop global warming, protect endangered species, or reduce the pollution of our planet's earth, air, and water.

Philosophers provide ways of thinking about things. We are also trained to identify errors in the words, concepts, images, symbols, and the like that guide the ways in which we already think about things. Although some positive theses will emerge toward the end, the main thrust of this paper is critical: I will argue that there are fundamental flaws in the conceptual structures that inconspicuously inform contemporary discourse about our environment.

The very word *ecology* is misleading and should be abandoned. The planet we inhabit is, indeed, our dwelling place, but it is not at all like a house. We build houses to protect ourselves from our surroundings. Most of the people who concern themselves about the environment spend most of their lives in structures designed to provide shelter from wind, rain, fire, and moving earth. Our primary habitat is that part of the world that has been tamed to be fit for human dwelling. David Abram, who knows about such things, tells me that people we regard as more primitive than ourselves and closer to nature also sometimes think of the world at large as a house or congenial dwelling place. Perhaps that is because they, too, have been reared to believe that a superior power created the earth to provide a place for us to live.

That belief reflects the familiar desire to influence by worship, supplication, and arcane rites the powers whose sendings take our destinies out of our hands. There are, indeed, awesome powers at work in the universe, but they did not contrive Being for human dwelling and do not operate by transforming the *logos* into reality—although it is well to employ *logoi* in the attempt to understand them. Anthropomorphic design, intention, and intelligence belong in the sphere of *anthropos*, which is but one part intertwined with others in the flesh of the world.[1] So, it would be wise and prudent to think and speak differently about the uncanny place mutating around us. *Ecology* is an inept neologism: what we need to develop has an older name. *Phronesis* resonates with the archaic motives of fear and arrogance, but in a more mature way, governed by a reality principle that seeks understanding. It is not latently informed by a metaphor based on primitive superstition.[2] *Phronesis,* or practical wisdom, is the endeavor to find out how the world works, and to incorporate that understanding in our actions with the hope that it will produce consequences more to our liking than those that follow from acting in ignorance. Or on the basis of superstition.

Merleau-Ponty writes about brute being, and uses terms like *wild* and *savage* to characterize the natural world into which we have been thrust. Unlike his sometime friend and colleague, Sartre, who argued that being could have only the significance we impart to it, Merleau-Ponty had a robust sense of the transcendence of the world. For him, being does not lack meaning and oppress us by being sheerly contingent and *de trop*; rather, it overflows with *sens* not all of which is congenial to human needs. The world limits our freedom and has its own transcendent fate, which we have no choice but to accommodate, even though we are largely ignorant of it and bereft of reliable information about any origin or destiny it might or might not have.

The French word *sens* can be translated into English as sense or meaning or direction. Direction is a spatial term, but as such, it refers also to time. A one-way street, in French, is *une rue sens unique,* a street with a specific direction of movement through time. My point here is that meaning, as Merleau-Ponty conceives it, is bound up with time, time that is inseparable from space, culture, and nature. Merleau-Ponty's ontology is an ontology of becoming; it asserts the reality of time, and in doing so denies the atemporality definitive of all ontologies of Being. This is a pivotal point in what I have to say, so I will take a moment to explain it.

Kant and his successors in the tradition of transcendental philosophy espouse various forms of the thesis of the ideality of time, that is, the thesis that time is a formal structure projected onto experience—in Kant's case, by the understanding informed by the pure forms of intuition and governed by the transcendental unity of apperception. Temporal categories should not be applied to the thing in itself because the thing in itself is defined by appeal to the *Ens Realissimus* or *Ens Perfectissimus*, which is atemporal. Derrida also asserts the ideality of time, but bases his grammatological account on *différance* and the play of signifiers: for him, it is by virtue of the *gramme* (rather than Kant's transcendental unity of apperception) that time is synthesized in human experience.

Merleau-Ponty is initially enticed by this transcendentalism with regard to time, but quickly moves away from it. He does assert the thesis of the primacy of lived time, that is, that all our objectifications of time are grounded in time as perceived, but goes on to acknowledge the reality of natural time. We conceive time as transcending our temporal experience. We think of a time that preceded us and will continue beyond us. And we are correct to do so: archeology and carbon 14 dating substantiate the transcendence of time; and evolution teaches us that a temporal process led us to perceive time and other things as we do, hence that our experience of time presupposes a passage of time that transcends us. This is not to say that the human apprehension of natural time is everlastingly true; quite the contrary, as it is with other things that transcend us, our understanding of time is finite, corrigible, and is being modified right now in physics labs. Nonetheless, our apprehension of natural time is, albeit finite and partial, an apprehension of time, itself, as it unfolds in the natural world. There is but one time as there is but one space, but there are many aspects of both, and many perspectives upon them, all of which both reveal and obscure the transcendent reality that grounds them.

At first, Merleau-Ponty designates the relationship between lived time and natural time with Husserl's term, *Fundierung*, but then subsumes it under his own notion of reversibility. We come to be in natural time and in that coming to be develop a capacity to experience it. Lived time, the time of perceptual unfolding, allows us to form an understanding of the time that transcends us, but is itself grounded in that time. Ultimately the two are intertwined in a process of genesis that does not permit the isolation of either in what Husserl called a fulfillable intention.

Given his understanding of time as both transcendental and real, as both immanent and transcendent, Merleau-Ponty is committed to an ontology of becoming: he rejects the belief subtending all ontologies of Being that time is but a human projection and ultimately an illusion.[3]

This ontology of becoming based on the thesis of the transcendence of time affects our understanding of ecology profoundly—all the way down. But I will start at the surface with the notion of protecting endangered species. Physicists tell us that the sun will burn out in ten to the whatever years. Some geologists tell us that another ice age is coming fairly soon. And other sciences of a softer nature predict an even sooner end: if thermonuclear warfare does not wipe us out, then biological or chemical warfare will. The best we can hope for is rearguard action that will save the whales and spotted owls for a little while longer. Now, why would we want to do that? Evolution tells us that species mutate, and that some mutations displace their ancestors: no more dinosaurs or three-toed horses. Does it make sense to try to interfere with this process, especially when we have a pretty good idea of our planet's destiny? Why not embrace the new species that emerge as life adapts to changes in global habitats?

Consider one endangered species, *homo sapiens*. We have come a long way from the Pleistocene. We are now civilized, in some measure, at least, and in some sense of the term. That is, we have adapted to living in cities, in the *cives*. Some of us tolerate smog, traffic, crime, police, noise, gang warfare, graffiti, ubiquitous filth, and so on, and in short, inure ourselves to close proximity to the other noxious creatures we call fellow human beings. Not only tolerate it, but actually prefer it. Is this a new species? Will it (or has it already) developed discernibly different DNA from persons who are descendents from an unbroken heritage of farmers? Which DNA will the longest survivors bear? Which species or subspecies would we prefer to survive? Note that the judgment to be made here is driven by preference, by the need to be lucid about what one wants.

Conservation, as the term is used in discourse about ecology, is a curious notion. The greens are typically regarded as left wing, not as political conservatives, who usually prefer capital profit to preserving the habitat of endangered species. People committed to preserving the environment typically repudiate all forms of power generation except some that are derived from sun, wind, and renewable resources. Why not develop supersafe nuclear generators? Because it cannot be done? Because the cost and the risk are too high? How would an environmentally friendly aircraft be powered? How would an environmentally friendly military go about its business? What is to be conserved? What is to be forsaken in the process of conserving what we choose to conserve? Do we deprive lumberjacks of jobs and Weyerhauser of profits for the sake of spotted owls? How does one make such decisions and defend them in rational ways? To conserve is to protect something from change: What can be protected from change?

Why would one want to do that? And how would we go about grounding our judgments about what to conserve and what to relinquish?

Note that the technical questions of how to deal with the ecosphere have given way to prior questions of a discernibly philosophical nature. What is worth saving? What is worth saving when every attempt at conservation is likely to involve forsaking something else some human beings value?

Surrounding the question of conservation is the question of restoration: patching the ozone layer, cleaning the land and water and air, replanting the forests, cleaning up the mess we have made. Well, then, what do we restore? The way things were back then. But when? Before there was nuclear waste? Before the industrial revolution? Before men and women devised means of exerting control over their surroundings, a process that always involves artifice, hence transformation of nature?

The ancient Greek poets were not the first to characterize their species as the intruder, the corrupter, the species that, by its very nature, upsets *moira*, the cosmic balance, but they provide a familiar exemplar. Is there a cosmogony that does not portray our species as the one that trashed paradise? As Anaximander said, we are the ones that change things: we upset the balance, and we pay penalties for doing so, according to the assessment of time (Kirk and Raven 1957, 107). Time. What goes around, comes around. Like it or not, the karmic debt will be paid. By our very nature, we provoke the nemesis. If you are a green and want to identify the enemy, look in the mirror.

This is a big idea. Our species is a curse on the environment. We are the species that fouls its own nest, its own *oikos*. We are the ones who, by nature, break natural law.

Three philosophers I know contest this view. The other two besides Merleau-Ponty are de Sade and Derrida. Derrida does not think there is such a thing as natural law, hence it follows that it cannot be broken. I could refute Derrida by strapping a scuba on him, taking him down sixty feet or so, and inviting him to defy Boyle's law by holding his breath and swimming to the surface. De Sade argued that everything we do occurs in nature, that, for example, the primordial prohibition of incest is regularly violated by us and other species, hence that nature permits libertinage—and anything else we natural beings are capable of doing. Merleau-Ponty argues along similar lines that we are worldly creatures, as natural as any others, not above or beyond nature. There is dehiscence of nature, differentiation within nature, of course, and we can distinguish ourselves as that part of nature that reflects upon the natural order. What does this have to do with ecology? In a word, everything.

Conservation and *restoration,* key terms in ecological discourse, both appeal implicitly to a natural ordering informed by design, by some sort of teleology, some sort of purposiveness. Ordering is for the sake of something. What is the teleology operative in ecological valuation? The de facto answer is a confused teleology. Confused because distinctions are typically not drawn between the different entelechies manifested by different species,[4] neither is the crucial distinction between divine and finite teleology given its due.

I believe, but do not have the space here to demonstrate, that much if not most of ecological discourse covertly presupposes some sort of appeal to a natural teleology that is onto-theological at its core. For example, the notion of a cosmic balance upset by self-seeking human projects that subtends the idea of karma as well as the fear of tampering with natural species through artificial manipulation of DNA is largely crypto-onto-theology. Balance is stasis, rest, and perfection, none of which is apparent in the turmoil of continental drift, global warming on the earth's surface, cooling at its core, and the chaos of weather. Suffice it to say that I believe that the teleologies implicit in projects of conservation and restoration should be made explicit. Let me, then, be explicit about my own standpoint on this matter.

First off, I believe in Boyle's law and other natural laws that articulate causal relations in the physical and organic world, but I do not believe that these laws serve a cosmic design or divine purpose that is discernible and serves to provide a measure for our values and decisions. Nonetheless I do believe that *our* purposes are served by discerning natural laws like the one discovered by Boyle and that they do provide a measure for our behavior (as I tried to illustrate with the example of scuba diving). The more you know about how the world operates, the better able you are to deal with it: ignorance is costly.

I also believe that the ends that teleology presupposes themselves presuppose needs and desires, and perfect beings have no needs or desires. Therefore, the very notion of cosmic teleology grounded in divine perfection is untenable. Finite beings, organisms, are all driven by goals, all behave purposively. We attribute to our own species some ability to set goals for ourselves in a deliberate way, but tend to think of other organisms as driven by instinct. A rough distinction can be made between those who incorporate the needs of species other than their own in their thinking about conservation and restoration, those who implicitly appeal to divine authority, and those who limit their concerns to their own kind (which may not and typically does not include all members of their species). Savers of whales and spotted owls belong in the first category, many of those who fear genetic engineering fall into the second, and some recent presidents of the United States belong in the third. Where do I belong? Definitely not in the second group.

The question underlying debates about conservation and restoration is always a question about competing goals, competing needs, desires, and values. That competition includes decisions as to the extent of one's concern for beings other than oneself. Do we do what we think is best for ourselves in the singular or in the plural? Do we prioritize the family, clan, state, species, vertebrates at large, or every living being except mosquitoes and slimy things that live under rocks? My answer to that is Dillon's law of proximity: the value, positive or negative, of other beings is a function of psychic and physical distance—we love and hate up close, and indifference sets in with remotion. I was more touched by the death of my cat last summer than I was by the famine in Somalia. How one limits the scope of one's concerns is no easy question to answer—think of Agamemnon and Iphigenia—and I will make no further attempt to do so here . . . except to say that in other work[5] I have argued that conflicts of interest are best addressed through the agon of expression and debate, and should whenever possible be adjudicated by appeal to the co-opting power of truth rather than by taking the always available last resort first. Violence will remain forevermore on the horizon, but the ability to contain it is the prime measure of civilization.

Let me now go directly to the overriding issue: How do we stand—how should we stand—with respect to the world in which we dwell?

In his influential essay "The Question Concerning Technology," Heidegger has both illumined and obscured this issue. The fulcrum of the essay is the distinction Heidegger draws between *techne* and *poiesis*. On the one hand, there is the self-dissembling horizon presupposed by our technological era in which we tacitly take the world for granted as *Bestand,* as standing reserve, as a resource to exploit in various modes of mastery and control. On the other, there is the listening or attunement to Being that he describes in terms of *poiesis, aletheia,* and *Gelassenheit.* Heidegger acknowledges that the two orientations, *techne* and *poiesis,* are related—*techne* is but one of the orientations revealed through the wonder of *poiesis*—but the thrust of his essay is that the hegemony of *techne* in our era poses a serious danger. The danger is that of closing us off from the wonderful and awesome aspects of Being that might be revealed were we to approach the world with wonder and awe. In sum, Heidegger argues that there is an intimate agon between *techne* and *poiesis,* that *techne* has supervened in our era, and that this supervenience constitutes a bad or dangerous state of affairs.

Contemporary readings of Heidegger frequently miss the point that he, like his prime mentor, Nietzsche, is a philosopher of transcendence, hence they miss the main point of the essay, the call to awaken to what lies beyond our daily concerns. That, in my view, is the message that resounds throughout Heidegger's *corpus,* a constant theme perduring through the many twists and *Kehren* of his writing. It is a message that needs to be heard. It is a message obscured by the onto-theological attempt to deliver it in bite-size pieces designed for comfortable consumption. It is the one thing that was right about old-time religion.

But Heidegger also erred in separating our daily concerns from our awe of transcendence. Erred in seeing the agon between *techne* and *poiesis* as abyssal. *Techne* is essentially a response to *poiesis* as houses are a response to brute being. Our houses have stout walls and roofs, but they also have windows, and we place them carefully in order to view what lies beyond. Anyone who has made it a project to find an appropriate *templum* for her dwelling place, anyone who has lived on the land before building her dwelling in order to sense the spirit of the place . . . any such person knows that *poiesis* informs *techne,* knows that the quality of what he makes depends as much on the quality of his listening as the respect he has for his materials and the mastery he has over his tools. You don't build an igloo in equatorial Africa. You do learn from the wisdom of generations of successful builders how it is done here, and why. And the why tells you how to do it better in the place you have chosen, which is equally a place that has chosen you.

In "The Question Concerning Technology," Heidegger momentarily forgot that the flight of *das Man* from transcendence is, itself, an awareness of transcendence in the privative mode. In issuing the wake-up call, Heidegger momentarily forgot that sleep, as opposed to death, always includes a tacit monitoring of the world from which it is seeking temporary surcease. If it were not, no call could interrupt the slumber, and Heidegger's writing would be sheer vanity.

There is an element of mastery implicit in *techne,* but that mastery is a bit more subtle than contemporary critics of mastery and power seem to realize. From farmers to heavy equipment operators to civil engineers, the ones who work the land know the land better than most of us who walk on it, even if we carry cameras. I have seen a dozer driver scoot out of a pond site he was excavating because he felt what was indiscernible to me, a little ripple in the hardpan that said he would bury his machine if he didn't get the hell out right now.

Men and women who go to sea in technical contrivances know the sea and sky, are attuned to their moods, sensitive to the inflections that betoken change, hence appreciative of the beauty that portends a fate. They are truly masters and wonderful to behold in action, but their mastery is full of respect: for the most part, they attempt to control themselves and their vessels, not the sea. Read Melville and Conrad and you will get a remote sense of this. Go to sea in rough weather with such a master and you will see it at secondhand. Try to do it yourself, and you will learn that *poiesis* drives *techne,* all the way from the design of the craft to the craft of handling it.

The sea can teach us much if we will listen. The first lesson is ceaseless motion and change. The earth is also restless, but, for the most part, moves more slowly and less dramatically than the sea; nonetheless it, too, is constantly becoming. In neither case is there any question of restoring the status quo ante or reaching equilibrium; that is a lesson the sea can teach us about the earth. Another is that neither earth nor sea provides a comfortable and secure habitat for our species, although the earth is somewhat more accommodating. Both earth and sea command respect and vigilance.

The sea feeds us, waters our crops, replenishes our lakes and streams; it also changes its boundaries, amps up our hurricanes, and regularly wrecks mariners who lack respect and prudence. When it seems calm, it is brewing its next storm. It is a mistake to regard the sea as anything other than implacable. The sea is not a woman. It has no human characteristics at all, although it is a fecund source of anthropomorphic metaphors.

The sea can be defiled and polluted. I have been sailing and diving the waters of the northern part of the western hemisphere for half a century, and I have seen it happen. Waterfowl and fish, coral reefs and shorelines, sheltered bays and ocean reaches—all bear traces of human waste. The sea transforms itself to accommodate our garbage. Some species of fish can eat the filters of our cigarettes and survive; others cannot. The sea will endure. Not forever. Only change is forever. But it will last longer than we will. It may have a different aroma; it may swell or shrink; it inevitably will breed different inhabitants in its depths and well beyond its shores.

What can we learn from this? We are the species that has evolved in such a way as to surpass all others in the capacities to calculate and to produce garbage. We are now wondering how to combine those skills. The answer to the how lies in reversibility.

To touch is to be touched. To pollute is to be polluted. We need to learn to calculate the positives and the negatives about wrapping things in plastic, driving cars and flying planes, generating energy this way and that, and in general, using the world for our purposes. That learning is best conceived as developing our capacity for *phronesis*. *Phronesis* is best conceived as the cure for dogmatic ideology. I doubt that we will ever stop generating garbage, but the answer to that problem does not lie in turning off our powers of calculation; it lies in tuning them up according to the revelations that come from *poiesis* or wonder, on one hand, and our penchant for comfort, on the other.

As it is with sea goers, so it is with earth movers, hunters, gatherers, and ironically, Heidegger's silversmith in "The Question Concerning Technology." The smith that crafts the chalice that beckons toward the unknown beyond must sense the beyond he is invoking, must listen to the silver and respect its limits as well as its beauty, and only then can he exert his power and ply his trade. If he cannot wonder, he cannot make; he can only duplicate.

How, then, do we stand—how should we stand—with regard to the world in which we dwell?

I have addressed two issues, both having to do with care. Who or what do we—should we—care about? And how do we exercise that care?

My answers lie in the questions themselves, as I posed them here: that is, both in the questioning of what to do or not to do, and in the questioning of the grounds that might serve to justify the judgments we make. Here, my belief is that the warrant for judgment is ultimately local. Judgment is bound to specific circumstances; it may be informed by one or more of the mixed bag of principles we confusedly call universal, but it cannot be derived from them, simply because one needs some warrant for appealing to this principle rather than that. Judgment, in classical terms, is the process of deciding what general category a particular thing properly belongs in. One has to attune oneself to the thing and then ask which among the competing categories it calls for. That query needs to be situated within the context to which the thing properly belongs, and ultimately within the context of one's sense of the global horizon. How would changing this thing resonate with its environs?

Interrogation, as Merleau-Ponty conceived it, is exactly the undertaking that does *not* blindly adhere to ideology and predetermine itself to an overriding dogma. Interrogation is oriented toward uncovering the truth of the matter at hand, and doing that with the hope and belief that the expression of truth will command assent among the parties in dispute. The choice here is between *phronesis* and violence as engine of change. And the problem is that wisdom and power do not always reside in the same place. Think of Lord Acton's famous dictum, "Power corrupts and absolute power corrupts absolutely."

Finally, I believe that the relevant categories are ultimately aesthetic, that is, based on desire. One has to determine what one wants. There are desires and needs that all human bodies have in common. There are others that are more particular. Identifying the basic needs for clean earth, air, energy, and water is the sometimes obscured *telos* of the ecological movement. The question of distribution of resources, however, will always involve conflicting local interests, and those issues point to the intersection of ecology and politics. Where incompatible aesthetics collide is the familiar battlefield of conflicting interests.

How will the eco-battles be resolved in the long run? Here are my speculations.

The losers will be members of that subspecies of the human order who, like myself, value privacy, personal autonomy, and individual responsibility. We are the endangered species that wants distance from the burgeoning mass of humanity, remotion from neighbors, and freedom to live as we choose. I currently live in the sequestered protection of a hundred or so acres of privately owned woodland. It is true that I have to get the permission of bureaucrats to build a house or a septic system, or to dam a stream to create a lake, or to kill a marauding bear or a succulent doe, to open a road or manage timber or . . . the list goes on. It is also true that the bureaucrats are free to condemn my property and appropriate it at their price to build roads they think are necessary for people I don't know or want to know, to cut down my trees or spray them with something that behaves like agent orange to protect their power lines and phone lines, and to tax me for funds to use as they see fit (including paying their own salaries and hiring more people like themselves).

Still, I am remote enough for the time being that nobody pays much attention, and I can do pretty much what I please as long as I do not annoy other people who will invoke bureaucratic retribution.

Nevertheless, it is inevitable that *das Man* will drive people like me into proximity with himself, just as my desire for telephone service and electricity entails submitting my trees to their defoliants and chainsaws. The needs of the many will continue to supervene over the desires of the few. Taxes alone will ensure the disappearance of my subspecies from its chosen habitat. My kind will be eased out of existence by legislation enacted for the sake of *das Man*. That is inevitable. It may even satisfy some variation on the theme of what is now being called "social justice." I am reconciled to it because I think I will beat them to the punch by dying before they encroach too much more than they already have. That is one consolation. Another is that becoming is as implacable as the sea: species change behavior or die out. I have that in common with the spotted owl. But the human species at large is resilient: *das Man* is, as Heidegger suggested, fairly close to being immortal, and will only die out or mutate beyond recognition when his own self-proliferation finally makes his planet unfit for habitation by anything resembling what I respect as human. *Das Man*'s contribution to the gene pool will engulf the DNA of the likes of me.

Subsequent generations will have intermittent access to places like the one in which I live if they are willing to pay an entrance fee to the public park, obey the signs that will be nailed to the trees, and pack out their own excrement. A half century ago I actually ate the fish I caught in the Potomac River a mile or so upstream from Watergate. A half century from now, my descendants may be able to eat the salmon they take from the sea, but they will have been bred in fish farms. A few generations further on, people will read in history books that humans used to feed themselves from the wild, and they will not know whereof they read, just as I can't quite imagine what it might have been like to live as Native Americans did when the woods and streams were rich with game. I can still hunt wild grouse and woodcock, but I stock my land with pheasants and chukkars bred in incubators, and fill my ponds with farm raised trout.

I think that *das Man* will have crowded my subspecies into extinction long before the sun burns out. And that might actually be a happier end to the brief chapter of human existence in the endless book of becoming than the far more likely scenario suggested by Freud in *Beyond the Pleasure Principle*. In that scenario, it is not the slow degradation of habitat that will kill humanity as we know it or morph it into some alien being that thrives on its own waste, but rather the bellicose nature of our own kind. In individual cases, *Thanatos* always prevails over *Eros*, and the same might well be true for the species. The greatest threats to the lives and welfare of people like ourselves do not come from recurrent catastrophes in the natural world, but rather from that part of the natural world we call human, that is, from the hostility and contagion of members of our own species. We are now learning what we should have known from the start, that nonproliferation treaties drafted by the possessors of nuclear, biological, and chemical warfare capabilities will be contested by peoples who do not belong to the club. The force and direction of the vector from battleaxes to stealth bombers to MRVd missiles is clear enough to see: the force is increasing and the direction is unwavering. Weaponry has always been at the cutting edge of technological development. There is no slogan for forging plowshares into swords, because the swords were always there first.

My guess is that, one way or another, and sooner rather than later, we will kill ourselves, and the world will have to chug along without us and the gods we invoke when, once again, we prepare to cut loose the dogs of war.

Or maybe *phronesis* will prevail. I'd like to think so.[6]

NOTES

1. *Flesh of the world* is Merleau-Ponty's term for the "element" of Being that is a "general thing," like earth, air, fire, and water, or "a sort of incarnate principle" that is "midway between the spatio-temporal individual and the idea . . ." (VI 1968, 139). Although I employ this term regularly to designate an ontological category patterned on the human body that undercuts the traditional bifurcation of mind and matter, body and world, by stressing that "there is reciprocal insertion and intertwining of one in the other," that, as incarnate, humans are part of the world, I am increasingly troubled by it. "Flesh of the world" suggests that the world is organic. Part of the world is organic, of course, but other parts are not, and it is a fundamental mistake to take the whole as an organism. Organisms are intentional, operate according to their own teleologies, and in that sense are purposive. Whether the world, writ large, is chaotic or governed by law, it is not driven by purpose. Water flows downhill, but it does not want to reach the sea. Eventually, of course, it does reach the sea. And stays there for a while.

2. Whether it is possible for one voice to change language I leave moot. I prefer to think in terms of *phronesis* and its derivatives rather than *ecology* and its derivatives, but will continue here to employ the term now in currency. It is hard enough to be understood.

3. Time, as Merleau-Ponty conceives it, cannot be a circle simply because its closure stops time. Much of time, as we live it, is indeed cyclical, but the successive times are different, as the second A in the principle of identity, A=A, is different from the first, hence nonidentical. Every summer is different.

This is perilously close to the domain of metaphysical gobbledegook, but here is the argument. Either the circle is closed or it is not. If it is closed, then time stops (actually never started). If it is open, it is not a circle. This is the *arhetos* of Hegelian thought.

4. We do not die after we spawn, as do salmon, although as Freud points out, we may both be driven by a compulsion to repeat rooted in a death-seeking teleology.

5. "Does Merleau-Ponty's Ontology Predelineate a Politics?" Posthumous publication in preparation.

6. Martin C. Dillon passed away after having made initial revisions in his essay. The editors, in consultation with Ms. Joanne Dillon, have made further revisions, though not in the substance of the paper.

REFERENCES

Heidegger, Martin. 1977. "The Question Concerning Technology." In *The Question Concerning Technology and Other Essays*. Translated and with an Introduction by William Lovitt. New York: Harper Torchbooks. Originally published as "Die Frage nach der Technik," in *Die Technik und die Kehre*. 1962. Pfullingen: Günther Neske. Reprinted in *Vorträge und Aufsätze*. 1954. Pfullingen: Günther Neske.

Kirk, G. S. and J. E. Raven. 1957. *The Presocratic Philosophers*. Cambridge: Cambridge University Press.

Contributors

David Abram is a cultural ecologist and philosopher, and director of the Alliance for Wild Ethics. He the author of *The Spell of the Sensuous: Perception and Language in a More-than-Human World,* which has been translated into many languages, and for which he received the Lannan Literary award for Non-Fiction. David lectures and teaches widely on several continents; he maintains a passionate interest in interspecies communication, and in the rejuvenation of oral culture.

Carol Bigwood is the author of *Earth Muse: Feminism, Nature, and Art* (Philadelphia: Temple University Press, 1993) and numerous articles on Merleau-Ponty and Heidegger. She entwines their philosophies with topics such as Blake's illuminations, gender theory, Sappho, and Naess's environmental philosophy. She currently teaches philosophy at Atkinson College, York University, Toronto, Canada.

Edward S. Casey is Distinguished Professor at SUNY, Stony Brook, where he was chairman of the department from 1991 to 2001. His books include *Imagining; Remembering; Getting Back into Place; The Fate of Place; Representing Place in Landscape Painting and Maps;* and *Earth-Mapping.* He is currently at work on a book whose tentative title is *The World on Edge.*

Duane H. Davis is Associate Professor of Philosophy at The University of North Carolina at Asheville. He is the editor of *Merleau-Ponty's Later Works and Their Practical Implications: The Dehiscence of Responsibility* (Amherst: Humanity Books, 2001). In addition to his work in Merleau-Ponty and phenomenology, he has published essays and translations on contemporary French thought, especially the work of Alain Badiou and Denis Guénoun.

Martin C. Dillon was a Distinguished Teaching Professor of Philosophy at Binghamton University until his death in March of 2005. He is the author of *Merleau-Ponty's Ontology, Semiological Reductionism: A Critique of the Deconstructionist Movement in Postmodern*

Thought, and *Beyond Romance.* At the time of his death there were two works in progress: *Phenomenological Foundations of Value,* and *Art, Truth, and Illusion: Nietzsche's Ontology.*

Jocelyn Dunphy-Blomfield studied with the late Paul Ricoeur, on whom she is completing a book long in preparation. She teaches in the School of Psychology, Psychiatry, and Psychological Medicine at Monash University, Melbourne. As well as French phenomenology, her research interests include process philosophy, issues of epistemology, and the field of action—from ethics and politics to the connections between the philosophy of mind, psychiatry and psychoanalysis.

Sally Fischer is a professor in the Philosophy Department of Warren Wilson College in Asheville, North Carolina. Her articles on Merleau-Ponty have appeared in *International Studies in Philosophy,* and in a forthcoming volume entitled, *Intertwinings: Merleau-Pontian Reflections on Body, World, and Intersubjectivity.* She is currently working on a book on Marcel, Irigaray, and Merleau-Ponty.

Maurita Harney is Senior Fellow in Philosophy at the University of Melbourne, and was formerly Head of Philosophy at Swinburne University. Her publications cover a range of topics, including phenomenology, hermeneutics, philosophical aspects of computing, and the philosophy of inquiry. Her book, *Intentionality, Sense, and the Mind* (Martinus-Nijhoff, 1984), explores the relationship between Husserl's phenomenology and the analytical tradition in philosophy.

Molly Hadley Jensen recently completed her Ph.D. in Religion, Ethics and Society from Vanderbilt University with a dissertation on "'Fleshing' Out a Relational Ethics: Merleau-Ponty's Contributions to Ecological Feminism." She has taught religion and ethics at Huston-Tillotson University, Southwestern University, and Austin Presbyterian Theological Seminary in Texas and is a contributor to the Encyclopedia of Religion in Nature (Continuum).

Hwa Yol Jung is Emeritus Professor of Political Science at Moravian College, Bethlehem, PA. He was trained in Western political theory. He has published numerous books and articles in multiple areas of Western political theory and philosophy, comparative philosophy, culture, and literature; communication theory, and environmental philosophy. Currently he is writing a book on Merleau-Ponty in addition to *The Making of Body Politics.*

Robert Kirkman is Assistant Professor of Philosophy with the School of Public Policy at the Georgia Institute of Technology. He is the author of *Skeptical Environmentalism: The Limits of Philosophy and Science* (Indiana University Press, 2002), as well as articles in environmental philosophy and the ethics of metropolitan growth.

Kenneth Liberman is Professor of Sociology and Religious Studies at the University of Oregon and has been teaching phenomenology for three decades. His most recent book is *Dialectical Practice in Tibetan Philosophical Culture: An Ethnomethodological Inquiry Into Formal Reasoning* (Rowman & Littlefield, 2004). He is presently working on *Husserl's Criticism of Reason, With Some Ethnomethodological Specification.*

Patricia M. Locke holds the Adolph W. Schmidt Chair at St. John's College, Annapolis. She is completing a book on Merleau-Ponty and architecture, *Recollecting Architecture: A Phenomenology of Ambiguity.*

John R. White is an associate professor of philosophy at Franciscan University of Steubenville, in Steubenville, Ohio. His research focuses on environmental ethics, on Continental philosophy, in particular the philosophies of Max Scheler and Maurice Merleau-Ponty, and on Medieval philosophy. He is currently working on a book-length study investigating the manner in which social practices associated with industrial capitalism affect environmental value experience and cognition.

Index

Aboriginal people: 40, 46

Abram, David: 10, 12, 143, 144, 194, 196, 197, 218, 253, n. 1; 259

actions: 9, 12, 14, 21, 23, 27, 31, 32, 73, 87, 89, n. 13; 97, 101, 119, 121, 122, 130, 133, 136, 139, 140, 142, 143, 167, 172, 196, 219; as ethical, 168, 199, 200; as habitual, 139, 213; Merleau-Ponty's philosophy of, 218, 225-231; in political life, 65, n. 19; 230; and reactions, 10, 20, 142, 179; and reflexes, 142, 224, 225, 226

agri-chemicals, 8, 75, 83

agriculture: 19, 34, n. 2; 84, 87, 98; 191

alienation: 11, 44, 45, 47, 113, n. 5; 160, 187, 197, 206, 240

anthropocentrism: 13, 38, 73, 182, 203, 249, 251

Arch, St. Louis Gateway: 81-84, 86-88, 90, nn. 23, 37

architecture: 7, 51, 54, 62, 141, 192, 200

art: 7, 53, 63, n. 2; 65, n. 17; 67, 70, 72, 100, 225, 227, 247; of construction, 8, 9, 96, 113, n. 5; of cultivation, 8-9, 96, 100, 211; as eco-art of everyday living (feng-shui), 13, 248, 249

agency, human: 6, 40, 41, 42, 48, 97, 108, 140

ambiguity: 6, 21, 29, 30, 31, 167, 214, 229, 232

animals: 7, 24, 51, 53, 55, 56, 57, 58, 59, 60, 63, n.2; 73, 88, 95, 96, 97, 98, 101, 107-111, 113, n. 5; 120, 124, 134, 138, 139, 159, 162, 177, 200, n. 2; 214, n. 3; 250, 251; and animality, 5, 11, 120, 165, 175, 177, 179, 187, 188, n. 10; communicative behavior in and signs, 134, 138, 141; disappearing species and diversity of, 191, 198; and ontology, 205, 249; and vital values, 178, 186, 188, n. 8

Bacon, Francis: 239, 240, 246, 249

being: 3, 4, 6, 7, 9, 28, 38, 40, 42, 44, 46, 52, 55, 56, 62, 93, 94, 95, 109, 113, n. 6; 119, 123, 127, 128, 131, n. 9; 137, 181, 194, 195, 196-200, 204, 205, 210, 214, n. 1; 217, 220, 223, 236, 237, 242, 248, 249, 252, 253, nn. 6, 7; 260, 261, 265, 266, 271; as "brute," "wild," 5, 39, 40, 41, 46, 47, 51, 52, 57, 61, 81, 97, 260, 266; as ecological, 107, 206, 251; as elemental, 93, 100; as gendered, 99ff.; as generative, 96, 97, 100; and human being, 9, 43, 56, 58, 95, 100, 103, 104, 107, 110,

124, 167, 169, 177, 186, 192, 193,
196, 197, 210, 243; and Interbeing,
248, 251, 253, n. 2; 254, n. 15; and
sexuality, 111-112, 113, n. 5; *see* also
home
Bergson, Henri: 15, n. 5; 42, 220
Bigwood, Carol: 8, 9, 253, n. 9
biosemiotics: 10, 134-144
body: 3, 4, 5 6, 7, 39, 57, 58, 59, 67,
95, 100, 101, 108, 109, 111, 133,
141, 142, 153, 162, 166, 172, 180,
185, 186, 187, 193, 194, 196, 197,
206, 207, 219, 220, 221, 222, 238,
239, 240, 242, 243, 243; as animal,
55, 97, 107 ff., 165; as body-subject,
133, 179, 209, 241; and bodily
praxes, 11, 180; as communicative,
206ff., 211; and consciousness, 3, 41,
133; and the earth, 41, 44, 163, 172,
241, 245, 254, n. 16; in Eastern
thought and geophilosophy, 246-250;
as ecological home, 8, 93, 94; and
ethics, 11, 178; and the "I can," 41,
108, 220, 223, 224; as gendered, 99
ff., 208, 245; as habitual, 139, 140;
as lived, 3, 4, 5, 11, 13, 68, 86, 177,
178, 183, 184, 185, 187, 206, 214,
n. 1; 240, 241; and mind-body dualism, 3, 94, 102, 133, 137, 156-157,
203, 204, 206, 239, 240, 246, 271,
n. 1; as my own, 4, 24, 25, 34, 43,
52, 62, 94, 95, 103, 105, 107, 109,
112, 136, 137, 139, 162, 167, 178,
193, 194, 196, 199, 205, 220, 224,
241, 250, 251; as objective, 3, 5,
136; as sentient and sensible, 5, 10,
11, 23, 103, 105, 156, 168, 194,
195, 196, 222, 242, 250; and
soul/mind, 4-5, 206, 242; in Tantric
Buddhism, 244-245
borders: 7, 8, 13, 58, 59, 65, n. 16; 67-
75, 77, 79-89, 237, 238, 251
boundaries: 7, 8, 57, 67, 69-75, 77, 79-
84, 87-89, 90, n. 24; 111, 121, 197,
205, 251, 267
Buddhism: 13, 244-245, 253, nn. 2, 3

capitalism: 11, 178, 184, 185, 186, 211,
226, 227
carbon dioxide, increasing atmospheric
levels of: 19, 26, 28, 29, 30
Cataldi, Suzanne L., 194, 196
Central Park: 8, 78, 79, 80, 81, 82, 84,
85, 86, 87, 88, 90, nn. 19, 20, 23; 91,
nn. 26, 31
Cézanne, Paul: 2, 225,
ch'i: 13, 247, 249
chiasm: 4, 5, 21, 102, 103, 105, 111,
112, 205, 208, 224, 242, 251
climate: 20, 27, 29, 34, 47, 61, 63, n. 1;
248; change in, 6, 19, 20, 21, 25-34
and n. 3; and the Intergovernmental
Panel on, 19, 34, n. 3; social and
political, 34, 184
communication: 10, 11, 12, 30, 56, 87,
95, 106, 111, 134, 135, 136, 140,
141, 142, 144, 168, 194, 196, 206,
209, 210, 211, 212, 223, 247, 248;
and communion, 107, 163
community: 11, 31, 54, 97, 99, 100, 103,
154, 155, 166, 175, 181, 198, 200,
211, 245; and ecocommunitarian politics, 12, 203-205, 210, 213 and n. 1
compassion, 9, 98, 113, 168, 169, 252
Confucianism: 13, 246, 248-250, 252
consciousness: 1, 2, 3, 41, 51, 68, 82,
89, n. 11; 103, 107, 108, 110, 128,
133, 137, 139, 168, 177, 178, 179,
182, 192, 195, 196, 198, 211, 223,
224, 230, 240, 241; in relation to
Nature, 220, 222; self-consciousness,
193, 195; time-consciousness, 67, 68;
and the unconscious, 34, 168, 223,
224
conservation: 14, 42, 262, 263, 264,
265
corporeality: 7, 10, 13, 41, 58, 62, 89,
nn. 5, 8; 99, 152, 167, 169, 206, 222,
248; intercorporeality, 6, 7, 11, 13,
37, 39, 41, 43, 44, 46, 47, 100, 113,
n. 4; 169, 196, 197, 205, 206, 207,
236, 238, 239, 242, 244, 245, 248,
250, 251

cyberspace: 10, 151, 152, 158, 164, 172, 174

death: 7, 20, 22, 24, 46, 58, 62, 83, 95, 122, 150, 172, 182, 224, 235, 265, 266, 272, n. 4
dehiscence: *see* differentiation
Deleuze, Gilles, and Félix Guattari: 85, 91, n. 27; 236, 239
depth: 5, 7, 22, 24, 26, 27, 29, 58-60, 62, 68, 84, 89, n. 1; 102, 104, 110, 122, 151, 163, 173, 179, 199, 212, 267
Derrida, Jacques: 261, 263
Descartes, René: 15, n. 5; 40, 77, 156, 220, 221, 239, 246, 134, 205; and the cogito, 3, 239, 243; and instrumental reason, 239, 249; non-Cartesian social world, 7, 51; and ontology, 134, 137; and scientific objectivism, 203 f.
development, environmental and scientific: 11, 12, 110, 151, 154, 157, 158, 184, 199, 217, 225, 271
differentiation: 9, 101, 103, 110, 111, 112, 128, 130, 195, 263
Dillon, Martin C.: 13, 14, 137, 199, 222, 223
divergence (*écart*): 9, 68, 103, 104, 127, 128, 205
diversity: 5, 11, 13, 98, 191-193, 196-200 and n. 3; 206, 231, 251; ethic of, 11, 191-201
dominance: 11, 12, 43, 44, 100, 155, 185, 186, 199, 207, 211, 240, 251

earth: 4, 6, 7, 9, 13, 14, 20, 27, 37-47, 51, 70, 73, 74, 82, 84, 87, 88, 90, n. 15; 91, n. 26; 121-123, 125, 149-153, 156, 162-165, 167-170, 172, 175, 191, 235, 236, 240, 241, 244, 245, 249, 250-253 and n. 9; 254, n. 16; 259, 264, 267-269, 271, n. 1; as house or home (oikos), 9, 13-14, 93-94, 102, 107, 111, 113, n.5; 259-260
ecology: 5, 7, 8, 10, 12, 13, 14, 42, 47, 77, 82, 84, 85, 87, 98, 100, 107, 133, 135, 141, 199, 200, 205, 207, 217, 218, 229, 231, 232, 235, 236, 249, 250, 252, 259-262, 264, 269, 271, n.2; deep ecology, 5, 7, 101, 229; and home, 93ff., 100, 250; as philosophical, 133-139; as social, 12, 203, 204, 206-208, 210, 212, 213, 231
ecological: balance, 7, 10, 75, 200; crisis, 13, 191, 235, 236; destruction, 13, 87, 98, 251; issues, 5, 83, 184; psychology, 142, 143; recovery, 45ff., 88, 89; systems, 12, 218; threats: 11, 20, 21; values: 10, 11, 177-180, 183-188, n. 11; 264; value cognition, 177, 179, 183, 187
economic destabilization: 12, 98, 217
ecosystems: 10, 150, 179, 183, 187
egocentrism: 13, 249, 251
ecofeminism: 8, 94, 101, 113, n. 5; 245
edges: 7, 8, 63, 67-71, 73-80, 85, 86, 89, 165, 191, 235, 253, n. 10; 271
Emerson, Ralph Waldo: 119, 122
empathy: 9, 10, 93, 100-102, 107, 110, 169
environment: 5, 6, 8, 9, 10, 11, 13, 21, 32, 34, 41, 44, 51, 55, 60, 62, 67, 72-74, 80, 84, 88, 89, 94, 114, n. 7; 117, 118, 119, 121, 123, 124, 130, 131, n. 2; 134, 135, 138, 139-142, 179, 180, 183, 186, 187, 217, 236, 237, 248, 252, 259, 262; issues concerning, 5, 37, 38, 44, 48, n. 1; 62, 75, 184, 186, 188, nn. 11, 15; 191, 192, 206, 210, 248, 262; threats to, 6, 12, 26, 29, 94, 96, 98, 186, 187, 197, 203, 217, 229, 263
environmental ethics, 5, 10, 11, 177, 187, 191-201, 254
essences: 1, 38, 41, 75, 127, 129
ethics: 5, 11, 38, 99, 166-170, 175, 181, 182, 186, 187, 188, n. 7; 192, 200, 207, 209-214 and n. 2; 227, 244, 252; of diversity, 11, 191-201; Kantian, 12, 15, n. 5; 40, 118, 123, 131, n.2; 192, 198; *see also* Kant
Eurocentrism: 13, 237, 238, 251

farming: 8, 9, 83, 96-98, 113, n. 3; 192, 210, 214, n. 3; 262, 267, 270; and violence, 8, 98

feminine, the: 96, 101, 208, 239, 243; see also flesh, logos, and ontology

flesh: 57, 107, 149, 162, 172, 197, 200, n. 1; 206, 209, 213, 224; and biodiversity, 198, 199; and the body, 4, 5, 6, 21, 34, n. 1; 46, 93ff., 103, 107, 109, 110, 112, 161, 162, 175, 240, 241, 244, 251; continuous fabric of, 8, 213; as empathic, 107, 110; and an ethic of diversity, 11, 191-201; as feminine, 102-107, 245, 252; flesh-to-flesh, 25, 47, 59, 103, 167, 168; as generativity, 8, 102, 111; and intercorporeality, 6, 207; and pregnancy, 111, 112, 199; and reversibility, 4-7, 51-53, 58, 62, 127, 129, 195, 205, 211; and sentience and sensibility, 11, 22, 52, 56, 105, 193-195; and sexuality, 113, n. 5; 208, 245; and silence, 39, 45, 106, 128, 246; and social ecology, 203-215; and suffering, 22, 25; and visibility and invisibility, 7, 23, 45, 222; and vulnerability, 22ff.; and wilderness, 45 f.; of the world, 4, 5, 21-23, 25, 28, 31, 43, 46, 58, 63, 68, 103, 104, 107, 128,133, 163, 192, 240, 241, 245, 251, 260, 271, n. 1; see also ontology

fossil fuels, combustion of: 19, 34, n. 2

freedom: 23, 211, 269; of being, 42, 95, 269; fragility of, 12, 229; limits to, 14, 150, 227, 260; and love, 228, 229; of movement, 72, 74, 77, 80, 87, 88, 152, 169, 227; of thought, 157, 227

Freud, Sigmund: 2, 222, 224, 228, 270, 272, n. 4

Galileo: 156, 157

generativity: 8, 48, n. 8; 94, 96, 97, 100-102, 110, 111

geophilosophy: 13, 237-240, 241, 245, 246, 248-252

global warming: 6, 19-20, 26, 34, n. 2; 259, 264

greenhouse gases and effect: 19, 28, 32, 34, n. 2;

habitat: 45, 62, 77, 165, 172, 252, 259, 262, 267, 270

Haida, the: 7, 51, 53-58, 60-63, 64, nn. 3-15; 65, nn. 16, 17, 19

Hamrick, William S., 229, 252

healing: 8, 9, 58, 96, 101-104, 110, 111, 245

Hegel, G.W.F.: 2, 203, 211, 220, 225, 226, 237, 253, n. 3; 271, n. 3

Heidegger, Martin: 8, 9, 14, 43, 44, 72, 94, 124, 180, 223, 248; on cultivating and constructing, 96, 97, 99, 249; on difference, 237, 238; on dwelling and home, 93-96, 130; earth and world, 8, 74, 84, 90, n. 15; 93, 102, 125; and the environment (Umwelt), 123-125, 217, 218; and the fourfold, 122, 123; on Gestell, 97, 98; and nature, 123-127, 129, 130; and techne and poeisis, 14, 93, 97, 113, n. 4; 265-267; and the transcendental, 118, 123, 126

history: 2, 10, 40, 56, 70, 74, 82, 83, 99, 109, 110, 211, 213, 226, 227, 235, 253, n. 11; and borders, 73, 74, 82; as conditioning perception, 81, 86, 210, 213; of consciousness, 107, 108, 211; of dwellings, 61, 100; evolutionary, 34, 98; and the French Revolution, 226, 227; and Marx, 225-227; of monuments, 83, 87; and modernity, 225, 226; and nature, 40, 56, 99, 110, 126, 203, 240, 270; of sex and gender, 113, n. 5; 208

home: 9, 44, 46, 75, 87, 96, 112; being at home, 8, 9, 93, 94, 95, 100, 102, 103, 107, 109-112, 119, 124, 125, 129, 130, 153, 160, 161; as dwelling, 85, 93-95, 100, 112; of the Haida, 54, 64, nn. 5, 6, 14; in nature, 9, 119, 124, 125, 129, 130; see also being and earth

horizons: 3, 22, 30, 62, 67, 69, 71, 74, 89, n. 8; 104, 123, 128, 138, 143, 151,

160, 168, 204, 265; of being, 44, 199, 221; and the earth, 165, 268; and gender, 208, 245; internal and external, 7, 52

Husserl, Edmund: 1, 2, 28, 51, 67, 75, 84, 105, 118, 123, 128, 133, 180, 217, 218, 220, 222-228, 261

individualism: 12, 203-205, 209

intentionality: 1, 10, 68, 118, 128, 130, 142, 203, 212; in Being, 127, 128, 131, n. 10; 133, 143, 204, 205, 253, n. 6; as biologically based, 133, 135, 139, 143, 220, 271, n. 1; as communicative, 12, 207, 210, 213; as latent, 9, 128-129; and signs, 140, 143, 220

interactions: 10, 102, 142, 143, 154, 157, 163, 167, 168, 200, 229 232, n. 3; in genetics, 155, 164; in plants and sunlight, 134, 138

intercorporeality: 7, 41, 46, 47, 100, 169, 248; and the earth, 37, 39, 41, 43, 44, 250; and flesh, 6, 207; and ontology, 13, 236, 251; with others, 11, 196, 197, 206, 251; in Tantric Buddhism, 244ff.

intersubjectivity: 12, 205, 208, 209, 211, 224

intertwining: 4, 5, 21, 57, 59, 97, 102, 104, 110, 165, 194, 197, 200, n. 2; 205, 223, 224, 231, 236, 240, 247, 251, 260, 261, 271, n. 1; see also others

Irigaray, Luce: 8, 12, 13, 93, 94, 100, 101, 106-110, 113, nn. 4, 5; 203, 204, 207-210, 212, 244, 245, 252

Kant, Immanuel: 211, 219, 220, 223, 224, 239, 260, 261; see also ethics

landscape: 6, 7, 8, 23, 33, 41, 42, 44, 46, 47, 51, 54, 56, 59, 62, 63, 71, 72, 75, 78-82, 84-86, 88, 124, 151, 161, 196, 207

language: 2, 3, 13, 20, 45, 51, 113, n. 5; 131, n. 11; 138, 142, 144 and n. 1; 155, 186, 188, nn. 6, 8; 194, 200, n.

3; 218, 222, 223, 240, 244, 246-248, 253, n. 1; 272, n. 2; and listening, 4, 124, 160, 175, 211, 265-268; and speaking, 4, 28, 42, 46, 67, 94, 95, 122, 124, 140, 144, 151, 155, 156, 194, 208, 221, 224, 241, 246, 248

Lévi-Strauss, Claude: 54, 56, 63, n. 2

life: 6, 7, 8, 24, 77, 85, 91, n.32; 98, 99, 100, 110, 120, 152, 153, 159, 169, 178, 185, 187, n. 1; 188, n. 6; 207, 227, 245; adult and child, 228-229; afterlife, 153, 172; conscious, 137, 179, 192, 205, 220; diversity of, 11, 191, 197, 198; everyday, 20, 27, 32, 74; as flourishing, 11, 185, 186, 199; forms of, 5, 183; and the Haida social world, 7, 51, 52, 54, 55, 58-60, 63, 64, n. 13; 65, n. 15; human, 1, 7, 153, 182, 198, 253, n. 10; interconnectedness of all, 101, 109, 110, 111, 197; online, 171, 173; our own, 20, 31, 32, 83, 108, 125, 151, 154, 155, 159, 205, 219, 219; political, 2, 12; sciences, 155, 221; and semiotics, 134 ff.; social, 100, 187; and vital values, 182ff., 188, n. 7, 188, n.8

logos: 131, n. 10; 211, 260; in the Feminine, 93, 95, 100; and nature, 94, 221; perception as nascent, 220, 240; rational logos of the state, 85; and Sappho, 95, 112

London, Jack: 37, 43

love: 12, 25, 107, 110-113, and n. 5; 162, 164, 187, 207, 209, 212, 217, 218, 228, 229, 232, n. 2; 244, 246, 265

Matisse, Henri: 70, 89, n. 5

matrix: 11, 86, 160, 174, 197

Mazis, Glen: 38, 40, 41, 45, 104, 110, 251

Matrix, The: 173-175

meanings: 2, 5, 8, 10, 14, 40, 41, 43, 51, 56, 64, n. 7; 70, 95, 102, 109, 110, 113, n. 5; 142, 173, 183, 209, 210, 214, n. 1; 219, 226, 227, 246; and the body, 94, 139ff., 178, 179; as essences, 1, 2, 14; generated from biological process, 135-136, 140, 143; and habit, 139, 140; in Haida images, 58-59; and ontology, 71, 222, 223, 249, 260; in relationship of organism and environment, 135, 139; and signs, 134-135, 138, 141; and temporality, 62-63, 260; and transcendence, 125ff., 260; and the transcendental, 121ff.; as "wild," 7, 51-52

metaphysics: 5, 12, 79, 124, 131, n.2; 204, 219

natural resources: 19, 186, 188, n. 15; 262, 265, 269

nature: 2, 3, 5, 6, 9, 12, 37, 40, 41, 45, 46, 60, 94, 95, 109, 117, 121, 125, 131, nn. 2, 9; 143, 239, 240, 244, 249, 252, 254, n. 16; 259, 263; at home in, 119, 125 ff., 129, 130; beauty of, 120; brute, "wild," 40, 47; cultural mediation of, 38, 48, n. 8; 65, n. 15; 81-82, 85, 88, 102, 133, 203, 245; cyclical rhythms of, 252, 253, n. 11; exploitative domination of, 44, 98, 130, 207, 240, 249; and environment, 117, 118; essences in, 127, 129; as event, 41ff.; as generative, 97, 100; Gestell of, 97; and humans, 110, 139, 200, n. 2, 231-232, 246, 250; Merleau-Ponty's concept of, 15, n. 5; 126, 218-225; perception of, 41, 93; as phusis, 94, 124; restoration of, 14, 264; signs in, 134, 138, 140, 141, 143, 144; Sinic aesthetics of, 13, 235; strangeness from, 9, 124; time in, 45, 260; as threat, 9, 47, 99, 125, 130, 236; transcendental approach to, 118ff., 125ff. see also consciousness, Heidegger, history, home, and logos

nurturing: 8, 9, 48, 55, 97, 100-102, 110, 199, 244

Nietzsche, Friedrich: 2, 120, 238, 266

Olmsted, Frederick Law: 85, 91, nn. 26, 28, 31, 32, 33; and Vaux, 78, 80, 86, 90, n. 21

ontology: 3, 12, 13, 33, 39, 93, 106, 117, 128, 131, n. 10; 180, 199, 204, 221, 223, 225, 229, 236, 259, 260; of becoming, 14, 260, 261; Cartesian, 134-139, 144, 221; of the feminine, 93, 208; of flesh, 5, 11-14, 21, 32, 103, 192, 196, 199, 204, 205, 271, n. 1; and Heidegger, 123, 124, 126, 218; and Husserl, 218, 220, 223, 228; and nature, 126, 127, 129, 206, 220, 224, 231, 249; and sexual difference, 207-209; and transcendental phenomenology, 118, 126, 129, 131, n. 2; see also animals, Descartes, flesh, and intercorporeality

openness: 9, 45, 104, 108, 125, 194-196, 223

organisms: 133, 150, 169; and biosemiotics, 134, 135, 140, 141, 142; biotechnological manipulation of, 98, 155, 172, 186; and environment, 5, 10, 31, 135, 139, 142; essence of, 127; and flesh, 6, 198; and synergy with others, 196, 207; and teleology, 264, 271, n. 1; threats to, 20-23, 26; see also communication

others: 209, 219, 220, 228; and the body, 10, 194, 195, 197, 242, 248, 250; the child's relations with, 12, 169, 170ff., 192-193, 200, 214, n. 2; 218, 223-224, 228, 229; dialogical relationships with, 203, 206, 207, 209, 210, 212-13, 217; diversity of, 11, 172, 196, 199; ethics and, 166-170; and globalization, 211-212; and intercultural relationships, 13, 214, n. 4; 251; interspeciesistic, 13, 197, 263, 264; and intertwining, 194-195, 197, 205, 260, 271, n. 1; isolation from, 199, 239, 269; love of, 228-229; and non-human, 74ff., 88, 97, 101, 121, 133, 139, 175, 182, 183, 192, 251; and pregnancy, 111-112; reciprocity with, 11, 57, 196-198; respect for, 210-213; and self, 4, 8, 12, 102; and social ecology, 12, 210ff.; and touch, 9, 23, 52, 103, 106, 110, 114,

n. 8; 194, 244; as threats, 23, 24, 26, 103, 262; threats to, 32-33; and visibility, 22-24, 34, n. 1; 44-45, 53, 63; vital values of, 182-187; *see also* intercorporeality *and* intersubjectivity

Paci, Enzo: 12, 217, 218
Peirce, Charles Sanders: 10, 134, 135, 138, 140, 144 and nn. 1, 4
perception: 3, 7, 25, 32, 33, 41, 43, 59, 71, 76, 93, 108, 111, 134, 164, 165, 179, 218, 225, 261; as action, 225, 227, 230; ambiguity in, 6, 31, 214, n. 2; and Being, 2, 253, n. 6; and body, 4, 21, 34, 39, 52, 58, 59, 136, 193, 196, 219, 220, 222, 240, 241, 251; of climate change, 26-28, 30; as communicative relation, 142, 206, 207, 213, n.1; and constitution, 57, 58; field of, 9, 46, 178; and flesh, 5, 11, 21, 34, n. 1; 107, 194, 241; and the imperceptible, 153, 181, 231; and the intentionality of consciousness, 2, 139ff., 142; and meaning, 51, 52, 140; and movement, 108-109, 113, n. 6; and the natural sciences, 6, 28, 32, 154, 156; of nature, 41, 99, 225; normal and pathological, 2, 142; of others, 196, 206, 210, 214, n. 3; and perceptual faith, 68, 131, n. 4, 219; and phenomenology, 3, 6, 12, 206, 218; primacy of, 10, 240, 247; and reversibility, 4, 6, 21, 58, 103, 143, 204, 224; of self, 192, 193, 196, 224; sense, 194, 195; of things, 55, 56, 103, 205, 240, 261; and values, 11, 178, 181, 186, 187, 213; "wild," 128, 149; *see also* being, body, *and* flesh
phenomena: 1, 2, 38, 69, 73, 122, 136, 142, 143, 157, 159, 167, 169, 169, 184, 192, 195, 211, 214, n. 2; 243, 247; and life-world, 1-3; and phantom limb, 137, 139; and phenomenal field, 67, 69
phenomenology: 6, 8, 14, 38, 39, 94, 123, 229; of the body, 222, 241, 247;

of climate change, 21, 32; and consciousness, 3, 224; and constitution, 1-2, 40; of denial, 33, 34; and Husserl, 1-2, 128, 218, 220 and intentionality, 1-2, 128, 203; ; as method, 2-3; and nature, 3, 38, 40-41, 222; and ontology, 3, 4, 40, 128, 129, 205; of others, 196-197; of rationality, 219, 240; and science, 2, 21, 28, 126, 221; of subjectivity, 205, 248; *see also* intentionality, ontology, *and* perception
phronesis: 14, 260, 268, 269, 271 and n. 2
Plato: 95, 152, 153, 172, 174, 245
political life: 2, 12; *see* actions
politics: 34, 72, 211, 227, 230, 236, 269; *see also* ecocommunitarian politics
power: 12, 14, 22, 30, 41, 51, 57, 58, 61, 67, 70, 74, 77, 87, 88, 96, 111, 124, 134, 154, 156, 179, 206, 224, 229, 230, 239, 240, 265, 269; of the body, 112, 220-222; higher, 14, 259; of humankind, 42, 144; of nature, 34, 104, 120, 122, 262; of other animals, 56, 97; social units of, 184, 185, 269 ; in techne, 266-267; of technological manipulation, 166, 173, 205, 262; of thinking, 221, 225, 226
psychology: 12, 126, 218-222, 224, 225, 229; *see also* ecological psychology
Pythagoras: 152, 153

reversibility: 42, 105, 206, 243, 261, 268; *see also* flesh
Ricoeur, Paul: 219, 222

sameness, logic of: 11, 199
Sartre, Jean-Paul: 4, 125, 188, n. 4; 226, 232, n. 2; 237, 260
Scheler, Max: 10, 11, 177, 180-184, 186, 188, nn. 4, 6, 7, 8, 9, 10, 188
skin: 7, 43, 44, 52, 58, 59, 102, 105, 109, 110, 162, 166, 244
science: 1, 2, 20, 34, 85, 86, 88, 111, 115, 143, 154, 165, 215, 262; life

sciences, 155, 221; method, 2, 21, 28;
modern, 34, 126; and philosophy, 2,
149, 223; natural, 6, 21, 25-27, 29,
30, 32, 40, 219, 220, 232, n.1; neuro-
science, 154, 155; social, 5, 126, 219,
222, 225, 226, 232, n. 1; and study of
the body, 136, 206; and technology,
28, 151, 155, 239; *see also* life *and* perception
sea, the: 7, 14, 19, 26, 51, 53, 55, 56,
59, 62, 63, 76, 83, 102, 107, 122,
267, 268, 270, 271, n. 1
self: 4, 11, 12, 46, 52, 56, 59, 94, 99,
124, 130, 149, 156, 158-160, 164,
167, 168, 172, 174, 175, 186-187,
193, 205, 209, 210, 212, 213, 217-
219, 242, 259, 262-264; consciousness, 193, 195; and difference, 198-
199; ecofeminist understanding of,
101ff.; as ecological, 2, 3, 245; as
embodied, 8, 11, 101, 103, 107, 192-
197; in self-identity, 44, 104; individualistic view of, 203; in movement,
113-114; as nurturing, 8, 97; and proprioception, 107ff.; as relational, 101,
102; and selfhood, 12, 195-197, 199,
204; in the touching-touched relationship, 58, 101, 106, 109; vital feelings
of, 182-183; and world, 102-103,
193; *see also* intercorporeality *and*
others
sentience and sensibility: *see* body *and*
flesh
Sheets-Johnston, Maxine: 94, 105-108,
110, 114, n. 8
signs: *see* animals, intentionality, meanings, *and* Nature
Sinism: 13, 246-248, 253, n. 2
Smithson, Robert: 85, 86, 91, nn. 26,
28, 32, 33
space: 20, 31,41, 85, 87, 89, n. 1; 102,
110,150, 152, 221, 241, 248, 260;
bodily, 137, 152, 169; Cartesian, 77,
79; cultural, 53, 55, 57, 59, 60,74,
90, n. 2; 91; cyber-, 10, 151, 152,
158, 164, 172, 174; natural, 20, 261;

outer, 125, 157; objective, 242, 253,
n. 5; and spaces, proliferation of,
158, 161
spatiality: 65, 77, 81,104, 123, 260;
bodily, 59, 60, 137, 248; cultural, 60,
63; of edges, 70-71; and pre-spatial
implacement, 71, 75
subjectivity: 1, 12, 41, 81, 102, 105,
130, 132, n. 12; 136, 143, 205, 206,
208, 209, 219, 222, 248; and subjectivism: 219, 232, n. 1; *see also* intersubjectivity
sympathy: 121, 184; as vital, 10, 182-
184, 187, 188, n. 10;

Taoism: 13, 246, 249
technology: 10, 12, 14, 28, 30, 32,83,
87, 96, 124, 149, 151, 155, 157, 158,
162, 165-168, 171, 172, 174, 175,
205, 217, 239, 240, 253, n. 5; 265,
266, 268, 271; *see also* dominance,
organisms, *and* science
temporality: 4, 14, 45, 53, 60, 77, 82,
104, 242, 248, 260, 261, 171, n. 1; *see
also* meanings
terrain: 6, 43, 102, 109, 151, 160, 161,
163-164, 168, 169
terrorism: 12, 231
Thoreau, Henry David: 9, 118-122, 125,
129
time: 20, 24, 52, 53, 68, 122, 241, 248,
253, n. 12; 271, n. 3; of climate
change, 27, 31; and cultural/historical
epochs, 7, 60, 63 and n. 2; 64, n. 9;
86, 93, 95, 99, 121, 223, 231, 232,
253, n. 11; as duration, 81, 83, 97,
120, 172, 173, 223; ideality of, 260-
261; as lived, 14, 45, 261; and monuments, 87, 88, 260; natural, 14, 28,
45, 63, 221, 260, 261, 263; vast scale
of, 31, 53, 157
Toadvine, Ted: 38, 41, 42
touching/touched: 4, 7-9, 22, 23, 34, n.
1; 52, 57, 58, 93, 103-105, 110, 143,
206, 222, 242, 268; *see also* others,
self, *and* flesh

transcendence: 9, 42, 117, 119, 122,
  123, 125, 127-129,137, 152, 212,
  250, 260, 261, 266
transcendentalism: 9, 117-119, 122,
  123, 125, 126, 129, 261
transversality: 13, 235-238, 240,242,
  251-253, nn. 3, 4
trust: 23, 30, 34, 39, 156, 165, 167

Uexkull, Jakob von: 134, 135, 144, n. 2;
  217
universality: 12, 13, 37, 37,47,184, 192,
  209, 211, 212, 222, 237, 238, 251,
  268; and universals, 13, 237

violence: 8, 68, 167, 169-171,174, 230,
  232, 265, 269; see also farming
visibility and invisibility: 4, 6, 7, 21-24,
  26-29, 33, 44-45, 52, 53, 56, 60, 62,
  63, 70, 72, 89, n.1; 90, n. 17; 105,
  106, 108, 109, 127, 144, 149,150,
  205, 207, 222, 242; see also flesh and
  others
vulnerability: 5-7, 9, 19-22, 24, 25, 31,
  32, 94, 96, 110, 125, 167, 171, 230;
  see also flesh

weather: 6, 27, 29-31, 59, 85, 88, 97,
  100, 138, 264, 267
Weber, Max: 184, 185, 188, n. 13; 226-
  228, 231
Whitehead, Alfred North: 5, 15, n. 5;
  217
wilderness: 6, 7, 37, 38, 39, 42, 45
Wilson, E.O.: 191, 197, 198
women: 9, 55, 64, n.13; 94, 96, 99-102,
  106, 113, nn. 3, 5; 140, 208, 214, n.

3; 239, 241, 244, 245, 263, 267
world: 22, 26. 27, 30, 41, 70, 78, 82, 86,
  101, 109, 110, 118, 119, 123, 125,
  133, 137, 149, 195, 197, 200, 204,
  211, 219, 220, 239, 243, 249, 252,
  259, 260, 263, 265, 266, 268; brute,
  39, 43; of the child, 224f.; as conceptual, 47, 219, 226; developed, 30, 32,
  96; dislocated, 217, 226, 228, 229;
  generativity of, 8, 101; globalized, 10,
  200; and intercorporeality, 38, 242;
  and interworld, 212, 242; of life (life-
  world), 1, 2, 3, 20, 39, 96, 142-143,
  154-155, 237; and liminal world of
  the Haida Indians, 51-65; mathematical, 152-153; and meaning, 10, 43,
  135, 143, 144, 219, 220; microscopic
  and macroscopic, 10, 154ff.; natural,
  40, 56, 57, 59, 63, 74, 75, 77, 124,
  125, 192, 197, 210, 213, 259, n. 1;
  260, 261, 271; noncorporeal, 151ff.;
  psychological, 216, 223; as objective
  scientific data, 10, 27, 28, 29, 40, 98,
  138, 143, 154-157, 165, 218, 264;
  perceived, 154, 174, 218, 240, 220,
  225, 231; preservation of, 37, 62, 191,
  192; and proliferation of worlds, 10,
  150ff., 157-161; relation of self to,
  102, 103, 197, 199, 205; revealed by
  body, 41, 42, 62, 101, 104, 109, 139,
  142, 144, 162, 172, 182, 195-196,
  203, 206, 214, n. 1; 219, 241; sensuous, 52, 59, 103, 152-154, 161-176;
  stable order of, 12, 225; working order
  of, 14, 185, 260, 264; and worldly
  asceticism, 185, 227; see also flesh,
  Heidegger, life, and self

Printed in Great Britain
by Amazon

52663308R00169